The Sociology of Anthony Giddens

Steven Loyal

Pluto Press

LONDON • STERLING, VIRGINIA

First published 2003 by Pluto Press
345 Archway Road, London N6 5AA
and 22883 Quicksilver Drive, Sterling, VA 20166-2012, USA

www.plutobooks.com

British Library Cataloguing in Publication Data
A catalogue record for this book is available from
the British Library

ISBN 0 7453 1781 2 hardback
ISBN 0 7453 1780 4 paperback

Library of Congress Cataloging in Publication Data
Loyal, Steven.
    The sociology of Anthony Giddens / Steven Loyal.
        p. cm.
Includes bibliographical references and index.
    ISBN 0–7453–1781–2 (hbk) — ISBN 0–7453–1780–4 (pbk)
    1. Giddens, Anthony. 2. Sociology—Philosophy. 3. Social structure.
4. Civilization, Modern. 5. Giddens, Anthony.—Contributions in
political science. I. Title.
    HM479.G54L69 2003
    301'.01—dc21

2003003645

10   9   8   7   6   5   4   3   2   1

Designed and produced for Pluto Press by
Chase Publishing Services, Fortescue, Sidmouth, England
Typeset from disk by Stanford DTP Services, Towcester, England
Printed and bound in the European Union by
Antony Rowe, Chippenham and Eastbourne, England

Contents

List of Figures

Acknowledgements

I am grateful to various publishers for allowing me to reproduce certain figures. The sources of the figures are: Figures 1 and 6, Giddens (1984) *The Constitution of Society*, Cambridge: Polity, p. 7 and p. 22; Figure 2, Giddens (1979) *Central Problems in Social Theory*, London: Macmillan, p. 56; Figures 3, 4 and 5, Loyal and Barnes (2001), Agency as a Red-Herring, *Philosophy of Social Science* volume 31, No. 4, pp. 509–11.

This book is based on a doctoral thesis submitted to the Department of Sociology, University of Exeter in 1997. My supervisor Barry Barnes was both a model academic and inspiring supervisor and he continues to be a source of encouragement and intellectual stimulation. This intellectual debt is clearly evident throughout the book. In addition, Chapter 3 contains material from a joint paper written with Barry. I would also like to thank a number of other people including friends and former colleagues for their comments and suggestions during the long gestation of this book: Paul Keating, Rene Spencer-Woods, E. Cockle, Neil Rolin, Louise Campbell, Stephen Quilley, Eric Dunning as well as the NUI publications scheme for their financial assistance and Pluto's Publisher, Anne Beech, and copy-editor Tracey Day.

Finally, I would like to dedicate the book to my grandmother, Kartar Kaur Rehal, my two brothers William and John and particularly to my mother and father Lakbhir Kaur and Harjit Singh Loyal who have always supported me in everything I do.

Introduction

Few would object to the view that Anthony Giddens is Britain's foremost sociologist. The recent publication of a four-volume book set dedicated to his writings shows that his work not only carries an intrinsic significance, but perhaps, more importantly, that it continues to exert a considerable theoretical influence on the direction and development of British sociology in general (Bryant and Jary 1997). Previous critiques of Giddens's sociological works have tended to focus on the formal concepts and ideas underlying his contributions to the subject. In this respect this book offers nothing new.

However, this emphasis on the abstract architecture of his work underplays the dynamic character of his texts and fails to elucidate the broader social and political rationale underlying his approach. This book seeks to fill this lacuna by focusing on the developmental nature of Giddens's work drawing sparingly upon the sociology of knowledge. In contrast to immanent ahistorical approaches, the intention here has been to elaborate the historical emergence, structure and direction of sociological knowledge in relation to group dynamics and political interests.[1]

The central argument of this book is that Giddens's sociology needs to be placed within the social, political and historical context within which it was constructed. His theoretical project makes sense only as part of a wider world-view which centres on an attempt to renew a progressive form of liberalism. The distinctive pattern of theoretical innovation, the eclectic derivation and combination of concepts, the inclusion and exclusion of certain principles and ideas, as well as the theoretical inconsistencies and contradictions which arise in consequence, derive ultimately from this commitment to progressive liberalism. Placing his ideas in a context of a broader political world-view allows us to make sense of a pronounced shift in the content of his work after 1989, in addition to his most recent and most overtly political work on the 'Third Way' – work which has served as both a basis for and a rationalisation of Tony Blair's politics. Although this study is primarily concerned with Giddens's structuration theory, it also incorporates an analysis of his work on modernity and politics, arguing for the interconnection of all three.

1

It will also be argued that, although Giddens attempts to move beyond certain traditional dualistic approaches by recognising, for example, that 'agents' only become 'agents' in and through 'social structures', one consequence of his world-view is a residual commitment to a form of epistemological individualism. Despite repeated reference to the importance of social practices, this unnecessary individualism effectively reproduces conceptual binaries relating to structure and agency.

The shape of my argument is as follows. Chapter 1 elaborates the social, political and historical context within which Anthony Giddens develops his sociological project. It is argued that his world-view provides a prescriptive rationale for the inclusion in his writings of a number of theoretical postulates and tenets. This 'world-view' is seen to represent a failed synthesis between liberalism and aspects of socialism in the guise of a libertarian-socialism. It is contended, following Mannheim, that Giddens follows a 'natural law' style of thought which draws heavily on the Enlightenment. Chapter 2 analyses the epistemological foundations of structuration theory which account for the basis of individual agency in relation to the 'knowledgeability' of actors. It is argued that Giddens's moral-political world-view requires a standpoint which aims, simultaneously, to rehabilitate the status of an actor's knowledgeability and to argue that this knowledge is fallible in relation to sociological critique. However, this uncomfortable synthesis oscillates epistemologically between foundationalism and a form of relativism. Chapter 3 examines Giddens's theory of action and agency. Giddens stresses two fundamental tenets in regard to actors: their *knowledgeability* and their *capability*. The former is demonstrated in terms of the actor's discursive and practical consciousness. The latter is indicated by the power of the agent 'to always do otherwise' as a result of his/her transformative capacity. Giddens's agent is seen to bear a strong imprint of his moral-political standpoint. Hence, the commitment to voluntarism implicitly demonstrates a desire for individuals to have the capacity to choose and to effect change in the existing order of things. His position on agency also contains deep theoretical flaws.

Chapter 4 evaluates Giddens's deployment and reworking of the concept of 'structure'. It will be argued that a central conflict in the agency/structure debate concerns the question of whether 'structure' should be regarded as a noun – referring to patterned social relation-ships – or as a verb, referring to generative rules and resources. It is posited that this division represents a displacement of the agency/structure couplet. After reviewing Giddens's novel conception of structure as rules and resources what remains unexplicated, yet intrinsic to this concept, are time and space. These concepts, as well as Giddens's proposal for a discontinuist view of history to supplant Marxism, are therefore analysed in Chapter 5. It is argued that the conceptualisation of time and space suffers from similar problems to those concerning the conception of structure as rules and resources. Moreover, Giddens's historical sociology contains a number of contradictory and dualistic value assumptions, again reflecting his world-view. Chapter 6 outlines Giddens's theory of modernity and focuses on empirical and theoretical problems associated with the concept of reflexivity. Chapter 7 discusses the concepts of rationality and reflexivity as a way of disclosing the political conundrum of the 'paradox of socialism' underlying his work. In Chapter 8, Giddens's political sociology, which he describes as 'Third Way politics', is elaborated in relation to his commitment to progressive liberalism. Attention is drawn to the inadequacy of his treatment of power and domination. Chapter 9 looks at the historical nature of the agency/structure debate and offers an alternative sociology. It is argued that these concepts represent a particular way of perceiving the social world and cannot provide the basis for a general sociology. Instead, a standpoint which originates in Aristotle but is carried forward by Marx and Durkheim and emphasises the social nature of humans will be proposed. Chapter 10 summarises the argument of the book.

1 The Political and Sociological Project

> In the contemporary world we are between capitalism and socialism in two senses, and any discussion of normative political theory must be concerned with both. In the shape of actually existing socialist societies, socialism is a reality, part of the power-bloc system that tenuously controls the anarchy of the world nation-state order. It is no longer plausible, if it ever was, to say that they are not really socialist at all or that their insufficiencies have nothing to do with Marxist thought in general. On the other hand, if socialist ideals retain any validity, we are between capitalism and socialism in the sense that such ideals seem capable of much more profound development than has been achieved in any society to date. (Giddens 1987, p. 181)

In this chapter, I aim to contextualise what follows in the rest of this book by examining Giddens's work in terms of a world-view.[1] Such a theoretical manoeuvre permits us not only to understand some of the contradictions which occur in his copious writings, but also to account for the shifts in his sociological perspective. More specifically, this chapter will look at how the practice of sociology within an academic field of production is conditioned by an intersecting political field.[2] It will be argued that Giddens's work has always embodied a political project characterised by an attempt to combine liberalism with aspects of socialism. In practice the emphasis on renewing liberalism has always overshadowed the residual commitment to any more radical socialist or libertarian project.

ANTHONY GIDDENS

Anthony Giddens was born in Edmonton, London in 1938. He was the son of a clerk employed by London Transport. He attended the University of Hull and graduated in 1959 with a combined honours degree in sociology and psychology. He went on to earn a Masters degree in Sociology at the London School of Economics and in 1961 became a lecturer in the Department of Sociology at Leicester University. Between 1967 and 1969 Giddens held a visiting Assistant Professorship at Simon Fraser University in Vancouver, Canada. After a short stint at UCLA, he went on in 1970, to become a lecturer at King's College Cambridge and attained a Professorship in 1986, having already become a director of Polity Press in 1985. Giddens eventually left Cambridge in 1987 to become Director of the LSE, a position that he currently occupies.[3]

Giddens's intellectual career can be analysed into five overlapping chronological periods, each marked by a distinctive set of theoretical preoccupations. The early work on suicide contains little of theoretical interest, although it does demonstrate the individualistic social psychological orientation which was to remain a continuing feature of his work.[4] It was not until his trenchant (and canonical) analysis of the work of Marx, Weber and Durkheim in *Capitalism and Modern Social Theory* (1971a) that he established his reputation as a major theoretical contributor to sociology. This was followed shortly afterwards by an attempt to re-evaluate the sociological conception of class in *The Class Structure of the Advanced Societies* (1973). These important works were then followed by a third phase in Giddens's work which was characterised by an attempt to 'transcend' a number of dualisms within social theory, most significantly, the opposition between agency and structure. In parallel with this theory of structuration was Giddens's attempt to rewrite and re-periodise human history through a critical encounter with historical materialism. Giddens's writings on ontology and substantive history spanned a decade, from the late 1970s to the late 1980s. The fourth substantive phase in his career was marked by an attempt to analyse the contours of 'late modern' societies – or what he referred to as 'modernity'. This prepared the way for his most recent and most overtly political writings, which have sought to transcend the dichotomy between left- and right-wing political ideologies. This attempt to extend the political horizon 'beyond left and right' has identified him firmly as the foremost intellectual spokesperson for the 'Third Way'. These five overlapping periods in Giddens's intellectual development are summarised below:

1. 1960–70: early writings
2. 1971–75: analysis of nineteenth-century social theory and its relevance
3. 1976–89: structuration theory and historical sociology

4. 1990–93: theory of modernity
5. 1994 to the present: Third Way politics

From this chronology, the broad contours of Giddens' intellectual career become apparent: from outlining and analysing the work of other theorists to the development of his own theory of structuration and history, followed by an analysis of 'late modernity'; and finally to a political analysis as overt political engagement. Presented in this way, it might appear that a practical orientation towards politics only figures rather late in Giddens's work. In this book, however, it is argued that a profoundly political or ideological dimension has been present in his work from the outset. Although his substantive theoretical concerns have changed, there remains an underlying progressive liberal 'world-view'.

THEORY AS WORLD-VIEW

Though encapsulating a diversity of competing and conflicting approaches to the study of knowledge and the social world, and including reference to figures as disparate as Marx, Durkheim, Mannheim, Lukacs, Goldmann, Scheler, Berger and Luckman, and Bourdieu and Foucault, the sociology of knowledge[5] is unified in virtue of its claim that knowledge is socially constructed. Following this line of thinking, it will be argued throughout this book that the totality of Giddens's work can also be examined in terms of a 'world-view' expressing social, ethical and political interests which act as causal determinations affecting the content and coherence of his work.[6]

In this chapter I shall outline the central political and intellectual contradictions which run through the whole of Giddens's work. I shall attempt to provide a framework through which this work can be contextualised. This procedure does not, however, simply mean furnishing a purely politically reductive history of Giddens's work, as is often a side-effect of the sociology of knowledge.[7] Rather, the political and the sociological moments will be regarded here, following Bourdieu (1977), as reflecting two analytically distinct fields with a corresponding habitus. That is, they represent two different social spaces to which correspond two homologous mental spaces (Bourdieu 1991). Nonetheless, although both of these fields possess a certain relative autonomy and follow a different 'logic', it is possible for one field to become translated into the other. In this case, reference to the political field allows us to explain both the internal theoretical anomalies *within* Giddens's work as a whole and the theoretical shifts in his writings. It is important to note, however, that it is not social influences *per se* that are the problem. The problems located in Giddens's work are not explainable simply by reference to their ideological, political and ethical underpinnings but, rather, these determinations result in a mode of analysis which is both sociologically and empirically inadequate. Such a procedure implicitly presupposes a view of knowledge which is both genetic and social and which regards knowledge as 'actively' and collectively produced by interacting and competing social groups, embedded in differential structures of power. As Barnes notes:

> Knowledge is not produced passively by perceiving individuals, but by interacting social groups engaged in particular activities. And it is evaluated communally and not by isolated individual judgements. Its generation cannot be understood in terms of psychology, but must be accounted for by reference to the social and cultural context in which it arises. Its maintenance is not just a matter of how it relates to reality, but also of how it relates to the objectives and interests a society possesses by virtue of its historical development. (Barnes 1977, p. 2)

Two main implications follow from such a viewpoint, both of which take us away from the notion of a self-sufficient and autonomous actor who individually 'creates' beliefs and theories. Firstly, as Mannheim and Elias both recognise, knowledge is not produced *de novo* by intellectuals but draws instead upon previously developed or extrapolated knowledge.[8]

Secondly, the subject of thought and action can be conceived neither as an isolated individual nor as a collective subject. This standpoint reflects the individual/society, agency/structure dualism which Giddens himself wishes to resolve. Instead, the subject of thought consists of networks of interacting social individuals, each of whom belongs to an array of different groups and networks and participates on an ongoing basis in a number of different social relations or fields (familial, occupational, national, friends and acquaintances, social classes, and so on). When the totality of these relations is combined in relation to a single concrete social individual, it forms a unique, complex and sometimes relatively contradictory 'individual' mental structure.

In addition to the social and historical nature of social reality postulated here, following Durkheim, Marx and more recently Goldmann and Bourdieu, the mental structures of social individuals should be understood as being homologous with the order of their social world: so that, as Durkheim famously noted, the classification of things reproduces the classification of people.[9] However, in contrast to the rigid use of classificatory and taxonomic metaphors by these thinkers, these mental structures can be regarded as being continually produced on an ongoing, finite and contingent basis.[10] Such mental structures can then be grouped according to what may be characterised as a 'world-view'. Expressing the consciousness of its members' affective, intellectual and practical orientation, a world-view guides and is moulded in response to the problems presented by interrelations with other groups and with nature.[11] On this basis we can analyse the forms of classification consciously and unconsciously employed by any individual thinker.

THE INTELLECTUAL FIELD

The Enlightenment

The *longue durée* of ideas which are rooted in the Enlightenment provides an overwhelmingly important intellectual context for Giddens's own project. *Capitalism and Modern Social Theory* (1971a) can be seen as his first major engagement with the sociological legacy of the Enlightenment. The ideas of the Enlightenment not only shaped the writings of Marx, Weber and Durkheim, but also expressed the contours of emerging political ideologies in the shape of liberalism, conservatism and socialism. The point of departure for understanding both classical and modern sociology is the combination of an emerging secular world-view and revolutions (specifically the French, American and Industrial Revolutions) in the political, social and economic orders in the eighteenth century. Sociology has always played interlocutor to the problems consequent upon modernisation. Both the scientific and liberal values of the Enlightenment, and the conservative and romantic reaction to the Enlightenment, framed the central problematics and theoretical agenda of classical sociology. However, it is important to remember that these ideas were taken up differently by different sociologists, often because of the historically divergent experiences and class configurations in different countries. If Britain is taken as the measure, neither France nor Germany achieved such industrial growth or internal political stability. Against Jacobin hopes, the Restoration in France re-entrenched reactionary interests. Germany, in contrast, prior to Bismark and Prussian unification, remained a loose aggregation of sovereign states under Junker hegemony. Hence the sociological revolution and its preoccupation with 'man' and community cannot be understood independently of any of these social, political, cultural and economic configurations or, more specifically, of the Enlightenment itself (Nisbet 1967, Hawthorne 1976, Seidman 1983).

The Enlightenment, as Cassirer, Gay and Goldmann have all pointed out, was in no way a simple or unitary phenomenon. The elasticity and differences within the movement were again reconfigured both by the national social, political and cultural differences between Britain, France and Germany – despite the reciprocity of influences among them – and by the broad historical span and diversity of political opinion which the concept attempts to capture.[12] As a result it may be more useful to talk of Enlightenment, or enlightenments, as some have argued (Foster 2001). Notwithstanding the fact that the Enlightenment was never a monolithic project, it always carried political consequences and those who have shared or rejected its intellectual and social implications have often done so for political reasons. In earlier times, immediately after its ascendence,[13] the Enlightenment was challenged by a conservative reaction. In more recent times, it has also been attacked by writers of a left-liberal persuasion, often influenced by Nietzsche or Heidegger (for example, Adorno, Horkheimer, Foucault and, more recently, by a number of postmodernist writers) who see the Enlightenment project as nothing short of a return to repressive forms of social bondage through the obliteration of difference and multiplicity.[14]

Although it reached its apogee in France (see, *inter alia*, Gay 1977), by championing what Gay calls the trinity of atheism, republicanism and materialism (ibid.) the paradigmatic expression of Enlightenment remains Kant's description of the Enlightenment as the emergence from infancy:

Infancy is the inability to use one's reason without the guidance of another. It is self-imposed, when it depends on a deficiency, not of reason, but of the resolve and courage to use it without external guidance. Thus the watchword of the enlightenment is: *Sapere aude!* Have the courage to use one's own reason! (Kant 1996, p. 54)

Enlightenment thinkers opposed the organisation of conduct and knowledge into closed and dogmatic systems which, according to its advocates, led to intolerance, fanaticism and authoritarianism.

Moreover, by seeing all individuals as equal because equally rational, tolerance was to be extended to other creeds and ways of life, and was to replace local historical prejudices which were not founded on reason. Hence Locke's noted essay on toleration argues for religious tolerance though, interestingly, not for atheism.

However, the Enlightenment was not only a battle against religious views, superstition and monarchical structure which were central characteristics of the feudal order.[15] It was also a positive attempt to replace these with a critical conception of the world: a way of seeing man's relation to the world in terms of rational knowledge. Again, Kant expresses this paradigmatically in his *Critique of Pure Reason*:

Our age is, in especial degree, the age of criticism, and to criticism everything must submit. Religion, through its sanctity, and law-giving through its majesty, may seek to exempt themselves from it. But they then awaken just suspicion, and cannot claim the sincere respect which reason accords only to that which has been able to sustain the test of free and open examination. (Kant 1997, pp. 100–1)

This was the basis for the scientific posture of the Enlightenment. Nature was no longer simply an expression of Divinity, but was regulated by an interlocking system of universal laws of which, in certain respects, 'man' formed a part. As Kant insisted, the world itself was ordered and logical and could become known through the rational activity of science, exemplified by Newtonian mechanics.

The writers of the Enlightenment always thought of knowledge in close connection with action. Human practice, however – both in its effects on nature and in its social and historical consequences – was generally regarded in terms of individual action, or as the simultaneous action of individuals in large numbers (exceptions to this individualism include Hume, Voltaire and Montesquieu), and also as the application of knowledge acquired by the intellect. As Goldmann notes:

For them [the Enlightenment philosphers], the mission of man, which gives meaning to his life, lies in the effort to acquire the widest possible range of autonomous and critical knowledge in order to apply it technologically in nature and, through moral and political action, to society. Furthermore, in acquiring his knowledge, man must not let his thought be influenced by any authority or any prejudice; he must let the content of his judgements be determined only by his own critical reason. (Goldmann 1968, p. 2)

Hence the eighteenth-century Enlightenment included various rationalist and empirical currents of thought which, despite their numerous differences, treated the individual as the point of departure for all investigation of knowledge and action. Rationalism, in the work of, for example, Descartes and Leibniz understood true knowledge as innate ideas existing independently of experience, whereas empiricists such as Locke and Bacon located the origin of knowledge in sense-perception, with the majority of Enlightenment thinkers occupying a position somewhere in between these extremes.[16]

While for many of these thinkers the free individual provided an obvious point of departure,[17] others, such as Rousseau, concurrently emphasised equality between individuals. The social contract, Rousseau argued, was an agreement between free and equal individuals, all willing to put themselves under the general will. Along with freedom and individualism there was also an emphasis on equality before the law.[18]

The Enlightenment did not originate only in the context of a reaction against Christianity's emphasis on God, religion and hierarchy but also in opposition to its pessimistic view of human nature, often rooted in the idea of original sin. According to many Enlightenment thinkers, human beings were by nature rational and good. Moreover, by systematically underemphasising the non-rational aspects of human nature – though the role played by sensuality and desire were acknowledged – the Enlightenment argued that individuals and humanity could strive toward perfection. An emphasis on progress and an orientation toward the future were the central hallmarks of this approach.[19]

As part of the emancipation from religious bigotry, therefore, the Enlightenment saw human beings as universally rational individual agents who act for reasons which are not determined by the influence of traditional political or religious authority. Rationalism meant above all freedom with regard to all external authority and constraint, and also freedom with regard to our passions. Yet in cases in which each individual, autonomously and independently of other men, decides what is true or right, the bond between the individual and the community is broken. The universe and the community become external things which can be contemplated or observed, but which no longer have any human and living relation to the subject. According to Goldmann, this chasm between individual freedom and community or universe became the central preoccupation of Kant's philosophy. However, as we shall see, its implications run through classical and modern sociology, too.[20]

Liberalism

As a political philosophy, liberalism[21] contributed heavily to Enlightenment thought, though the latter remains a more capacious term. Like the Enlightenment, there is no straightforward standard definition of liberalism. As a doctrine spanning over 300 years it contains numerous strands and various arguments that have changed from generation to generation according to an array of social, political and geographical vicissitudes. Nevertheless, the distinguishing feature of liberalism as a world-view is the value it places upon 'man' as individual and upon freedom (Goldmann 1971, p. 26), whether as freedom from coercion, moral self-determination, or as the right to individual happiness. Liberals have sought to defend individual freedom through a variety of discursive idioms – for example, the doctrine of natural rights (Locke), utilitarianism (Bentham), moral idealism (Kant), historicism (Humboldt), or fallibilism (Mill). Liberalism originally arose as a reaction against a static, religious, hierarchical and fixed absolutist order, which maintained various obstacles to individual liberty through customary privileges. In contrast, early forms of liberalism spearheaded an attempt to universalise a number of liberties for every citizen. These included freedom of speech and of assembly, religious toleration, freedom from arbitrary arrest or imprisonment, and freedom to vote and exercise a democratic choice. Liberals championed the cause of freedom on the assumption that individuals were rational enough to shape their conduct and beliefs with minimum interference from either state or Church. They sought to conduct authority away from these central agencies of society in order that its members might exercise a degree of self-government or personal responsibility. This thinking often presupposed a strident emphasis on secularisation.

Since many of the earlier liberals believed that liberty flourished in a free economy that imposes few restrictions on the accumulation of private property, liberalism became inextricably tied to *laissez-faire* capitalism, and was seen as an ideology of the new middle class as it rose to political dominance. Liberalism may have begun as an ideology against tradition, but it was to later gain meaning in contradistinction to conservatism and socialism.[22]

Towards the end of the nineteenth century certain forms of social liberalism modified the commitment to a minimal state and instead came to emphasise state responsibility for the poor. The rationale for this more interventionist stance hinged on the capacity of poor people to exercise their own liberty. In addition, as Robert Eccleshall (1986) notes, running through liberalism is a persistent conviction that political stability presupposes a moral community of individuals who cooperate in the pursuit of common objectives. Liberals confronted aristocratic paternalism with an alternative meritocratic social ideal of the self-made man whose wealth and status were achieved rather than conferred by birth. Liberals wished to make the working classes virtuous. In becoming thrifty, prudent and self-reliant they would alleviate their condition, and so free themselves from dependence upon aristocratic benevolence. Such law-abiding citizens would abandon any illusions that their future lay in class warfare. Again, liberals endorsed policies intended to universalise bourgeois virtues as a means of promoting the moral elevation of the labouring classes. Notwithstanding inequalities of income, which came with the diversity of individual talent and achievement, the liberal desire was to create a one class society through common habits of self-discipline and citizenship.

Since many of the radical ideas of these liberals have been taken up by other parties – ideas such as civil liberties, representative and accountable government, democracy and even social welfare and the mixed economy – the lines of demarcation between liberals, social democrats, those in the centre or right of the Labour Party and even the 'wet wing' of the conservatives are constantly being blurred.[23] Liberalism has always contained many progressive impulses, which socialists have taken up and attempted to radicalise.[24] This will become clearer when we look at Weber, Durkheim and, most importantly, Giddens. However, before we do so, we can usefully extend this analysis of the Enlightenment and liberalism by drawing on the work of Karl Mannheim. As a leading sociologist of knowledge, Mannheim identifies the production of knowledge by referring it to its sociological context through his concept of 'existential determination' or *Seinsverbundenheit*.[25] In his essay on conservatism, Mannheim (1986) identifies specific thought styles, a notion which he takes from the history of art.[26] Here he aims to describe two styles of thought in the specific context of early nineteenth-century Europe and to identify their social carriers – the rising bourgeoisie and the conservative reaction to the Enlightenment. The two starkly opposed styles of thought he identifies are the natural-law or bourgeois thought-style, which originated in France and held sway up to and just after the Revolution, and the conservative thought-style, which originated in Germany between 1800 and 1850 (Barnes 1994).

Notwithstanding certain lacunae in his standpoint,[27] Mannheim's approach still offers a fruitful way to proceed. The philosophical and political reaction to both liberalism and to the Enlightenment and its embodiment in the French Revolution, as Mannheim points out, was overwhelming. Its two fundamental representatives were conservatism and, to a lesser extent, romanticism. The conservative style of thought arose explicitly in diametric opposition to all the central characteristics of natural-law thinking. For Mannheim, the core of conservatism was that it was 'traditionalism become reflective'. In contrast to the codified and reflective natural-law style of thought, it was external to the conservative form of life and opposed the former on all fronts. It was empirical as opposed to rationalistic, cautious as opposed to optimistic, concrete as opposed to abstract, holistic as opposed to atomistic (Barnes 1994). In many circumstances, it sought to preserve the status quo rather than transform institutions wholesale.[28] In addition to a pessimistic view of human nature based on egoism, power and mutual suspicion, it normatively postulated a stratified social order where 'communal' property explicitly carried differential privileges, rather than expressing the relationship of an individual to an alienable commodity. Conservatism sought to valorise the actions and thoughts of everyday life rather than criticise them. For conservatism, experiencing and thinking are connected to what is immediate and concrete in a practical way, it is against progressive action that is animated by a consciousness of what is abstractly possible or speculative.[29] The emphasis is in life over reason, practice over norms and being over thought (Bloor 1983, p. 162). For Mannheim, this conflict can be represented in a series of binary opposites which is represented in Table 1.1.

Table 1.1   Styles of thought

Natural law	Conservative
Based on reason	Based on history
Abstract	Concrete
Quantitative	Qualitative
Universal validity	Local validity only
Generalising/socialising	Embedded/particular
Deductive	Anti-deductive
Inference from general principles to particular cases valid	Deductive inference – impossible/invalid
Atomistic	Holistic
Mechanical	Organic
Static	Dynamic
Criteria of validity – eternal/absolute	Criteria of validity – in process of change
Non-dialectical	Dialectical

Source: Barnes (1994, p. 67), adapted from Mannheim (1986, pp. 107–9).

In addition to a generalised conservative attack upon the Enlightenment and its liberal preoccupations, there arose a romantic response to its rationalism. Many romantic writers questioned the emphasis placed by the Enlightenment on the rational basis of human action. As a result, there were some overlapping tendencies between conservatives and romantics.[30] Expressed in terms of oppositions, romanticism also emphasised the concrete over the abstract, variety over uniformity, nature over culture, the organic over the mechanical, freedom over constraint, the emotional over the logical. In contrast to conservatism however, the unique individual was paramount for romanticism.[31] Its emphasis was on the organic whole and the world as some spiritual unity which had been shattered by the modern capitalist world in which individuals became divorced from themselves and, more importantly, from nature.

The conflict between traditionalism and modernism and the contradictions thrown up by the French Revolution and Industrial Revolution emphatically defined the parameters and dilemmas of sociology. Industrialism threw up problems relating to the condition of labour, the transformation of private property, urbanism, technology and the factory system. The democratic revolution highlighted problems relating to centralisation, egalitarianism, secularism, bureaucracy, individual rights and the moral reconstruction of the family, church and property. The intellectual elements of sociology were therefore refractions of the same forces and tensions that also produced liberalism, socialism and conservatism. As Nisbet (1967) notes, the nature of community, the location of power, the stratification of wealth and privilege, and the role of the individual in emerging mass society are all issues which sociologists attempted to confront. An index of such changes was provided by the proliferation of new words and concepts. Hence terms such as industry, democracy, class, ideology, rationalism, atomistic, masses, collectivism, egalitarian, liberal, conservative, capitalism and bureacracy all emerged as linguistic currency.

The major ideas and frameworks in sociology therefore have roots in both moral and political aspiration. The major sociologists, both classical and modern, have consequently been preoccupied with the implications of Enlightenment thought and with its critics (Callinicos 1999, p. 3). Sociologists including Marx, Weber and Durkheim all sought to transcend a number of dualisms bequeathed by Enlightenment and counter-Enlightenment thinkers (Seidman 1983). Nevertheless, the Age of Reason characterised by ideas such as the individual, progress, contract, nature, reason, did not simply disappear after the conservative challenge during the nineteenth century with its emphasis on traditionalism, communalism and the non-rational. Hence, although the conservative thought-style made a big impact in the social sciences and was partly taken up in the work of Marx, Durkheim and in a different way in Weber,[32] the individualism of the Enlightenment and liberalism remained paramount. The Enlightenment and liberalism furnished and continue to furnish the basis for the dominant epistemological framework which characterises the modern order in both the natural and social sciences.[33] Such a framework not only attempted to provide a neutral description of social reality, but often incorporated within such descriptions an evaluative moral scheme. In the social sciences, this was often typified by an emphasis on individualism, on universals, on explicit normative codes, on abstract forms and by the denigration of tradition, custom and particularity.

The modern context[34]

Having outlined, in terms of the Enlightenment and its reaction, the broad sociological and intellectual legacy which Giddens confronts, as well as the political context which underpinned it, it is also important to examine the immediate political context which shaped Giddens's political habitus or world-view.

From its inception in the 1920s onwards, sociology retained at its foundation a strong liberal viewpoint. As Turner (1992a) argues, many British intellectuals saw their role as educative and opinion forming. Hence, the influential sociological writings of Leonard Hobhouse, Morris Ginsberg, T.H. Marshall and Percy Cohen contained a strong impulse towards political liberalism which was expressed in their emphasis on individual and ethical responsibility and their strong aversion to evolutionary and structural models of social change (Studholme 1997). Nevertheless, following the Second World War, British sociology, reflecting its intermediary position – in historical, cultural and linguistical terms – between the United States and Continental Europe, was formatively shaped by the contextual dynamics of Cold War politics. As Anderson (1977) notes, within this global context, left-liberal intellectuals maintained a peculiar combination of tension and dependence in their relation to both the Soviet Union and capitalism. The Soviet Union represented the only significant breach in an unjust and unequal capitalism in the twentieth century, at one stage encompassing over one-third of the globe. Yet, its 'barbarities', civic and political repression and bureaucracy offered little hope for an increase in human freedom. Conversely, contemporary capitalism, while championing individual freedom as its baseline, generally ignored issues relating to social equality.

Such a political context was refracted through the institutional and curricular development of sociology in Britain within a general context of growing university expansion.[35] The period between the 1950s and 1960s has been characterised by Giddens as one of an 'orthodox consensus' (Giddens 1972c, 1978). Though this characterisation exaggerates the unity of the sociological curriculum, it still has a degree of validity and usefully shows Giddens's own perception of the sociological world. For Giddens, the orthodox consensus embodied two main strands. In contrast to traditional society, it posited a theory of industrial society where class and conflict were disappearing and models of functionalism incorporating unfolding models of social change, progress and order, and a form of naturalism which drew attention to strong parallels between the social and natural sciences (Giddens 1977b, Abrams et al. 1980, p. 4). In this respect Giddens highlights the pivotal role of Talcott Parsons, whose dominance was such that any attempt to come to grips with social theory necessitated a critical engagement with Parsonian functionalism.

As Bourdieu rightly observes, the intellectual field is never a homogeneous social space and, understood as a constellation of relational positions, it is often characterised by differences of power and authority expressed through the opposition between orthodoxy and heterodoxy. Here the distribution within the field corresponds very closely to the distribution of political positions.[36]

In the United States, within a context of growing political radicalism, such a frontal assault on the Parsonian orthodoxy had come earlier, both from the radical left and from the liberal centre. Liberal reworkings of functionalist theories had been initiated by Merton and subsequently pressed further by a more radical Garfinkelian ethnomethodology as well as by writers from the symbolic interactionist tradition inspired by Schutz (Merton 1949, Berger and Luckmann 1966, Garfinkel 1967). For sheer oppositional force and virulent theoretical and political excoriation, the work of two American left-wing radicals, C. Wright-Mills (1959) and Alvin Gouldner (1971), stood out above others.[37] Similarly, in the UK, the most vociferous criticisms of Parsons's work came from 'conflict theorists' – most notably those advanced by Rex (1961), Dahrendorf (1958) and Lockwood (1956). Two major critical themes ultimately emerged from this motley of theoretical standpoints, both of which reflected the political context of rising social conflict, the eruption of student radicalism and a concomitant re-emergence of Marxism.[38] Ethnomethodological and symbolic interactionist critiques focused on the knowledgeability and reflexivity of actors. More overtly political critics on the left emphasised questions of power, conflict and interest.[39]

It is in relation to these writings, which reasserted both the importance of the individual and of power as domination, within a context of growing student radicalism, that Giddens initiated his own criticisms of Parsons's work.[40] His first attack on Parsons constitutes one of his earliest papers (1968b) and derived largely from a 'conflict' theory perspective (Parsons 1967). Giddens's choice of subject was by no means accidental. As Clegg (1989, p. 135) notes, 'Parsons' application of his general analytical framework to the concept of power was a particularly choice target for anyone who wished to score a decisive hit on the corpus of functionalist theory.' His next theoretical challenge was in a series of essays (1970a, 1971b, 1971c, 1972c) and in his first major book, *Capitalism and Modern Social Theory* (1971a), which I will now examine.

SETTING THE SCENE: CAPITALISM AND MODERN SOCIAL THEORY

Perhaps the most crucial text amongst all of Giddens's writings is *Capitalism and Modern Social Theory: An Analysis of the Writings of Marx, Durkheim and Weber*, which sharply refracts the social, political and theoretical dimensions outlined above. This book, as well as defining or setting the scene for the whole of his subsequent *oeuvre*, is in many ways Giddens's best work. It combines acute scholarship with a systematic attempt to place each of these thinkers in the social and political context within which they wrote.[41]

The implicit frame of reference in *Capitalism and Modern Social Theory* was the ongoing critique of Parsons's substantial writings. In his paper '"Power" in the Recent Writings of Talcott Parsons', Giddens had already argued that

> What slips away from sight almost completely in the Parsonian analysis is the very fact that power, even as Parsons defines it, is always exercised over someone! By treating power as necessarily (by definition) legitimate and thus starting from the assumption of consensus of some kind between power-holders and those subordinate to them, Parsons virtually ignores, quite consciously and deliberately, the necessarily hierarchical character of power, and the divisions of interest which are frequently consequent upon it. However much it is true that power can rest upon 'agreement' to code authority which can be used for collective aims, it is also true that interests of power-holders and those subject to that power often clash. (Giddens 1968b, p. 265)

Giddens's next theoretical attack in *Capitalism and Modern Social Theory*, though less explicit in reference, was eminently more thorough and biting. It attempted to displace the Parsonian canon by undermining its roots. Parsons's first book, *The Structure of Social Action* (1937), had laid the foundation for his subsequent theoretical reputation. Its central argument concerned the convergence thesis: that the classical sociological figures, Weber, Durkheim and Pareto, all converged in regard to a 'voluntarist theory of action'.

It was upon this premise that Giddens focused his critique. Although not referring to Parsons directly, *Capitalism and Modern Social Theory* clearly invokes the Parsonian trinity. However, Giddens's reworking of the canon replaces Pareto with Marx and questions the voluntarist framework. He also rejects the narrow interpretation of Durkheim and Weber.[42] As he notes in the Preface,

> This book is written in the belief that there is a widespread feeling among sociologists that contemporary social theory stands in need of a radical revision. Such a revision must begin from a reconsideration of the works of those writers who established the principal frames of reference of modern sociology. In this connection, three names rank above all others: Marx, Durkheim and Max Weber. (Giddens 1971a, p. vii)

In addition, Giddens argues that most of the dominant branches of modern social theory can be traced with some modifications and extensions to these three authors:

> Marx's works, obviously, are the primary source of the various forms of contemporary neo-Marxism; Durkheim's writings may be identified as the dominant inspiration lying behind 'structural-functionalism'; and at least some of the modern variants of phenomenology derive, directly or indirectly, from the writings of Max Weber. (ibid., pp. xi–xii)

Thus Giddens introduces Marxism as the central interlocutor for social theory and attempts to merge its insights with what he calls the 'bourgeois sociology' of Weber and Durkheim.[43] He therefore sets out not only to provide a comprehensive analysis of the sociological ideas of each of these three authors, but also to re-examine some of the main points of convergence and divergence between them by using Marx as the principal point of reference. That is, he attempts to evaluate the relationship between Marxism and bourgeois sociology which had come to represent a significant debate in sociology in the 1960s.[44]

The debate during the 1960s incorporated two polarised standpoints. According to the first position, adopted by many Western sociologists, Marx's work belonged to a 'pre-history' of social thought and sociology properly began only with the generation of Durkheim and Weber. The second Marxist position held that the works of this subsequent generation should be seen as a bourgeois-liberal ideological response to Marxism. However, for Giddens both positions were 'dangerously misleading'. Giddens argued that even Marx's own epistemology avoided such a naive reductionism since it accepted many aspects of bourgeois theory as valid whilst also recognising its limitations. For Giddens, therefore, even though Durkheim and Weber were committed to a 'bourgeois' political position, this is not an adequate basis for dismissing the content of their writings. In addition, Weber's critique of Marxism reached conclusions which were in some aspects closer to the original Marxian dialectic than the deterministic doctrines of some of Marx's declared followers.

Giddens argued that the political views of Durkheim and Weber are difficult to categorise in terms of the traditional divide between liberalism and socialism. And, although Weber's methodological position is more 'individualistic' than Durkheim's, both, like Marx, rejected the individualism of the utilitarians and with it certain of the suppositions of nineteenth-century political liberalism. The social and political background to these arguments can be understood in terms of the social and political development of Britain, France and Germany in the latter part of the nineteenth century. This provides a context both for the critiques of Marx put forward by Durkheim and Weber respectively, and for the main points of difference between the latter two authors. The result is that:

> Marx's writings share a good deal more in common with those of Durkheim and Weber than was apparent to either of the latter two authors; in perceptible measure, the polemical foils of the three writers were the same, since Marx's works, like those of the two later writers, constitute an attempt to transform and supersede both Romantic conservatism (in German philosophy) and Utilitarianism as manifest in classical economics. (Giddens 1971, p. 244)

Rather than converging upon the idea of an implicit Hobbesian 'problem of order', these theorists, according to Giddens, were instead all concerned with the profound rupture between capitalism and earlier feudal or traditional social forms:

> it is a basic contention of this book that the overwhelming interest of each of these authors was the delineation of the characteristic structure of modern 'capitalism' as contrasted with prior forms of society. (ibid., p. xvi)

Marx, Durkheim and Weber, rather than giving voice to a sharp distinction between socialism and liberalism or Marxism and bourgeois sociology, all sought, in different ways, to effect a synthesis between liberalism and revolutionary or radical forms of thought. Their shared intention was therefore to realise the progressive potential and the commitment to autonomy and democracy central to the idea of liberalism. In conjoining liberal and romantic styles of thought, Marx saw freedom and equality in terms of self-realisation and sought the realisation of this idea through the abolition of the institutions of private property and division of labour.

The social and political structures of each of the three major countries of Western Europe had changed considerably since the time of Marx's writings. In both France and Germany, working-class movements of a potentially revolutionary nature came to play a leading role in the political system. However, the influence of these radical movements was counterbalanced by a rise in nationalism.

In relation to these social changes, the sociology of Durkheim and Weber did not simply represent a bourgeois response to Marxism and socialism, but incorporated into its analysis aspects of the critical and constructive project of the revolutionary tradition. The absence of a strong democratic tradition in Germany led Weber to adopt a positive attitude towards Marxism in order to compensate for the shortcomings of German liberalism. Marxism represented both a theoretical alternative to the idealist tradition and a democratic alternative to Prussian conservatism and the anti-democratic liberalism of the middle classes. Hence, from his earliest investigations to his trenchant criticisms of historical materialism, Weber's work used Marx as a critical foil against the reactionary aristocratic Junker class and the Lutheran Church's ideology, from the standpoint of a nationalistic liberalism.

Durkheim's sociology, though not shaped in the same way by a direct and explicit encounter with Marxism, emerged within a socio-historical context marked by a crisis of liberalism. In this case, the French liberal order was struggling to achieve stability in the face of severe attacks from both left and right. Durkheim sought to unite various progressive social forces in the shape of a democratic liberalism capable of supporting the Third Republic against anti-modernist and irrationalist attack from both left and right. This progressive project combined the individualism, pluralism and secular modernism of liberalism with the egalitarianism, communitarianism and critical rationalism of the revolutionary tradition.

Marx's writings constitute an analysis and critique of early capitalism. He provided his successors in the field of sociology with a formidable analysis of the contradictions between the universalist claims of bourgeois politics and the one-sided character of their material and economic interests. Both Durkheim and Weber attempted to reinterpret the claims of political liberalism in a manner which steered a course between hypernationalistic romantic conservatism, on the one hand, and revolutionary socialism, on the other. They sought to modernise liberalism by acknowledging its failure both to recognise the legitimate rights and demands of the working classes and to extend these rights universally.

Certain differences notwithstanding, both Weber and Durkheim re-emphasised the sociological importance of rational thinking and moral autonomy as a basis for reinvigorating liberalism as a social, political and moral force in the European social order. It is the central argument of this book that Giddens's work continues this project of reinvigorating liberalism by engaging with its detractors. That is, Giddens seeks to undertake a project analogous to the attempt by Weber and Durkheim, to marry liberalism with aspects of socialism in order to reinvigorate the former:

> In important respects, this [book] represents a return to the issues which were of over-riding significance in the writings of the three authors discussed in this book. Their works must still form the main point of departure if this is to effect an important reorientation of social theory. It may be granted that Marx's model of capitalism, in its entirety, is inappropriate to the post-bourgeois industrial society in which we live ... It does not follow from this that some of the major elements of Marx's analysis of bourgeois society are not of considerable significance today. This does not imply the reiteration of the familiar theme that Marx accurately 'predicted' some of the important characteristics of contemporary societies, or that others of his supposed 'pre-dictions' have subsequently been falsified. It is to hold that Marx's analysis poses issues which must be regarded as problematic for modern sociology: exactly the same is true of the writings of Durkheim and Weber. To argue that it must be one of the main tasks of modern sociology to revert to some of the concerns which occupied its founders is not to propose a step which is wholly regressive: paradoxically, in taking up again the problem with which they were primarily concerned, we may hope ultimately to liberate ourselves from our present heavy dependence on the ideas which they formulated. (Giddens 1971a, p. 247)

We can pass over the question here of whether Marx, Weber and Durkheim were predominantly concerned with understanding capitalism *per se*, rather than modernity more broadly conceived. The dominant figure in this political project of uniting liberalism with aspects of socialism continues to be Weber rather than Durkheim.[45] Giddens, as we shall see, draws heavily on Weber's individualism, his notion of rationalisation and the search for meaning in a meaningless universe. Habermas also plays a major role in Giddens's work.[46]

Just as the work of Weber and Durkheim is informed by the problem of constructing stable liberal national polities at the end of the nineteenth century, so Giddens carried the baton in the context of an ossifying state socialism and the cold war. It was in relation to the actually existing politically opposed coordinates of state socialism and industrial capitalism that Giddens developed his ambivalent political ideology. That is to say, this bipolar world with its corresponding habitus constituted the political field within which Giddens was immersed. It was this ambivalent, dualistic political field, reproduced as a dualistic mental space or habitus, which was subsequently reconstituted into the sociological field and expressed in the majority of his writings. More precisely, Giddens's position as a social theorist reflected the standpoint of a Western left-liberal intellectual, isolated from any working-class practice or party.[47] As an intellectual, he confronted the ideal of a socialism which had degenerated into a bureaucratic and repressive state practice, yet which represented the only significant buffer against, on the one hand, an unegalitarian capitalism, and a morally redundant modern capitalism, on the other. It was in relation to this ambivalent social and political situation that Giddens attempted to criticise simultaneously the alienation and inequality engendered by modern capitalism and the bureaucracy and repressive 'unfreedom' which characterised actually existing state socialism. He made this attempt in the name of the universal human value of the self-realision of free *and* equal individuality, which he characterised in terms of a synthesis of aspects of the political ideologies of liberalism and socialism: a political standpoint that may be characterised as 'libertarian socialism'. This standpoint attempted to embody the positive aspects of both of these political doctrines: the conccomitant championing of freedom – a central value of liberalism – and the lauding of equality, a core postulate of socialism.[48] However, as Kilminster (1991) rightly argues, rather than giving both of these values of freedom and equality equal weight within his world-view, Giddens prioritises the concept of freedom, particularly in relation to the individual agent. Thus the European liberal focus on the freedom of the individual as a spontaneous agent capable of choice, particularly in relation to the constraining power of the state, constitutes the core tenet of Giddens's political viewpoint. This is also the basis for Giddens's exaggerated emphasis on individualism, in spite of his frequent references to interaction and social practices. As a thought-style, therefore, Giddens's sociology continues to embody a number of the intellectual hallmarks of natural-law theory. Thus, in practice his thought, as we shall see, is individualistic, rationalistic and deductive; it generalises and universalises, employing fixed criteria of validity. Giddens takes the isolated rational individual as the basis for his whole sociology. Ontologically, the individual is a free, creative, autonomous agent. Epistemologically, such an individual is in a position to identify correct applications of knowledge and to act accordingly, simply by virtue of his/her reference to an external reality through the use of his/her rational capacities. Substantively, the world is always open to transformation by adequately informed actors. Yet Giddens also draws on romantic, conservative and radical strains of thought, construing the social world as one in which individual freedoms are hampered, meaninglessness and cognitive dissonance are pervasive, and inequality is rife (see Giddens 1972b, 1973). His ontological and epistemological account is therefore implicitly normative. It is not simply a description of the social world but an evaluative claim about it and, as we shall argue throughout this book, one that creates a host of unresolved problems not least because of the failure to tie the loose threads of various world-views together.

Given that liberalism and socialism have long been antagonistic intellectual, moral and political traditions – expressed largely, though not solely, in the incompatibility of their points of departure concerning the individual and the social, respectively (Anderson 1992c) – Giddens's attempted synthesis remained problematic. This impasse did not simply result from the different starting points of these political traditions and the difficulty in reconciling them, but also stemmed from a theoretical failure to examine the socio-genesis of the concepts of individual and social. Thus, instead of examining how the concept of the 'individual' arose as a historical expression of social beings, Giddens reifies the concept and treats 'individuals' as enclosed entities or what Elias (1978) calls *homo clausus*. He then conjoins this reified notion of the individual, given expression within the political tradition of liberalism, with aspects of socialist thinking – hence his standpoint of 'libertarian socialism'. The result is an ambiguous world-view in which Giddens moves from one political position which is based on the individual, to another which presupposes a fundamentally social conception of humans. This ontological vacillation grounds his sociological writings, in particular his theory of structuration. That is, it is on the basis of this failed attempt to synthesise liberalism and socialism that Giddens constructs a whole series of unresolved dualisms in his ontology, epistemology, methodology and subtantive writings.

The political dualism which underlies Giddens's theoretical sociological work neither remains static nor does it characterise the totality of his writings. Rather, since the dualism itself is an historical expression of the bipolar socio-political relations between capitalism and state socialism, it follows that, when this context disappeared, as it did with the fall of the socialist states following the 1989 revolutions, so too did the corresponding political dualism which underpins Giddens's world-view.

Thus, as the Soviet Bloc disappeared and socialism ceased to be a widespread ideal, with Marxism no longer representing a dominant feature in the culture of the left, Giddens's work took on a new shape. Hence, it is only after 1990 that many of these sharp dualisms are either reconfigured or entirely disappear. This complex displacement or theoretical reconfiguration remains, however, firmly within a liberal framework. As a result of the demise of state socialism, Giddens's subsequent work on modernity and politics tends to focus upon the liberal dimension of his original libertarian socialist political dualism. This direction is revealed in Giddens's accentuated emphasis on the idea of freedom so central to liberalism with its correlates of individual spontaneity and choice, in opposition to the socialist principle of equality and social regulation.

THE THEORY OF STRUCTURATION

The theoretical background to Giddens's work on structuration can be found in a series of developments which took place in the social sciences over the past five decades. Following the Second World War, the 'orthodox consensus' represented a fairly broad, though consensual, paradigm, in terms of the nature and goals of the social sciences. However, the rise of a number of alternative and competing theoretical perspectives during the 1960s saw this overarchingly positivist paradigm increasing challenged not only by interpretivist and phenomenological sociologies, but also by Marxism. The result was a Babel of theoretical voices with numerous dialects all competing for the title of representing a new orthodoxy.

However, this plethora of competing theoretical approaches could be forced into either of two camps in sociology in terms of how they conceived the fundamental ontological relation concerning people constituting society or social formations constituting human agents. Counterposed to approaches which concentrated on the individual agent and stressed the centrality of intentionality and understanding in explaining the construction of the social world – for example, phenomenological and intepretivist approaches – were approaches which sought a structural explanation for the construction of the social world. These latter theories – for example, structuralist and functionalist sociologies – also regarded unknown, unperceivable and sometimes macro forces as shaping and controlling the actions of agents. Onto this dualism of agency and structure, other oppositions – for example, those of individual and society, voluntarism and determinism, subject and object – were easily mapped.

In sociology, the theoretical antecedent of the voluntarist and phenomenological approaches was usually regarded, with some degree of caricature, to be Weber, whereas the theoretical forerunner of the structuralist approaches was frequently thought to be Durkheim. The work of Marx, however, was spread evenly over both camps. Thus, in France, for example, Sartre's phenomenological Marxism stood squarely opposed to Althusser's structural variant. According to Anderson, these dualisms could be traced to the work of Marx himself:

> the permanent oscillation, the potential disjuncture in Marx's own writings between his ascription of the primary motor of historical change to the contradiction between the forces of production and the relations of production, on the one hand ... and to the class struggle, on the other hand ... The first refers essentially to a structural, or more properly intrastructural, reality: the order of what contemporary sociology would call system integration (or for Marx latent disintegration). The second refers to the subjective forces contending and colliding for mastery over social forms and historical processes: the realm of what contemporary sociology would call social integration (which is equally disintegration of reintegration). How are these two distinct types of causality, or principles of explanation, to be articulated in the theory of historical materialism? (Anderson 1983, p. 34)

However, from the outset, representations of both positions were extensively criticised on the grounds that both agency and structure were indispensable for any adequate sociological explanation. Notwithstanding certain attempts to transcend the agency and structure dualism in the late 1960s and early 1970s (Berger and Luckmann 1966, Berger and Pullman 1966, Dawe 1970, 1978), more profound attempts to do so came during the mid-1970s (Bourdieu 1977). One such attempt to reconcile the agency-structure dualism was made by Anthony Giddens in his work on the theory of structuration.

The central ambition of structuration theory has been to address the most fundamental and familiar problems of the social sciences by providing an account of the constitution of social life and of the nature of social action and social systems. In his theory of structuration, Giddens argues that the traditional dualisms between agency and structure, individual and society, voluntarism and determinism, and subject and object cannot be overcome merely by bringing these rival types of approach together, conjoining one to the other. Instead, a fundamental reconceptualisation of the debate in terms of duality is required:

> In place of each of these dualisms as a single conceptual move, the theory of structuration substitutes the central notion of the duality of structure. By the duality of structure I mean ... structure is both the medium and the outcome of the reproduction of practices. (Giddens 1979, p. 5)

It is according to the notion of the duality of structure that Giddens attempted to transcend the dualisms of traditional social theory and provide an answer to the conundrum of how human beings make history whilst society makes human beings.

> If interpretive sociologies are founded, as it were, upon the imperialism of the subject, functionalism and structuralism propose the imperialism of the object. One of my principal ambitions in the formulation of structuration theory is to put an end to each of these empire-building endeavours. (Giddens 1984, p. 2)

For Giddens, the theory of structuration achieves this aim not only by positing a duality, but also by synthesising a number of insights derived from a variety of otherwise flawed perspectives.

2 Knowledge and Epistemology

Since its foundation in the work of Comte, sociology has regarded itself as a science. Epistemological considerations concerning how knowledge is possible and how we acquire it, however, continue to form a central part of the discipline. Disputes between empiricism, rationalism, idealism and materialism and between positivism and hermeneutics have continued unabated. As we shall see, the lack of resolution between these diverse positions also becomes apparent in Giddens's epistemology. There are essentially two distinct though connected areas that stand out in his theory of knowledge. Firstly, those relating to the scientific status of sociology as distinct from 'common sense' or everyday lay beliefs; secondly those that concern what actors 'know' and what they can come to 'know'.

A HERMENEUTICAL STARTING POINT

Giddens characterises structuration theory as a 'hermeneutically informed social theory', and there is little doubt that he wishes to consciously incorporate a sharp distinction between the natural sciences and the social sciences within his framework:

> We have to take up a series of issues that stem from the profound differences which separate the social from the natural sciences. Sociology, unlike natural science ... deals with a pre-interpreted world, in which the meanings developed by active subjects actually enter into the actual constitution or production of that world. (Giddens 1976, p. 146)

Elsewhere he writes:

> The social sciences, unlike natural science, are inevitably involved in a 'subject–subject' relation with what they are about. The theories and findings of the natural sciences are separate from the universe of objects and events which they concern. This ensures that the relation between scientific knowledge and the object world remains a 'technological' one, in which accumulated knowledge is 'applied' to an independently constituted set of phenomena.

29

But in the social sciences the situation is different ... The implications of this are very considerable and bear upon how we should assess the achievements of the social sciences as well as their practical impact upon the social world. (Giddens 1984, p. 348)

It is partly in relation to this distinction between the natural sciences and the social sciences that Giddens argues for the crucial hermeneutical premise of the knowledgeability of agents.

As will be elaborated in the next chapter, an agent's consciousness is organised in terms of three sets of relations: the unconscious, the practical consciousness and the discursive consciousness. The unconscious is largely comprised of desires. In contrast, practical consciousness contains what Schutz referred to as 'stocks of knowledge', or what Giddens (1984) prefers to call 'mutual knowledge'. Despite its immediate unavailability to the discursive consciousness of actors, for Giddens practical consciousness plays a crucial role in explaining action by permitting agents to 'go on' within the routines of their everyday social lives. As a result, the content of this practical consciousness is generally non-propositional and consists of taken-for-granted, tacit knowledge which forms the 'background' to social encounters:

I use the term 'mutual knowledge' to refer generically to taken-for- granted 'knowledge' which actors presume others possess, if they are 'competent' members of society, and which is drawn upon to sustain communication in interaction. This includes 'tacit knowledge', in Polanyi's sense; mutual knowledge is 'configurative' in character. Even the most cursory verbal interchange presupposes, and draws upon, a diffuse stock of knowledge in the uptake of communicative intake. [Moreover], Mutual knowledge is 'background knowledge' in the sense that it is taken for granted, and mostly remains unarticulated; on the other hand, it is not part of the 'background' in the sense that it is constantly actualised, displayed, and modified by members of society in the course of their interaction. (Giddens 1976, p. 107)

Finally, discursive knowledge refers to knowledge that is generally propositional in form and immediately available to the consciousness of the actor. Although an important form of knowledge, discursive knowledge receives little attention in Giddens's approach, since he presumes that it constitues the paradigmatic form of knowledge in most social theory. The stratification model of agency allows Giddens to argue that actors are highly knowledgeable agents: 'As a leading theorem of the theory of structuration, I advance the following: every social actor knows a great deal about the conditions of reproduction of the society of which he or she is a member' (Giddens 1979, p. 5).

However, this knowledgeability is always bounded. For Giddens, this boundedness takes two major forms. Firstly, the spatial breadth of an agent's knowledge is circumscribed. Since agents only spend a certain amount of time in specific environments, they become unaware of what goes on in other spheres of social life. This applies not only 'laterally', in the sense of a spatial separation of social environments, but also 'vertically', in cases in which, in larger societies, for instance, those in elite groups or in less privileged sectors may know little about each other's lives.[1] Secondly, an agent's knowledgeability is bounded by both the unacknowledged conditions of action, which include both unconscious and practical knowledge, and by the unintended consequences of action. As a result, the primary task of the sociologist for Giddens is to uncover the boundedness of the actor's cognitive penetration of social reproduction.[2] Thus the vocation of the sociologist is to elucidate human actions not only in terms of their intentionality, but also in terms of their motivation and subsequent effects.

GIDDENS'S EPISTEMOLOGY

In order to reveal how the sociologist can elucidate the boundedness of an actor's cognitive penetration of social life, it is necessary to examine the connection that Giddens makes between the technical concepts of the social sciences and the concepts of ordinary language.

According to Giddens, two major interpretations have been put forward of the connection between ordinary language and the technical concepts of the social sciences, the first deriving from Schutz and the second from Winch. The Schutzian approach incorporates a 'postulate of adequacy', whereby two different orders of relevance are said to exist between social-scientific language and the concepts of ordinary language. For Schutz, the social sciences can only meet a 'postulate of adequacy' in relation to lay discourse if they can be translated into the latter. Thus, only if the 'second order' constructs of the social scientist can be translated into the 'first order' constructs of lay discourse, so that they can be understood by the lay actors themselves, can a 'postulate of adequacy' be said to have been met. However, for Giddens, this approach is 'hardly defensible' since it fails to specify how or why the premises regarding 'adequacy' are desirable in the first place. A second, contrasting, 'logical tie' approach derives from Winch. According to Winch (1958), the concepts of the social scientist presuppose a mastery of the concepts belonging to the social agents themselves. Although Giddens regards this as a more fruitful standpoint, he argues that a consequence of accepting the concepts of lay agents at their 'face value' is a 'paralysis of the critical will' (Giddens 1979, p. 250).

Giddens outlines his own position in contrast to both these standpoints. In his view, there is not only a 'logical tie' between the concepts of lay members of society and the social scientific community, as Winch argues, but also, a two-way relationship in virtue of which the concepts of the social scientist can be appropriated by lay actors themselves and subsequently reapplied as part of their discourse. The theories and the findings of the social sciences necessarily filter into lay discourse and become part of that discourse, thereby altering it irrevocably. Giddens refers to this process as 'the double hermeneutic'. The implication of this position is that consciousness, or, more precisely, reflexive self-consciousness, is an irreducible ontological form which separates the social sciences from the natural sciences by promoting a two-way 'dialogical' relationship between subject and subject rather than a unidirectional 'technological' relation between a subject and an independently existing object. As he notes:

> The point is that reflection on social processes (theories, and observations about them) continually enter into, become disentangled with and re-enter the universe of events that they describe. No such phenomenon exists in the world of inanimate nature, which is indifferent to whatever human beings might claim to know about it. (Giddens 1984, p. xxxiii)

For Giddens, a number of significant consequences follow from the double hermeneutic. Firstly, the possibility of establishing universal laws within the social sciences becomes problematic:

> There are no universal laws in the social sciences, and there will not be any – not, first and foremost, because methods of empirical testing and validation are somehow inadequate but because, as I have pointed out, the causal conditions involved in generalisa-

tions about human social conduct are inherently unstable in respect of the very knowledge (or beliefs) that actors have about the circumstances of their own action. (ibid., p. xxxii)[3]

"Third way"

Secondly, the political and practical consequences of the double hermeneutic are that sociology, as an academic discipline, necessarily and unavoidably has to adopt a critical outlook:

> it becomes clear that every generalisation or form of study that is concerned with an existing society constitutes *a potential intervention within that society*: and this leads through to the tasks and aims of sociology as *critical theory*. (Giddens 1979, p. 245)

This transmutation of sociology into critical theory is not an option, but an obligation:

> But, given the significance of the 'double hermeneutic', matters are much more complex. The formulation of critical theory is not an option; theories and findings in the social sciences are likely to have practical (and political) consequences regardless of whether or not the sociological observer or policy-maker decides that they can be 'applied' to a given practical issue. (Giddens 1984, p. xxxv)

However, if sociology is intrinsically critical as a result of the 'double hermeneutic', the form it must take to accomplish this critical task needs to be established. It was noted earlier that for Giddens the role of sociology is to highlight the boundedness of an agent's knowledge. As a result of their boundedness, agents possess an incorrect or partial view of the social world. Hence, although Giddens accepts a Winchian starting point – that the condition of producing valid descriptions of a form of life entails being able in principle to participate in that life – he wants to claim in addition that the concepts that lay agents deploy in engaging in their form of life can also be subjected to critical scrutiny in terms of their boundedness or limitations.[4] Thus, although Giddens retains a hermeneutic starting point in respect of the agent's knowledge, he maintains that this knowledge must also be subjected to sociological critique in order to avoid 'a paralysis of the critical will'. Such a critical standpoint can be adopted, according to Giddens, if a distinction is made between 'mutual knowledge', which is found at the level of practical consciousness and conceived as 'respect for the authenticity of belief', and 'common sense':

> A way out of this impasse can be found by distinguishing mutual knowledge from 'common-sense'. The first refers to the necessary respect which the social analyst must have for the authenticity of belief or the hermeneutic *entrée* into the description of social life. 'Necessary' in this statement has logical force to it. The reason why it characteristically makes more sense to speak about 'knowledge' rather than 'belief' also speaking of how actors find their way around the contexts of social life is that the generation of descriptions demands the bracketing of scepticism. Beliefs, tacit and discursive, have to be treated as 'knowledge' when the observer is operating on the methodological plane of characterising action. Mutual knowledge, regarded as the necessary mode of gaining access to the 'subject matter' of social science, is not corrigible in the light of its findings; on the contrary, it is the condition of being able to come up with 'findings' at all ... In distinguishing mutual knowledge from common sense I mean to reserve the latter concept to refer to the propositional beliefs implicated in the conduct of day-to-day activities. The distinction is largely an analytical one; that is to say, common sense is mutual knowledge treated not as knowledge but as fallible belief. However, not all mutual knowledge can be expressed as propositional beliefs – beliefs that some states of affairs or others are the case. Moreover, not all such beliefs are capable of being formulated discursively by those who hold them. (Giddens 1984, p. 336)

For Giddens, such a distinction can be effected by means of an analytical operation which involves relabelling 'mutual knowledge' as 'common sense' and by examining the latter in terms of its logical rigour and empirical belief claims, in light of the findings of the social sciences.[5] Following Bhaskar, Giddens adds that the discovery of inadequately grounded or false beliefs (logically) necessitates a transformation in action related to those beliefs.[6]

As Giddens (1984, p. 340) acknowledges, this position concerning beliefs, their situatedness and their critique presumes 'that it is possible to demonstrate that some belief claims are false, while others are true'. However, rather than offering an epistemological grounding for this position, Giddens instead reorients his analysis towards the development of a social ontology. Nevertheless, he does make some occasional references, largely in interviews or in passing comments, which point to an unelaborated position regarding epistemology. Hence when asked in an interview with Bleicher and Featherstone how he would ground a critical social science, Giddens responds by proposing a course which avoids two rival strategies:

> one is the strategy of trying to have a secure epistemology or a secure normative theory from which you can issue forth and study the social world. I think that's got to be futile. On the other hand the opposite strategy is also futile, which is to reject epistemology and the possibility of any coherent normative theory which means you've got to have a very strong sociological theory ... Each looks for two kinds of certainty; on the one hand the certainty of a philosophical kind, on the other some kind of sociological certainty. (Bleicher and Featherstone 1982, p. 72)

In contrast, Giddens argues that he aims to pursue a 'middle strategy' which involves:

> firing critical salvos into reality ... and work[ing] within a sociological conception which would seem to me to suggest that some things are clearly noxious and other things are clearly desirable and that it isn't necessary to ground them in order to proclaim this to be so. (ibid.)

In a different metaphor, he describes his position as moving between two houses, one factual and the other moral: 'I want to set up the idea of two houses, neither of which is a safe house, the factual house and the moral critical house, that you move between' (ibid., p. 74)

IDEOLOGY

Giddens then asserts that 'all these phenomena have to be related to the problems of ideology' (ibid.). Notwithstanding this claim, his references to ideology also remain scant, infrequent and largely confined to his paper 'Ideology and Consciousness' (see Giddens 1979, ch. 5; 1983). There, Giddens identifies two basic approaches to the problem of ideology which he argues have constantly reappeared within the relevant literature. The first approach turns on a contrast between ideology and science, while a second contrasting approach operates around a polarity which ties ideology to sectional interests.

Out of the two approaches, Giddens considers that the latter 'sectional interest' approach is more plausible since 'to locate the theory of ideology primarily in terms of the sectional interests/ideology differentiation *is to insist that the chief usefulness of the concept of ideology concerns the critique of domination'* (Giddens 1979, p. 187). This leads to his definition of ideology:

> As I conceptualise it, ideology refers to the *ideological*, this being understood in terms of the capability of dominant groups or classes to make their own sectional interests appear to others as universal ones. Such capability then is one type of resource involved in domination. (ibid., p. 6)[7]

Ideology operates at two different methodological levels according to which different analyses must correspond: a strategic level and an institutional level (see Chapter 5 for a fuller discussion). At the strategic level, ideology involves the 'use of artifice or direct manipulation of communication by those in dominant classes or groups in furthering their sectional interests' (ibid., p. 190). In contrast, at the second, institutional level, ideology involves showing how symbolic orders 'sustain forms of domination in the everyday context of lived experience' so that to study ideology in this way 'is to seek to identify the most basic structural elements which connect signification and legitimation in such a way as to favour dominant interests' (ibid., p. 191).

EVALUATION

Though his work on knowledge and epistemology is far from comprehensive, the important contribution that Giddens has made to the study of knowledge and beliefs, particularly as a result of his emphasis on the central role of hermeneutical analysis in social life, has rightly been acknowledged by many sociological commentators. The concept of the 'double hermeneutic' and its call for the sociologist to adopt a critical standpoint towards the social world can be seen as a complex and nuanced contribution in the debate concerning the role of the sociologist. Giddens's conception of social science as critique is, however, incomplete and shot through with 'confusion and sharp conflicting tendencies' (Bernstein 1989, p. 28). It was noted earlier that the theme of an actor's knowledgeability resonates with a host of political implications. Therefore, the amount of knowledgeability consigned to an actor in social theory is not merely a theoretical or empirical question, but one containing a number of moral and political ramifications. Giddens is clearly aware of this:

> It is an essential emphasis of the ideas developed here that institutions do not just work 'behind the backs' of the social actors who produce and reproduce them. Every competent member of every society knows a great deal about the institutions of that society; such knowledge is not incidental to the operation of society, but is necessarily involved in it. A common tendency of many otherwise divergent schools of sociological thought is to adopt the methodological tactic of beginning their analyses by discounting agents' reasons for their action (or what I prefer to call the rationalization of action), in order to discover the 'real' stimuli of their activity, of which they are ignorant. Such a stance, however, is not only defective from the point of view of social theory, it is one with strongly defined and potentially offensive political implications. It implies a *derogation of the lay actor*. If actors are regarded as cultural dopes or mere 'bearers of modes of production', with no worthwhile understanding of their surroundings or the circumstances of their action, the way is immediately laid open for the supposition that their own views can be disregarded in any practical programmes that might be inaugurated. This is not just a question of 'whose side (as social analysts) are we on?' – although there is no doubt that social incompetence is commonly attributed to people in lower social economic groupings by those in power-positions, or by their associated 'experts'. It is no coincidence that the forms of social theory which have made no or little conceptual space for agents' understanding of themselves, and of their social contexts, have tended greatly to exaggerate the impact of dominant symbol systems or ideologies upon those in subordinate classes: as in Parsons or Althusser. A good case can be made to the effect that only dominant class groups have ever been strongly committed to dominant ideologies ... because all *social actors*, no matter how lowly, have some degree of penetration of the social forms which oppress them. (Giddens 1979, pp. 71–2)[8]

The normative implications that underlie and explain Giddens's championing of knowledgeable human agency also allow us to understand many of his views on epistemology. Following Enlightenment thinking, structuration theory as a critical theory endeavours to extend the bounded, discursive and reflexive penetration of agents into the twin realms of the unacknowledged conditions and unintended consequences of their actions. Its intention is to maximise an agent's knowledge of the unknown conditions (unconscious and tacit knowledge) and consequences of his/her actions, in order to enhance the agent's capacity for self-regulation and political action. Giddens's general sociological aim is a moral-political one, based on a liberal desire to educate through sociological discourse and to create reflexive individual agents who, having recognised their conditions of social reproduction, will subsequently act according to more enlightened ends. As he notes in another context:

> Change in typically established connections tying unacknow-ledged conditions, the rationalisation of action, and unintended consequences, into modes of social reproduction results in potential alteration of the causal relations specified by a law or laws: and such alteration can stem from coming to know about such a law or laws. Once known – by those to whose conduct they relate – laws may become applied as rules and resources in the duality of structure. (ibid., p. 244)[9]

For Giddens, then, the social sciences are characterised by an intrinsically critical aim: the identification and elucidation of the cognitively limiting unacknowledged conditions and unintended consequences of actions as a means of eventually increasing human autonomy and self-regulation.

By introducing a triadic separation of knowledge in terms of unconscious, discursive and practical knowledge, Giddens endeavours to reach an appropriate balance between conceiving agents simply as 'cultural dupes', as they are often represented in structuralism and functionalism, and of seeing agents as excessively knowledgeable, as they are portrayed in phenomenology. His solution is to emphasise practice and practical consciousness, terms that are ubiquitous in Marxism, ethnomethodology and Wittgensteinian philosophy.[10] The main implication of practical con-sciousness is that actors know a great deal more about social life than they can articulate: they possess a tacit and active knowledge of 'how to go on' in social life: what cannot be said is simply done.

Although Giddens's claim that agents possess tacit or practical knowledge is attractive, albeit by no means novel,[11] the precise value of the triadic distinction he makes between unconscious knowledge and practical, discursive knowledge remains unclear. If the unconscious, as he asserts elsewhere (see Chapter 3), includes both agents' desires and their interests, does this mean that agents do *always* not have knowledge of their desires and interests as a basis for their motivations? If this is so, then this markedly detracts from their knowledgeability. His discussion of motivation is also undeveloped, since his singular reference to ontological security (see below) bypasses any sustained discussion of social interests or needs as factors influencing the constitution of social life.[12] Giddens's triadic distinction amounts to the claim that, on the one hand, agents know a great deal more about the social world than they can express, while they know little of their motivations and interests, on the other. However, this claim has negligible empirical backing.[13]

In addition, how Giddens grounds an individual agent's knowledge invokes a problematic concept that runs throughout his entire work: the notion of ontological insecurity. Since this will be discussed in more detail in Chapter 3, it will only be sketched briefly here. According to Giddens, agents possess a largely unconscious basic security system that requires the management and control of tension and anxiety, which is achieved by following routine. Giddens then ties this notion to mutual knowledge:

> In most circumstances of social life, the sense of ontological security is routinely grounded in mutual knowledge employed such that interaction is 'unproblematic', or can be largely taken for granted ... It is not difficult to see why there should be a close relation between the sustaining of ontological security and the routinised character of social life. Where routine prevails, the rationalisation of conduct readily conjoins the basic security system of the actor to the conventions that exist and are drawn upon in interaction as mutual knowledge. (Giddens 1979, p. 219)

Moreover, he adds in respect to the basic security system:

> The 'security of being' which is largely taken without question in most day-to-day forms of social life is thus of two connected kinds: the sustaining of a *cognitively* ordered world of self and other, and the maintenance of an 'effective' order of want management.

> Tensions and ambivalences in motivation can derive from either
> of these sources. (Giddens 1976, p. 118)

There is for Giddens an inherent connection between ontological
security and mutual knowledge, or 'a cognitively ordered world of
self and other'. Moreover, the former is a basis for the latter. Though
the concept of ontological security is derived from Sartre and Laing,
such an argument has many parallels with that of Garfinkel, whose
discussion of breaching and trust Giddens draws on sparingly.
However, rather than basing his explanation on the moral
expectations agents have of one another, as Garfinkel does (see
Heritage 1984, pp. 97–101), Giddens explains the social and cognitive
order in terms of psychological needs based on maintaining routine.
Giddens, like Garfinkel, sees the world as a collective accomplishment, but their respective accounts of how it is accomplished differ.
In contrast to Garfinkel, Giddens offers an individualistic account in
which ontological security instils in individuals a disposition towards
sustaining the everyday lifeworld and its constitutive knowledge. His
account also diverges from Durkheim's, who not only emphasised
our sociality as human beings, but also both authority and experience
as foundations for sustaining forms of knowledge (Durkheim 1976).
In explanatory terms, however, the need to maintain ontological
security offers a very fragile (because individualistic) basis for the
acquisition and sustenance of cognitive order, shared knowledge and
a singular cosmology. Since I will discuss this in more detail in the
next chapter, I will simply assert here that a high degree of collective
uniformity in the social world, despite the multiplicity of beliefs
people hold and the variety and disparate contexts within which
people act on an ongoing basis, cannot be explained by referring to
an individual psychological need for routine. The notion of creating
and maintaining routine in this account is simply taken for granted,
it is *ex post facto*. The willingness of individuals to cooperate, and to
coordinate and continuously align their cognition is a product of
their innately social nature. And it is only on this basis that shared
knowledge and cognitive order can be sustained and transmitted.[14]
A more robust account needs, I think, to re-emphasise the inherent
and active sociality of human beings as a basis for the contingent
development of knowledge instead of looking simply to individual
psychological dispositions to maintain cognitive order.

Furthermore, there are a number of misleading normative
asumptions underlying Giddens's theory of ideology. It was noted

above that Giddens – rightly – moves away from a conception of ideology contrasted with science, to a notion tied to social interests. However, within this conception, he goes on to assert some dubious logical and substantive claims, many of which presuppose a moral-political rather than a straightforwardly sociological grounding. Thus, he argues that 'the chief usefulness of the concept of ideology concerns the critique of domination' (Giddens 1979, p. 119). The implication in the rest of his essay on ideology is not just that beliefs are maintained to suit particular social interests, a plausible enough conception, but the more restricted claim that only dominant social groups have interests in influencing knowledge. Although this claim is logically acceptable, it requires some empirical or theoretical justification. The question of why only dominant groups and not those in subordinate positions have localised interests affecting cognitive claims remains unanswered. This ungrounded theoretical position is re-expressed in his belief that those in subordinate positions possess a 'greater penetration' into the nature of social reality:

> A good case can be made to the effect that only dominant class groups have ever been strongly committed to dominant ideologies. This is not just because of the development of divergent 'subcultures' – for example working-class culture as compared to bourgeois culture in nineteenth-century Britain   but also because all social actors, no matter how lowly, have some degree of penetration of the social forms which oppress them ... *it is not implausible to suppose* that, in some circumstances, and from some aspects, those in subordinate positions in a society might have a *greater* penetration of the conditions of social reproduction than those who otherwise dominate them. This is related to the *dialectic of control* in social systems. (ibid., p. 72; my italics)

Such a view found its consummate expression in Lukacs's notion of the proletariat as the identical subject-object of history, but also more recently in Standpoint Epistemology (Harding 1996). Such an argument is not unfeasible, provided it is based on ontological or epistemological grounds. However, Giddens provides no equivalent logical or empirical warrant for his claim; it remains merely an assertion.

However, the most far-reaching criticisms of Giddens's work on knowledge have to be reserved for the multitude of aporias that pervade his account of epistemology. Giddens's hermeneutic starting point betokens an ontological hiatus between the social sciences and natural sciences. Conciousness, as well as material reality, is constitutive of society; as he notes, 'social beliefs, unlike those to do with nature, are constitutive elements of what it is they are about' (Giddens 1984, p. 340). However, rather than regarding the constitutive role of consciousness as posing an acute dilemma in terms of how to account for the problem of grounding 'true' and 'false' beliefs, Giddens instead regards it as an opportunity to develop his theory of the 'double hermeneutic'. A consequence of the double hermeneutic is that the findings of the social sciences necessarily filter into lay discourse, and this makes it incumbent upon social scientists to maintain a critical posture. As Bernstein (1989, p. 3) rightly argues, however, Giddens confuses 'the issue of the practical consequences of social science on the social world with its critical impact'. Moreover, it is not made clear why the findings of the social sciences *must* filter into lay discourse. Again Giddens provides few empirical examples of the double hermeneutic, though he does cite Machiavelli's theory of the state. However, even in this example, he insists that sociology *may* constitute a *potential* intervention. There is then no logical force behind his claim, only a normative 'ought'. That is, the ideas of social theorists *may* filter down into lay discourse or they may not. Given the current extensive and protracted development of a mental–manual division of labour within modern society, this seems on balance highly unlikely.[15] There is, then, no logical or empirical basis as to why sociological viewpoints must enter into everyday discourse, only Giddens's normative standpoint which steers the argument towards this outcome.

Again, in relation to the double hermeneutic, although Giddens draws upon Bhaskar to support his claim that the discovery of a false belief necessitates a practical intervention with regard to transformative action linked to that belief, he fails to recognise the different epistemological and ontological background which gives Bhaskar's critical realist argument some validity. Thus Bhaskar (1979) argues for the existence of deep structures and, correspondingly, a distinction between essence and appearance. However, although Giddens is generally sympathetic to Bhaskar's work, he does not fully share the latter's view,[16] nor for that matter does he agree with Habermas's attempt to ground theory through reference to an 'ideal speech situation'.[17]

A related difficulty in Giddens's writings on epistemology concerns his attempt at sociological critique through the distinction of 'mutual knowledge' from 'common sense'. Mutual knowledge, which has certain affinities with Schutz's notion of 'stocks of knowledge', exists in a tacit form and conforms closely to Wittgenstein's formulation of knowing a rule. In contrast, however, to the position adopted by theorists such as Wittgenstein, Garfinkel and Winch, such knowledge is not exempt from critical scrutiny. By conceptually imposing a 'methodological bracket', 'mutual knowledge' can be distinguished from 'common sense' and opened up to sociological appraisal:

> It is *only* the methodological bracketing mentioned above that separates mutual knowledge from what I want to suggest can be called 'common sense'. By 'common sense' I refer to the un-bracketing of mutual knowledge: the consideration of the logical and empirical status of belief-claims involved (tacitly and discursively) in forms of life. Common sense *is* corrigible in the light of findings of social and natural science. (Giddens 1984, p. 252, my italics)[18]

However, such a distinction between 'mutual knowledge' and 'common sense' remains opaque and undeveloped. How is it possible, and for that matter what does it mean, to 'un-bracket' mutual knowledge? As Giddens admits, this distinction is largely an analytical one: 'common sense' is 'mutual knowledge', treated not as knowledge but as 'fallible belief'. This however, presupposes an epistemological basis for distinguishing between 'fallible' and 'unfallible' knowledge. Instead of providing such a basis, Giddens flippantly announces that:

> it is particularly at this juncture that a specific epistemological standpoint is presupposed. It presumes, and I presume, that it is possible to demonstrate that some belief claims are false, while others are true, although what 'demonstrate' means here would need to be examined as closely as would 'false' and 'true'. It presumes, and I presume, that internal critique – the critical examinations to which social scientists submit their ideas and claimed findings – is inherent in what social science is as a collective endeavour. I intend to risk the disfavour of the philosophically sophisticated by asserting, without further ado, that I hold these things to be the case. In a different context, however, it would clearly be necessary to defend such contentions at some considerable length. (ibid., p. 340)

This extraordinary evasion of a crucial though difficult question risks disfavour not only from the *corps d'élite* of the philosophically 'sophisticated'. It is striking that Giddens scarcely attempts even the most cursory analysis of the problem. That he can evade such an important question with a few throwaway remarks is one index of the social position he holds as a major social theorist within the academic establishment.[19] Needless to say, despite the prompting of numerous 'differing contexts' and the publication of additional books, Giddens has failed to delineate any comprehensive epistemological basis for his position. One sympathetic commentator, Ira Cohen, attempts to provide a rationale for the failure of Giddens to deal with epistemological issues. Cohen argues that these issues are of little consequence to Giddens, working as he does within a post-empiricist tradition that is more concerned with elaborating a robust social ontology. Giddens's work should instead be read in terms of an 'ontology of potentials' (Cohen 1989, pp. 12–18). Although Cohen is undoubtedly right to argue that there has been a return to questions of ontology in social theory, he fails to acknowledge that, in contrast to Giddens, other writers, such as Bhaskar (1979), have also gone to some length to outline an epistemological basis for their work.[20] Moreover, such a strict separation of ontology and epistemology must be seriously questioned at the outset. Given their intrinsic connection, it seems highly unlikely that it is possible to build a useful sociology solely on ontological premises without relying on epistemological and empirical checks. The lack of an epistemological framework may provide Giddens an opportunity to develop a wide range of ontological themes, but it also provides a green light for metaphysical excesses of the worst sort. I will discuss the sociological implications of such a rationalist detour in Chapter 5.

It may be inferred that Giddens's abstention from developing an epistemological exposition is connected with the difficulty of achieving a foundational critical epistemology whilst simultaneously championing a hermeneutical post-empiricist standpoint. Thus, although Giddens desires a fixed epistemological foundation or Archimedean point from which to generate his critical theory, the uncertainty of achieving such a foundationalism within the context of a post-empiricist philosophy of science which emphasises a constitutive as well as a referential role for knowledge, has hindered such an enterprise. We can examine this dilemma through the prism of the self-fulfilling prophecy as a sociological phenomenon.[21]

SOCIETY AND THE SELF-FULFILLING PROPHECY

In order to explain the difficulty of establishing a foundationalist and critical position within social science, while at the same time stressing the constitutive role of consciousness in social life, it may prove worthwhile to digress from Giddens's work and look to the nature of self-fulfilling prophecy as a sociological phenomenon. Robert Merton begins his justly celebrated paper on 'The Self-Fulfilling Prophecy' (Merton 1957, pp. 475–90) by citing the 'Thomas theorem', according to which, 'if men define situations as real, they are real in their consequences'. For Merton, this illustrates that 'men respond not only to the objective features of the situation, but *also*, and at times primarily, to the meaning this situation has for them' (ibid., p. 475; my italics)

Merton then goes on to expound the now infamous sociological parable concerning the collapse of the Last National Bank, run by Cartwright Millingville. On Black Wednesday, 1932, the Last National Bank, a flourishing institution, is beset by a crisis as the result of a 'false rumour [in its] insolvency'. Due to this false rumour, a belief in the viability of the bank's assets and its solvency is replaced by a belief in its financial unworthiness. For Merton, this initiates 'a run' on the bank and, ultimately, its collapse:

> The stable financial structure of the bank had depended upon one set of definitions of the situation: belief in the validity of the interlocking system of economic promises men live by. Once the depositors had defined the situation otherwise, once they questioned the possibility of having these promises fulfilled, the consequences of this *unreal* definition were real enough. (ibid., p. 476)

This quotation from Merton indicates the way in which the introduction of an 'unreal definition' or false belief into social life creates discordant and chaotic consequences which could have been avoided, had that false belief been prevented from entering into the social framework in the first place. This view is reflected in Merton's definition of the self-fulfilling prophecy:

> The self-fulfilling prophecy is, in the beginning, a *false* definition of the situation evoking a new behaviour which makes the originally false conception *come true*. (ibid., p. 477; my italics)

According to Merton, the consequences of a self-fulfilling prophecy are nearly always tragic. The poignant parable of false beliefs leading to the ruination of a bank can also be used to explain racism against Jews and Blacks.[22] Thus, for Merton, the self-fulfilling prophecy refers to circumstances in which a true or real definition of a social situation is replaced by an alternative false or 'unreal' definition of that situation. This almost always results in the false definition of the situation becoming true. The self-fulfilling prophecy is seen by Merton as a 'nuisance' which engenders troublesome consequences in social life, though not in the world of nature.[23]

In a seriously neglected paper, Daya Krishna (1974) points out that, although Merton recognises that the phenomenon of a self-fulfilling prophecy is peculiar to human affairs, he fails to enquire why this is so. Had he done so, Krishna argues, Merton would have discovered that the natural world is impervious to the meanings and hypotheses which are applied to it (except in the technological sense), whereas the social world is comprised of self-reflective, conscious beings who can become aware of what is thought or postulated about them, and on the basis of which they may alter their original thoughts and actions. It is this self-consciousness which constitutes the condition of possibility of the self-fulfilling prophecy.

Moreover, if the role played by the 'causal power' of beliefs in the constitution of social life is accepted, a substantial difficulty which Merton overlooks becomes apparent. That is, beliefs have consequences in social life, not because they are *true* or *false*, but because they are *beliefs*. Therefore, Merton's argument that self-fulfilling prophecies are only possible in cases in which agents possess a 'false definition' of the situation involves a restricted conception of the self-fulfilling prohecy. This argument is equally applicable to his use of the predicates 'real' and 'unreal' in defining the circumstances characterising the situation of the bank. Furthermore, and this is crucial, it is impossible collectively to define beliefs as true or false (or as real and unreal) when these beliefs do not exist independently of what they refer to in social life, but instead themselves partially constitute that very life. Thus, if a belief in a bank's credit structure is an essential constituent in establishing it as a 'bank' through the notion of a credit and financial structure, it is impossible to designate a competing definition as 'unreal' or 'false', since there is no independent criterion by which to judge it as such – that is, there is no independent index or standard of correctness (Wittgenstein 1969b).

The implications of this view, as Giddens acknowledges, highlight the peculiarity of the social sciences in contrast to the natural sciences. The argument illuminates the fact that consciousness, beliefs or even imaginings enter essentially into the reality studied by the social sciences. This has to be contrasted with the natural sciences, where much of the knowledge produced about 'nature' refers to entities which ultimately remain independent of, or separate from, this knowledge, and thus remain generally unaffected by it.[24] Unlike the knowledge of natural, independently existing objects, the study of self-conscious human beings in the social sciences and, by implication, the study of the social order refers not to entities which are independent of these beliefs, but rather, as Barnes (1988) notes, back to themselves: to social beliefs.[25]

Many positivistic approaches in social theory have failed to acknowledge the problematic nature of ascribing false and true beliefs to actors in social situations. Rather, social relations are somehow seen to exist independently of what is thought about them. In part this mirrors a view of language as referential rather than also as performative or constitutive.[26] As a result, many positivistic approaches concerned with the study of society, such as Merton's, have failed to recognise the crucial role of self-consciousness in regard to the study of social life in comparison with the examination of the world of nature. On the contrary, when the self-consciousness of human actors is acknowledged, it is regarded as a subjective nuisance in contrast to the direct 'objective' observation, which on this view has to replace it.

It is precisely in order to distinguish his position from positivism that Giddens takes as his point of departure the hermeneutic conception of knowledgeable agents. Such a standpoint recognises social beliefs as fundamental components in social life. Thus, in a discussion of self-fulfilling prophecies, Giddens notes that:

> the orthodox consensus was familiar with the mutability of laws in the social sciences in the form of 'self-fulfilling' and 'self-negating prophecies'. But here the relation between the reflexive appropriation of knowledge and the conditions of action is apprehended, first, only as a 'problem' confronting the social investigator; and second, only as affecting the mobilisation of evidence for generalisations, rather than as broaching epistemological issues relevant to the very character of the generalisations themselves. Self-fulfilling or self-negating prophecies, in other words, are seen as predictions

which, by the very fact of their announcement or propagation, serve to create the conditions which render them valid, or alternatively produce the contrary consequence. The 'problem' they pose is that of marginalising the noxious effect which such nuisances have upon the testing of hypotheses. But if the mutable character of all social scientific generalisations is acknowledged, we must conclude that such a standpoint is quite inadequate. Rather than attempting to marginalise, and treat purely as a 'problem', the potential incorp- oration of social scientific theories and observations within the reflexive rationalisation of those who are their 'object' – human agents – we have to treat the phenomenon as one of essential interest and concern to the social sciences. (Giddens 1979, pp. 244–5)[27]

Giddens remains acutely aware of the significance of beliefs in social life and criticises positivistically inclined sociologists for their insufficient attention to beliefs. Thus, he criticises what he calls 'revelatory' naturalistic approaches precisely for promoting the view that a cumulative and 'objective' scientific grasp of an independ- ently existing world is possible. In contrast, Giddens argues that a consequence of the fact that beliefs are partly constitutive of the social world is that the findings of the social sciences often appear trivial or 'already well known and familiar' to lay actors: a phenomenon which he refers to as 'the lay critique of sociology'.[28] However, although Giddens distinguishes his approach from positivistic approaches, he nevertheless still wishes to retain a positivistic foundationalist position on which to base an argument that lay actors can be mistaken about the social reality of which they form a part. He believes that only a foundationalist standpoint permits us to avoid 'a paralysis of the critical will' and allows the possibility of social critique.

Yet, at the same time, Giddens continues to recognise the hermeneutical postulate that since beliefs are partially constitutive of social life, a sociological perspective which allows for a multiplicity of readings and interpretations of social life must also be accepted. As a result, he attempts to forge a standpoint which pursues a middle position between a solid social scientific epistemological foundation and a relativistic view which accepts the importance of the constitutive role of beliefs in social life. Thus he talks of 'firing critical salvoes into reality' or 'moving between a factual and a moral house'.[29] However, although such a middle position is enticing, it is difficult to develop and remains absent from his work. Giddens implies, as he does throughout his work, that there is a 'third way' to be found between an epistemological foundationalism which permits the possibility of sociological critique and a relativism which recognises the constitutive character of beliefs in social life. But he fails to outline such a position, restricting himself instead to a few cavalier remarks concerning epistemology. Hence, Giddens's theoretical hermeneutical starting point, with its emphasis on the knowledgeability of actors, points towards a relativism, while his political position seeks a foundational or 'objective' platform for a social critique. His attempt to marry liberalism with the transformative aspects of socialism expects both: the knowledgeability of actors and social critique.[30] Giddens follows a middle path: a hermeneutical position which is simultaneously critical – the double hermeneutic. Nonetheless, the epistemological basis of this critique remains absent, not least because of the problems involved in attaining to an Archimedean position located outside of the collectively held beliefs of socially and historically embedded actors. In sum, Giddens accepts neither position completely but oscillates between the two.

At times then, Giddens clearly recognises in his epistemology the practical and tacit nature of conciousness and, like Garfinkel, the openness and contingency of knowledge. In some ways his epistemological position dovetails into a conservative thought-style rather than natural law thought-style. As Mannhein notes, the idea of knowledge as something one possesses or owns is part of the bourgeois natural-law style of thought which emerged with seventeenth-century capitalism and private property. Such a reified and fixed or closed notion of knowledge can be contrasted with the conservative approach, which represented knowledge processually as incomplete and provisional. Knowledge is something open and passed through tradition selectively through immersion. It is multiple and fractured, concrete and incommensurable. It is not a tool of reason and reflection, as it had been for the thinkers of the Enlightenment, but a pragmatic part of people's everyday lives and needs. Nor is it an individual possession, but socially shared, albeit hierarchically. In sum, it is not a commodity owned by each individual, but a collective process that is socially negotiated in particular contexts on an ongoing basis. However, despite sharing an elective affinity with the conservative view of knowledge, the overall character of Giddens's epistemology remains within an overwhelmingly individualistic and reified framework. That is, although

Giddens formally acknowledges the social nature of knowledge, in practice he often reverts to an individualistic perspective.

In many respects Giddens's stance on epistemology remains wedded to a subject–object dualism characteristic of much Enlightenment and post-Enlightenment thinking. The Enlightenment position presupposes that, in order to achieve a critical position in social theory the adoption of a foundationalist perspective is necessary (see Hekman 1990). It follows that relativism is incompatible with social critique and that normative judgements, along with all statements classed as knowledge, must be universally grounded (ibid.). However, such a standpoint is mistaken. It is not necessary to hold a foundationalist position in epistemology in order to be critical. To admit that social life is historical does not in itself preclude social and historical criticism if a distinction between epistemological and judgemental relativism is accepted.[31] Moreover, such a distinction itself, as Elias (1987) notes, only becomes possible within definite social and historical conditions with corresponding personality structures.[32]

Conversely, it may be asked whether it is even necessary for sociology to be inherently critical (in the Marxist rather than Kantian sense). The adoption of a critical standpoint has frequently resulted in sociological explanation confusing the world as it 'is' with how it 'ought' to be. It could be argued, therefore, that more 'detached' accounts of the social world are in some ways preferable to theories which overtly refer to themselves as 'critical' in order to avoid an excessively normative bias (Elias 1987). Such accounts would provide an explanatory perspective on the social world and would leave it to the readers of that viewpoint or description to 'decide' its social and political implications. This is brilliantly illustrated in Goffman's (1961) work on asylum, which avoids yielding to normative judgements throughout the explanatory analysis. Yet such a naturalistic analysis contains numerous normative implications. Sociologists could do well to heed Gramsci's remarks, though meant in a different spirit, concerning the 'pessimism of the intellect and the optimism of the will'.

The roots of Giddens epistemological failure are then both political and sociological. With regard to the former, liberal-socialist normative impulses underwrite his epistemology. With reference to the latter, Giddens retains an inadmissable dualism between ontology and epistemology and refuses to establish his ontology within a firmer epistemological framework derived from a sociology of knowledge.

3 Agency

action

How actions are to be understood in terms of intentionality, goals and ends, freedoms and constraints, are issues that are central to philosophical discussion. The concept of action and its correlate, agency, has, however, also remained a central feature of sociological analysis, particularly since the writings of Weber. To what extent social actors create the world or are instead productions of it, how we conceptualise or dissect actions has clear normative implications concerning social change and individual responsibility. As a result of such normative implications, 'agency' remains a 'contested concept' (Gallie 1995).

Central to Giddens's sociology is the emphasis on human beings as active agents. However, as we shall see, despite his claim to provide a sociological account in which a delicate balance between agency and structure is reached, Giddens's agent remains the sovereign autonomous agent of liberalism: one who is both rational and creative. In examining Giddens's conception of actor and agency, it is useful to divide his work into two major areas: (1) the stratification model of consciousness and action; (2) the conception of agency as related to power.

THE STRATIFICATION MODEL OF CONSCIOUSNESS

Giddens develops his account of the actor or agent in order to transcend what he regards as the limitations of previous approaches to the analysis of social action. Both positivistic, structuralist and functionalist accounts of the agent, on the one hand, and accounts rooted in phenomenology and philosophy of action, on the other, are seriously flawed. Positivistic approaches not only 'derogate' lay actors in terms of their knowledgeability, but also posit an overly deterministic account of social life. Actors are seen as unthinking 'cultural dupes' who are the playthings of social forces greater than themselves. Phenomenological approaches, by contrast, although capable of dealing with these criteria of knowledgeability and capability, suffer from a failure to theorise problems concerning institutional analysis, power and the unintended consequences of action, which the former positivistic approaches are able to incorporate. In attempting to synthesise these two approaches, Giddens in the first place initiates a structuralist move away from a 'centred' Cartesian *cogito*, which he believes characterises phenomenological, interpretivist and hermeneutical approaches. He does this by 'decentring' the agent through language:

> To relate the 'I' to agency, it is necessary to follow the detour suggested by structuralists in respect of the decentring of the subject ... The constitution of the 'I' comes about only via the 'discourse of the Other' – that is, through the acquisition of language. (Giddens 1984, p. 43)

Yet, simultaneously Giddens continues to insist on the knowledge-ability and capability of the human agent in order to avoid the objective reductionism of structuralism. The result is what he calls 'a stratification model of the actor'.

For Giddens, an actor's consciousness has three strata. By drawing upon the Freudian triadic schema represented by the id, ego and superego, which he replaces with the concepts of unconsciousness, practical consciousness and discursive consciousness, Giddens seeks a delicate balance between the Scylla of subjectivism and the Charybdis of objectivism. The unconsciousness, like the Freudian id, represents forms of cognition and impulsion which are either fully repressed or appear only partially, though in a refracted manner, in the other forms of practical and discursive consciousness. It is here that the motivational components of action, as well as the seat of memory, reside. These concepts will be discussed shortly. Practical consciousness, a concept that originates in the phenomenological and ethnomethodological traditions, is like the unconscious in that it is not immediately accessible to the discursive conscious awareness of the agent. Instead, practical consciousness represents tacit or 'mutual' knowledge, which is employed in the enactment of courses of conduct providing agents with the ability to 'go on', in terms of rule-following in social life, Finally, discursive consciousness refers to the agent's ability to articulate his knowledge or 'to be able to put things into words' (ibid., p. 45). The relationship between these three strata of consciousness varies, so, although there exists a 'bar' between the unconscious and the practical and discursive consciousness which is expressed through cognitive repression, the line separating the practical consciousness from the discursive consciousness is a 'fluctuating and permeable' one (see Figure 3.1).

Discursive consciousness

\-

Practical consciousness

Unconsciousness

Figure 3.1   Giddens's three strata of consciousness

Source: Giddens (1984, p. 7)

Loosely corresponding to this triadic division of the consciousness, agents are described in terms of reflexive monitoring,
rationalisation and motivation of action. The reflexivity of action
refers to the process whereby individuals reflect upon, monitor and
modify their actions on an ongoing basis and is generally associated
with the domain of discursive consciousness. The rationalisation of
action refers to the process whereby agents 'routinely and for the
most part without fuss, maintain a continuing theoretical understanding of the grounds of their activity' (ibid., p. 5). This is, on the
whole, associated with practical consciousness. Following Garfinkel,
individuals are able to judge one another as 'competent' and
'accountable' in terms of the rationalisations they provide for their
actions. Social action is processional: it unfolds as a continuous flow,
each 'act' overlapping and in part constituting the subsequent act.
Our perception of discrete unconnected units of action is *post hoc*
and results from a Schutzian moment of 'reflective attention' which
breaks into this flow. Agents' rationalisations of action should not,
however, be equated with the discursive giving of reasons for
conduct, though many actors are capable of furnishing such reasons
if asked. Giddens builds upon the standard Enlightenment account
of the human as a rational individual agent and asserts that reasons
should be regarded as causes.

> I propose simply to declare that reasons are causes, accepting that
> this no doubt implies a non-Humean account of causality. More
> properly put, in the terminology I have introduced: the rational-
> isation of action is causally implicated, in a chronic manner, in
> the continuation of day-to-day actions. (ibid., p. 345)

He adds that 'reasons are causes of activities which the individual
'makes happen' as an inherent feature of being an agent' (ibid.).
However, Giddens qualifies this assertion with another. The

Reasons or causes but id agents may not know the reason

individual agent does not necessarily know the reasons for an action and it is here that one has to distinguish the reflexivity and rationalisation of action from its motivation; the latter is found in the unconscious. Motives supply overall plans, or, following Schutz, 'projects' within which a range of actors' behaviour is conducted.[1] Although competent actors are normally able to report their intentions discursively and to provide reasons for acting as they do – even though 'most elements of social practices are not directly motivated' (Giddens 1979, p. 128) – they cannot account for their motives, which always remain opaque.

Giddens substitutes Freudian motivational drives contained within the id with a 'basic security system'. This represents a pre-linguistic mechanism found in the unconsciousness of the agent and established during the early years of childhood. Drawing sparingly upon the work of the ego/object-relations psychologists Erikson, Kardiner and Stack-Sullivan, he argues that the essential function of the basic security system is to generate feelings of trust in the social world, the formation of which requires the provision of predictable and caring routines by parental figures. Repeating Erikson's typology concerning the stages of personality growth from infancy to adulthood, Giddens argues that in all societies the early nurturing of the infant is dominated by the mother figure and focused on the development of the unconscious. The mother provides protection for an infant who exists within an unfamiliar environment. As a result of the infant allowing the mother figure temporarily out of sight, a form of trust is created by the predictability of her return. Giddens ingeniously relates the formation of trust to his time-space analysis: '"Trust" (here conceived as a trait of personality) is understood as psychologically "binding" time-space by an initial awakening that a sense that absence does not signify desertion' (Giddens 1984, p. 53).

Moreover, with time the child becomes more autonomous as he/she learns to adapt to longer and longer absences of the mother. Here, the infant employs what Goffman terms 'protective devices' which extend the autonomy of the infant. In time, the trust–mistrust polarity gives way to the developmentally superior polarity of autonomy versus doubt or shame. This, for Giddens, is expressed through the 'holding on and letting go' phase of childhood. Again, by connecting Erikson with Goffman, Giddens argues that shame in the infant is related to bodily posture which is divided into 'front' and 'back' regions. To avoid the anxiety of shame and embarrassment in social life, a child learns to sustain a 'front'. This stage in turn gives way to a third developmental phase which revolves around the polarity of initiative versus guilt, and is marked by the mastery of syntactically developed language. According to Giddens, the Oedipal transition allows the child to make the move from family to peer relationships as well as to constitute him-/herself as an autonomous 'I'. This, however, can occur only at the cost of the child experiencing repression and forms of anxiety and guilt. These three developmental phases represent a progressive movement towards autonomy for the infant and form the foundation for the reflexive monitoring of action.

The central mechanism employed by an agent in order to avoid anxiety and guilt is routine, which is in turn grounded in the basic security system:

> Routine is integral both to the continuity of the personality of the agent, as he or she moves along the paths of daily activities, and to the institutions of society, which are such only through their continued reproduction. An examination of routinisation, I shall claim, provides us with a master key to explicating the characteristic forms of relation between the basic security system on the one hand and the reflexively constituted processes inherent in the episodic character of encounters on the other. (ibid., p. 60)

As a result of this basic security system, agents aim to maintain a high degree of 'ontological security' by following daily conventions and accepted routines and by avoiding actions which involve radical change:

> Actors' wants remain rooted in a basic security system, largely unconscious and established in the first years of life. The initial formation of the basic security system may be regarded as involving modes of tension management, in the course of which the child becomes 'projected outwards' into the social world, and the foundations of ego-identity created. It seems plausible to suggest that these deep-lying modes of tension management (principally reduction and control of anxiety) are most effective when an individual experiences what Laing calls ontological security ... Ontological security can be taken to depend upon the implicit faith actors have in the conventions (codes of signification and forms of normative regulation) via which, in the duality of

structure, the reproduction of social life is effected. In most circumstances in social life, the sense of ontological security is routinely grounded in mutual knowledge employed such that interaction is 'unproblematic', or can be largely 'taken for granted'. (Giddens 1979, pp. 218–19)

A disruption of routine is inevitably followed by a 'critical situation'[2] whereby the anxiety controlling mechanisms of the basic security system are no longer able to contain feelings of anxiety. This argument draws upon Laing and Garfinkel, but also upon Bettleheim's discussion of the experiences of inmates in the prison camps of Dachau and Buchenwald where prisoners regressed mentally and behaviourally as a result of living through a phase of radical ontological insecurity (Giddens 1979, pp. 125–6).

For Giddens, an agent is an intentional, purposive and, on the whole, rational being who behaves according to what he/she knows or believes will be the outcome of his/her action. Intentional acts, however, often produce consequences for which the agent had not originally accounted. These unintended consequences in turn become for the agent the unacknowledged conditions of future actions. This is represented in Figure 3.2.

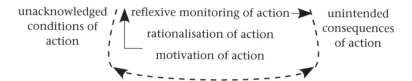

Figure 3.2   The stratification model of action

Source: Giddens (1979, p. 56)

AGENCY AND POWER

Giddens regards the individual agent as an embodied unit possessing causal powers which she may employ by intervening into the ongoing sequence of events-in-the-world: 'I shall define action or agency as the stream of actual or contemplated causal interventions of corporeal beings in the ongoing process of events-in-the-world' (Giddens 1976, p. 75). Furthermore, and this is crucial to Giddens's whole argument, 'it is analytical to the concept of agency that a person [that is, an agent] "could have acted otherwise"' (ibid., p. 76). This contention ties 'agency' to 'power':

> What is the nature of the logical connection between action and power? ... to be able to 'act otherwise' means being able to intervene in the world, or to refrain from such intervention, with the effect of influencing a specific process or state of affairs. This presumes that to be an agent means to be able to deploy (chronically, in the flow of daily life) a range of causal powers, including that of influencing those deployed by others. Action depends upon the capability of the individual to 'make a difference' to a pre-existing state of affairs or course of events. An agent ceases to be such if he or she loses the capability to 'make a difference', that is, to exercise some sort of power. (Giddens 1984, p. 14)

Following Kant he argues that it is the ability 'to act otherwise' (and thereby to 'make a difference') which distinguishes humans from nature. All humans are active agents, and society their achievement, just as ethnomethodologists claim: 'the social world, unlike the world of nature, has to be grasped as a skilled accomplishment of active human subjects' (ibid., p. 155). It follows that an agent ceases to be such if she loses the ability to 'act otherwise'. However, this is rare, since there always exists a 'dialectic of control' built into the very nature of agency.[3] The implication of this dialectic is that all power relations involve the interplay of autonomy and dependence, or a reciprocal and two-way relationship between actors, no matter how asymmetrical the distribution of resources between these individuals.[4] The type case of the dialectic of control is the labour movement, which succeeded in turning a labour contract under which individuals had only their labour power to sell as a commodity, into a resource which could be collectively withheld.

Giddens then attempts to reconcile this freedom of choice and the 'ability to do otherwise' intrinsic to agency with the pattern and predictability which is evident in human social life. He achieves this by arguing that ontological security presses upon agency to invoke routine and pattern to social life. In addition, Giddens highlights various other types of constraint on the individual. In *The Constitution of Society* he highlights three major types of constraints on choice: material constraints which derive from the limits imposed by the physical capacity of the body and features of the physical

environment;[5] constraints deriving from sanctions which are related
to power; and most importantly, structural constraints.

Structural constraints both limit the possibility for action and
appear to the agent as pre-structured enablements associated with
opportunities for action. As a result, such constraints only make sense
when an individual's pre-structured options are taken into account,
that is to say, structural constraints are possible only when the agent's
motives, wants and needs are recognised.[6] This distinguishes
structural constraints from the constraints which operate in nature:

> It is of the first importance to recognise that circumstances of social
> constraint in which individuals 'have no choice' are not to be
> equated with the dissolution of action as such. To 'have no choice'
> does not mean that action has been replaced by reaction (in the
> way in which a person blinks when a rapid movement is made
> near the eyes). This might appear so obvious as not to need saying.
> But some very prominent schools of social theory, associated
> mainly with objectivism and with 'structural sociology', have not
> acknowledged this distinction. They have supposed that
> constraints operate like forces in nature, as if to 'have no choice'
> were equivalent to being driven irresistibly and uncomprehend-
> ingly by mechanical pressures. Even the threat of death carries no
> weight unless it is the case that the individual so threatened in
> some way values life. To say that an individual 'had no choice but
> to act in such and such a way', in a situation of this sort evidently
> means 'Given his/her desire not to die, the only alternative open
> was to act in the way he or she did'. (Giddens 1984, p. 175)

It is on this basis that Giddens interprets references to structured
constraint in the work of Marx:

> Marx says that workers 'must sell themselves' – or, more accurately,
> their labour power – to employers. The 'must' in the phrase
> expresses a constraint which derives from the institutional order
> of modern capitalist enterprise that the worker faces. There is only
> one course of action open to the worker who has been rendered
> propertyless – to sell his or her labour power to the capitalist. That
> is to say, there is only one feasible option, given that the worker
> has the motivation to wish to survive. (ibid., p. 177)

EVALUTION   *Quite good*   *Not so good*

Giddens's theory of <u>social action</u> and of the <u>agent</u> has much to
commend it. It emphasises both the processual and tacit nature of
action and the complex interweave between intended, unintended
and unacknowledged conditions of action. His attempted synthesis
of diverse writers such as Goffman, Garfinkel, Schutz – and seemingly
antipodean philosophical traditions such as Wittgenstein, Bhaskar
and the psychoanalytical traditions of Freud, Erikson and Laing –
has done a considerable service in highlighting major theoretical
problems which still undermine the prospects for a 'general theory'
in sociology. Ultimately, however, the synthesis fails for two reasons.[7]
The first criticism concerns the decentring of the subject and the
stratification model of action and relates to the *knowledgeability* of
the agent; the second criticism concerns the *capability* of the agent.
It is upon these twin pillars that Giddens constructs his theory of
the actor and agency.

THE STRATIFIED AGENT

It was stated at the outset that Giddens undertook a post-Cartesian
critique of subjectivity by embracing what Gustav Bergmann has
called the 'linguistic turn' in philosophy. Thus, Giddens writes:

> the term 'I', whilst seeming to refer to the most essential conditions
> of human subjectivity, is in fact a linguistic term like any other,
> which therefore has to be understood in relation to the remainder
> of the terminology built into language. The 'I' is in linguistic terms
> a shifter, which has no content in relation to its referent any more
> than the term 'tree' has in relation to the object which it 'stands
> for'. (Giddens 1986, pp. 534–5)

Notwithstanding this structuralist decentring, Giddens equally wishes
to avoid yielding to an objectivism in which the subject as a knowing
and capable actor disappears altogether. His solution to this dilemma
is to adopt the concept of practical consciousness drawn from ethnomethodology and from Wittgenstein (see Wittgenstein 1958; also
Polanyi 1967), and to stress that an agent is capable of 'always doing
otherwise'.

Giddens, in contrast to post-structuralist thinkers, holds that
meaning cannot be traced to a referent or to a system of differences

which constitutes languages as a semiotic system, but only to the methodological apparatus contained in practical consciousness embedded in ethnomethods or in the routines in everyday life. As a result, the agent is reintroduced as a knowledgeable actor rather than as a passive unknowing effect of discourse.[8] Although Giddens correctly counterposes Wittgensteinian philosophy to post-structuralism in his analysis of subjectivity and meaning, his work on this area is far from unambiguous. For Wittgenstein – who represents, as I shall later argue, a more conservative style of thought – meaning and subjectivity are rooted in collective social practices such that the actor becomes fully decentred in social interactions. However, Giddens often reverts to a theory of a centred abstract agent, particularly in his discussions of rule-following (for a fuller discussion see Chapter 5) but also in relation to his analysis of agents as acting, choosing individuals who 'exercise' autonomy. In these discussions the social negotiation of constraint generally disappears. Such a centred agent is also implicit in Giddens's use of Erikson's rigid and unhistorical developmental schema to characterise an agent's maturation.

Wagner (1993) makes a similar point in his critique of Giddens on subjectivity. Giddens's work, he argues, reverts to a classical conception of identity in which there exists a subjective presence prior to and removed from all play of difference.[9] Although Wagner regards this is a result of Giddens's use of Heidegger's notion of *Dasein* as a starting point for his work, I think a more adequate interpretation of this position would see it as an effect of Giddens's unwillingness to abandon the subject completely *à la* (post-) structuralism, given that to do so would militate against his political and ethical liberalism. This political standpoint requires a knowledgeable, freely acting and self-determining agent. In his comments on Foucault, Giddens notes his wariness in relation to dissolving individuals into discourses:

> That 'history has no subject' can be readily accepted. But Foucault's history tends to have no active subjects at all. It is history with the agency removed. *The individuals who appear in Foucault's analyses seem impotent to determine their own destinies.* (Giddens 1987, p. 98; my italics)

In addition, by introducing a stratified conception of an agency, Giddens aims to produce a precarious, though delicate, balance between three forms of consciousness. However, rather than resulting

in a successful synthesis, his merging of Freud's and Erikson's use of
the unconscious with Wittgenstein's concept of practical consciousness, and these in turn with Habermas's employment of discursive
consciousness, yields a conception of personality that both lacks
depth and is highly formalistic in its characterisation of the relation
between the three spheres of consciousness. This is partly the result
of his decontextualised use of these concepts from the broader theory
within which they take on meaning and explanatory force. For
example, the Freudian psychology which Giddens draws upon
embodies a tense and explosive view of the unconscious – in which
libidinous drives constantly seek satisfaction and therefore often
disrupt the balance between ego and superego. Giddens's albeit
modified use of the Freudian unconscious is tame and undynamic
in comparison, and lacks the latter's explanatory power (Craib 1992).
The same applies to practical and discursive consciousness and to
their broader use in the work of Wittgenstein and Habermas
respectively.

Moreover, as was noted in the previous chapter, how or whether
motives enter into discursive or practical consciousness remains
unclear. If an agent's motives are unconscious, the knowledgeable
agent which Giddens champions is greatly compromised. In addition,
if these unknown motives are only biologically based, in terms of
the agent's basic security system, then what role do social factors
play in influencing or motivating actions? Finally, if, as Giddens
suggests, 'most actions are not directly motivated' then what
motivates them or how do they arise?

Overall, and despite his intentions to the contrary, Giddens's
discussion of the psychological structure of the individual agent tends
to remain within a discursive field that is disconnected from his
analysis of social structures. Rather than explaining how social
structures are lived through the psyche, through emotions and
various cultural identifications, the individual psyche follows its own
developmental logic. There is a failure to systematically analyse the
relationship between the structure of the personality and the social
structure other than by vague references to Erikson's work. As a result,
it appears that the steering of the individual by the unconcious
impulses of the ontological security system has a form and destiny
of its own, independently of the broader shifting social relations
which it undoubtedly informs. The individual basic security system
remains socially unprocessed and without a history; it has no
connection with the socio-genesis of structural social relations. As

Elias (1994, p. 488) rightly notes, 'a real understanding, even of the changes of ideas and forms of cognition, can be gained only if one also takes into account the changes of human interdependencies in conjunction with the structure of conduct'. This is equally the case with the relationship between the discursive consciousness, practical consciousness and the unconscious. Though the relationship between the former two fluctuates, the relations between all three concepts generally remain rigid and fixed with little psychogenetic analysis of their shift. This produces exactly the dualism which it is designed to avoid.

Free or determined action?

A further problem vitiating Giddens's conception of action stems from his definition of agency as the 'ability to do otherwise'. In recent sociological literature, the meaning of the concept of agency is usually derived by contrasting it with the idea of social structure. To the extent that individuals are said to have agency, they are capable of acting independently of, and in opposition to, structural constraints and may (re)constitute social structures through their freely chosen actions. The converse implication is that a human being without agency would be an automata whose action was determined by external social structures. Dawkins's metaphor of organisms as lumbering robotic vehicles for genes comes closest to such a perspective, although in this case the biological structures (genes) are internal to the organism, if external to consciousness. Through the issues it raises, the debate on agency resonates with a host of other important moral and political questions. The notion of a freely acting individual has occupied a central place in classical liberal theory since the late sixteenth and early seventeenth centuries. It is also, of course, a central tenet of capitalism. Equally, 'free' agents, capable of transforming their surroundings through active intervention, can be of theoretical value in the context of a socialist politics.[10]

Indeed, it is these political ramifications which underlie and explain Giddens's theory of agency. We can develop this argument by comparing his work to that of Talcott Parsons. In *The Structure of Social Action* (1937), Parsons set out what became a key reference point for all further analyses of action within social theory. Central to the analysis was his account of a 'unit act':

1. The act implies an agent, an actor.
2. The act must have an end, a future state of affairs toward which the action is orientated.

3. The act must be initiated in a situation in which intervening action is necessary to bring about the state of affairs which is the agent's end. This situation can in turn be broken down into two kinds of elements: those over which the actor has no control and those over which he/she has control. The former are the conditions of action and the latter the means of action.
4. The means and ends of action are to be understood by reference both to *individual* factors (wants or need dispositions in the case of ends, individual rational calculations in the case of means), and to a *social, normative* element involved in their constitution.

We can begin by examining the first *three* aspects of the 'unit act'. The agent seeks to realise ends in a situation in which given material conditions are to be taken into account and possible physical means of realising the ends are available. The situation in many ways mirrors a rational-choice account and Parsons refers to it as a 'utilitarian' approach. But Parsons regarded such an approach as 'reductive'. The ends or wants which prompt action here, whilst internal to the individual body, are nonetheless *external* to the individual's acting self or ego and operate causally upon it. The result is not true action, but rather something analogous to animal behaviour in that it is determined and not chosen (see Figure 3.3).

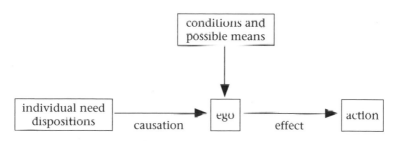

Figure 3.3   Utilitarian approach to the explanation of action

Source: Loyal and Barnes (2001, p. 509).

Parsons was not only intuitively averse to a 'reductive' utilitarian approach to the explanation of action, but he had a powerful argument against it: if 'egoistic' ends caused actions, there could be no social order such as we manifestly observe. Here he cited Hobbes's famous argument, that human beings who act simply to fulfil egoistic desires will merely produce 'a war of all against all'. Such a state of war can be overcome only if individual egoism is overridden. Evidently, that egoism is overridden – but by what? At this point the fourth aspect of action mentioned by Parsons enters: the agent has a 'normative orientation': he/she acts according to social norms as well as to individual desires.

Parsons believed that shared norms and values were internalised by the individual during socialisation and subsequently constituted an alternative basis for action to that offered by individual desires. In so far as a significant amount of action was oriented to social norms rather than to individual desires, a social order could be enacted and a Hobbesian war avoided. The individual, caught between the urges of egoism and the prompting of internalised norms (both internal to the individual but external to the acting self or ego), had only to act sufficiently often in relation to the latter for Hobbes's problem to be solved.

How individual ends and social norms press upon the centre of action in the individual could perhaps be represented by a simple extension of the initial illustration as in Figure 3.4, wherein the actor is caused to act in the way required by the stronger of two opposing pressures.

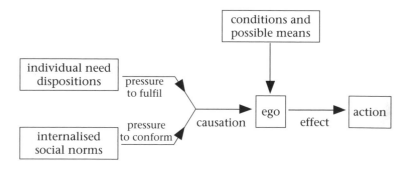

Figure 3.4   Utilitarian approach with normative orientation

Source: Loyal and Barnes (2001, p. 510)

Nevertheless, the idea of the individual acting in the direction of the 'stronger' cause is just as 'reductive' as that of the individual acting in response to a single cause, and Parsons preferred instead to represent matters as in Figure 3.5:

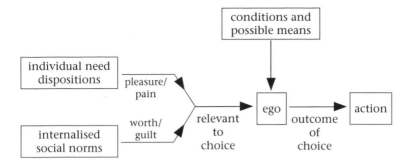

Figure 3.5   Parsons's voluntaristic theory of action

Source: Loyal and Barnes (2001, p. 511)

Figure 3.5 summarises Parsons's *voluntaristic* theory of action. While adding social norms to individual ends as factors impinging on action, Parsons took the opportunity to change the relationship between the factors and the action from one of causation to one of choice. The actor *cannot* choose the pains and pleasures associated with action, but *can* choose how far to take account of them when acting. Naturally, as the pain of deviating from norms increases, the actor will choose conformity more frequently, but it is choice nonetheless which results in action. Action is now voluntary, not determined, with the choosing agent placed between two kinds of pressure: action must always be thought of as involving a state of tension between two different orders of elements, the normative and the conditional (Parsons 1937, p. 732).

Parsons recognised, of course, that individual actors are moved to conform to norms by both external and internal pressures. The sanctions of others will also press upon the individual to conform to norms. But these sanctions are secondary and derivative supports of the normative order and have no independent significance.[11] Thus, in the last analysis, for Parsons, the amount of action generated in conformity with a norm will vary according to how strongly and extensively the norm is internalised, how strong the desire to realise individual ends which oppose it, and how much work and effort is entailed in conforming to the norm. According to his voluntaristic account (Figure 3.5), people will freely choose how to act whilst taking all of these factors into account. However, each factor can also be thought of bearing on action as *causes*, with what is actually done being determined as that which maximises the net cost-benefit of action, as in Figure 3.4. And, above all, there is no evident means of distinguishing the account implicit in Figure 3.4 from that implicit in Figure 3.5. Although Parsons could have asserted freedom of will and denied outright the predictability of action in order to avoid a reductive account of action, instead he systematically linked action to two antecedents: individual ends and social norms. Parsons wanted choice but he wanted predictability as well. And to maintain choice, he denied that ends and norms, the predictive factors in this scheme, were *causal* factors, the result of which would *determine* action. Instead he gave a (functionally equivalent) account of ends and norms as factors in relation to which actions are 'chosen'. But no fact of the matter will allow a distinction between this voluntaristic account and a causal one. Indeed, the many critics of Parsons who have read his account as a causal one are correct at least in this: there is no sociologically interesting difference between his voluntarism and a causal equivalent such as that represented in Figure 3.4. The tension between ends and norms in inspiring action may therefore be represented either voluntaristically or causally without implications for Parsons's basic sociological purposes. Nor is an understanding of deviance, social change, conflict or any of the other phenomena commonly held to cause difficulties for Parsons's account, affected by which alternative is selected.

In his theory of structuration, Giddens has argued that Parsons's 'voluntaristic' theory of action is in truth merely a version of determinism.[12]

> The use of the term 'voluntarism' suggests that Parsons wished to try and build into his own approach a conception of the actor as a creative, innovative agent, thus seeking to break with schemes in which human conduct is not conceptually differentiated from the explanation of the movement of objects in nature. For Parsons the very same values that compose the consensus universal, as 'introjected' by actors, are the motivating elements of personality. If these are the 'same' values, however, *what leverage can there possibly be for the creative character of human action as nominally presupposed by the term 'voluntarism'?* Parsons interprets the latter concept as referring simply to 'elements of a normative character'; the 'freedom of the acting subject' then becomes reduced – and very clearly so in Parsons' mature theory – to the need-dispositions of personality. In the 'action frame of reference', 'action' itself

enters the picture only within the context of an emphasis that sociological accounts of conduct need to be complemented with psychological accounts of 'the mechanisms of personality'; *the system is a wholly deterministic one.* Just as *there is no room here for the creative capacity of the subject on the level of the actor,* so there is a major source of difficulty in explaining the origins of transformations of institutionalised value-standards. (Giddens 1976, pp. 95–6; my italics)

This, however, is an inaccurate picture of Parsons's theory: it makes no mention of *effort*; nor does Giddens acknowledge the gap between acting in one of the many ways which conform to a norm, and being completely determined by it; nor is there any attention to the differences (represented above in Figures 3.4 and 3.5) between causation and the conditioning of choice on which Parsons places so much emphasis.

The above passage, however, provides an insight into the nature of what is in effect Giddens's own voluntarism. Giddens characterises the power of agents to intervene as a transformative capacity. Such a view suggests that the power to intervene amounts to a power to bring about social change or transformation. But, of course, this power might be equally well used to intervene in a situation that otherwise would change in order to maintain it. Hence what Giddens calls 'transformative capacity' could equally well be called 'stabilising capacity'. It covertly implies connection between activity and change, and, correspondingly, between passivity and stability. It is notable of course, in addition, that an individual power to intervene is only rarely a power to transform – transformation often requires a number of individuals acting together. There also remains a collective action problem in Giddens's account.

It appears that Giddens wants people to have choice because he wants them to be capable of effecting change in the existing order of things. He thinks that only a 'voluntaristic' theory, one that is stronger and more comprehensive than Parsons's, will permit him this capacity. Following the ethnomethodologists, Giddens allows his agents discretion over what in Parsons's view presses upon them (and, as Giddens sees it, determines what they do): agents can exercise discretion with regard to norms and rules. But in thus asserting the freedom of agents both from direct determination by rules/norms and from the guilt feelings inspired by rules/norms which, according to Parsons, constrain and press upon choice,

Giddens casts aside all the predictive/explanatory features of Parsons's theory. However, Giddens does recognise that routine rule-following is indeed very much the most common form of human action and acknowledges the need to account for why this is so.

Here Giddens faces just the same problem as Parsons had faced earlier: that of reconciling choice, with pattern and predictability in human action. His solution is, formally, the same as Parsons's. Giddens draws on the concept of *ontological security*. Just as norms press on choice in Parsons, so ontological security presses upon choice for Giddens. Just as for Parsons an action may be understood as the result of a choice based on the avoidance of the pain of guilt, so it may be understood for Giddens as a choice made to avoid the anxiety of ontological insecurity. And, just as a direct causal impact of norms is an alternative formulation to Parsons, so the need for security is an alternative to Giddens's account. Like Parsons, Giddens's sociology is 'complemented with psychological accounts of "the mechanisms of personality"' (Giddens 1976, p. 96).

As a result, Giddens ends up with a theory which is formally identical to Parsons's voluntaristic position. His theory starts with an insistence on choice, and then, in order to allow for patterns and predictability in action, introduces constraints on choice – factors which render intelligible the fact that choices will be of one kind rather than another. The account of constrained choice in Parsons was indistinguishable in its empirical implications from an account of directly (causally) constrained action (see Figures 3.4 and 3.5). The same kind of alternative formulation can be made of Giddens: that needs – notably the need for ontological security – and, similarly, constraints – notably the constraints of structure – may operate upon human beings in a causal sense, with action being understood as the effect of the overall impact of all the various causes. Indeed, there is no formal difference here between Giddens (or Parsons) and mundane rational choice theory, which quite explicitly uses the language of choice to describe human actions as in principle highly predictable.[13] These approaches share a conception of agency characterised in terms of the powers of independent human beings. That is, they embody a metaphysical individualism in their accounts.

Giddens speaks of actions which 'could be otherwise' in order to stress how actions are never wholly determined by 'structural constraints', but few sociologists have in any case ever believed in *complete* determination of this kind, and this position is readily opposed by the view that, if structural constraints exist, they merely

(handwritten margin notes: "Giddens position", "tending towards determinism")

feature among the many necessary causes of action rather than counting as sufficient causes of it. There are also times where Giddens adopts a rationalistic approach close to that of Habermas, and treats reasons as having the potential to inspire 'creative and innovative actions' which depart from routine. But it is perfectly possible to think of being given a reason to act as a causal intervention: if an agent is told that there is cyanide in the water and as a result does not drink it, it might be said that the proffered reason made him/her choose not to drink, or alternatively that the given reason caused him/her not to. Again, to what extent the agent 'could have done otherwise' in the given circumstances, having been told about the cyanide, is unclear and not amenable to empirical investigation.

Both Parsons and Giddens espouse choice/agency and oppose determinism with much the same kind of end in view, one that is not sociological in a narrow sense. Parsons seeks an actor capable of struggling against self-interest and 'animal' drives. Analogously, Giddens needs an actor capable of struggling against the status quo and its constituent routines. The intention is to produce a sociologically realistic yet politically optimistic picture of the human condition. However, evidence for such a picture, and in particular for the role of agency within it, is not supplied. There is no need for assertions of choice and/or agency here in order to be sociologically realistic. It is perfectly possible to produce empirically plausible accounts of the relationship between actions and self-interest or the social status quo without using such a vocabulary (Davidson 1980). Nor is this vocabulary especially appropriate to the expression of political optimism and the conviction that human beings may act in ways which overcome external pressures and restraints. A voluntaristic style of discourse may suit the liberal socialism of Giddens, but it has equally suited the objectives of repressive political and religious regimes which have sought to constrain their 'subjects' precisely by stressing their freedom of action and rendering them responsible and accountable for their actions – in some cases with their lives. Conversely, fully causal accounts of action, for example those in the various theological doctrines of predestination and divine determination, have been adopted by collectives concerned precisely with ignoring and contravening the authority of Church and state, and even with actively opposing and overthrowing them. Through and beyond the Reformation it suited creative and resourceful opponents of the political and institutional status quo to hold that, of themselves, they could not have acted otherwise.

There is no one-to-one exclusive correspondence between the characterisation of action as either 'voluntaristic' or 'determined' and its political and social accountability. When a human being acts, it may be regarded *either* as the implementation of choice *or* as the effect of a cause. Any action can be understood either according to the vocabulary of the institution of responsible and chosen action, or according to the vocabulary of the institution of causal or determined action. While there may exist obvious patterns with respect to the manner in which lay individuals use the two institutions (Barnes 2000, Loyal and Barnes 2001), there is no fact of the matter which serves to make sense of these patterns.[14] Notions of voluntarism and determinism refer to invisible theoretical entities – to beliefs and internal, inaccessible psychological states or powers – with no explicitly recognisable signs or indicators for their hidden existence. There is no empirical 'fact of the matter' with which to distinguish the two accounts. It is not possible to examine the antecedents of actions and find a feature of 'caused' actions that is not similarly possessed by 'chosen' actions. It is because of this that a number of Giddens's critics have concluded that his conception of structuration is too voluntaristic (Layder 1981, Archer 1982, Callinicos 1989, Clegg 1989), whilst others have seen it as overly deterministic (Bertillson 1984, Thompson 1989).

Given the problem of distinguishing voluntarist and determinist accounts of action, it may be more useful for sociologists to examine what gets done in and through such discourses; how, through communicative interaction, interdependent human beings regulate and coordinate their conduct and align their cognition and understanding in everyday life. Such a sociological viewpoint was established by Wright-Mills (1940) and has recently been taken further by Barnes (2000; see also Manis and Meltzer 1967). This approach redescribes voluntary actions naturalistically within an idiom of causation, yet in line with a compatibilist account, also acknowledges everyday uses of agency. As profoundly social interdependent actors, individuals draw on discourses of voluntarism and choice in order to assign rights and responsibilities to each other as independent moral entities. Not only does this standpoint reintroduce the importance of the modality of the social for sociological analyses of agency, but it is also grounded empirically.

4 Social Structure

In sociology the concept of social structure has had a varied, vague and shifting use. According to Lemert (1997, p. 127), generally speaking, structures have at least two defining characteristics: they 'make order out of some set of things' and this order has a degree of permanence. In sociology structures were usually conceived as objective features of social organisation which exist independently of social actors' cognitive beliefs and to some extent they shape and determine their conciousness and action (Rubinstein 1986). Structure was seen as external to, independent of and determinant upon, a freely acting agent. Many sociological approaches had, as a result, unwittingly affirmed the object over the subject, structure over agency, society over the individual, or determinism over free action. The overall effect was a 'derogation of the lay actor' in which social agents were reduced to unthinking 'cultural dupes' or passive, derivative effects of adamantine social structures. In his theory of structuration, Giddens reconceptualises structure in order to remedy its problematic dualistic sociological usage.

STRUCTURE

According to Giddens, the three prior theoretical applications of the term 'structure' – in functionalism, Marxism and structuralism – are all problematic. The orthodox functionalist approach defined structure either in terms of the law-like regularities which govern the behaviour of social facts, or as the aggregated patterning of social behaviour over time. In functionalism structure was generally understood descriptively, often in terms of visual analogies such as that of the girders of a building or the anatomy of a body. This denotation of structure deferred any explanatory role to the concept of function. When the two concepts of structure and function were combined they were referred to by 'system', often conceived in terms of a biological or organic analogy.

By contrast, Marxist approaches tended to retain an explanatory role for patterned social relationships, though there were often functionalist hybrids such as in the work of Althusser. An inevitable result of both usages was, for Giddens, the creation of a dualism in which

71

structure came to be regarded as both external to human agency and constraining upon it. As he notes: '[s]uch conceptions are closely connected to the dualism of subject and social object: "structure" here appears as "external" to human action, as a source of constraint on the free initiative of the independently constituted subject' (Giddens 1984, p. 16).

Interesting

Structuralism offered a fundamentally different understanding of 'structure' to both of these theoretical frameworks. As in Marxism, structure was accorded an explanatory role, though this was not in terms of the causal power of social relationships but premised upon the idea of transformation. For Lévi-Strauss, drawing on the Saussurian distinction between *langue* and *parole*, structure could be mapped by constructing models which penetrated beneath the surface manifestations of society to reveal its underlying codes or ordered relations. In this usage structure represents a shift from patterned and relatively permanent sets of social relationships to abstract models in the form of binary oppositions and dual relations which lived in and through human beings. In addition, structure did not exist in time and space, but only in terms of relations of presence and absence. This approach, however, is also problematic since there remains an 'ambiguity as to whether structures [refer] to a matrix of admissible transformations within a set or to rules of transformation governing the matrix' (ibid., p. 17).

structure collated with language

In addition to the above, all three approaches also share three major difficulties: firstly, the commitment to a distinction between synchrony and diachrony; secondly, the preoccupation with 'systems' as well as 'structures'; and finally, the failure to deal adequately with human agency.[1]

Despite these problems Giddens draws upon all three perspectives.[2] Structuralism in particular he argues, provides a 'more interesting' notion of structure 'as an intersection of presence and absence' through its Saussurian distinction between *parole* (the speech of the actor) and *langue* (the language structure drawn upon). Giddens then proceeds to present his own novel definition of structure by collating it with language:[3]

> An approach to the analysis of structures in sociology can be made by comparing what I will now simply call 'speech' (action and interaction) with 'language' (structure) the latter being an abstract 'property' of a community of speakers. (Giddens 1976, p. 118)

He adds:

(a) Speech is 'situated', i.e. spatially and temporally located, whereas language is, as Ricoeur puts it, 'virtual and outside of time'.

(b) Speech presupposes a subject, whereas language is specifically subject-less – even if it does not 'exist' except in so far as it is 'known' to, and produced by, its speakers.

(c) Speech always potentially acknowledges the presence of another. Its relevance as facilitating communicative intent is fundamental, but it is also the intended medium, as Austin makes clear, of a whole host of other 'illocutionary effects'; (natural) language as a structure, on the other hand, is neither an intended product of any one subject, nor orientated towards another. (ibid., pp. 118–19)   *Wittgenstein may not agree.*

In this formulation, structures like language are 'virtual' since they exist 'outside of time and space', are 'subject-less', and for the most part, are unintentionally reproduced. By comparing structure with language, Giddens introduces a social, contextual and generational relationship which is analogous to that between speech and language. Just as language is a structure which forms a condition of possibility for speech (agency), so more generally social structure provides the conditions of possibility for social action. By using this analogy, Giddens believes he achieves three things. Firstly, structure is no longer simply constraining but is also enabling. With language, structure not only limits speech in terms of syntax, but also permits the generation of that speech – it both enables and constrains, in the same way that social structures enable/constrain social action. Hence '[s]tructure thus is not to be conceptualised as a barrier to action, but as essentially involved in its production' (Giddens 1979, p. 70).

In the second place, structure is both the medium *and* the outcome of action. What Giddens labels 'the duality of structure' involves a movement from a dualistic rendering of structure as independent of agency to a duality in which it is integral to agency: 'structure is both medium and outcome of the reproduction of practices ... and "exists" in the generating moments of this constitution' (ibid., p. 5). Giddens is thereby able to argue that every act of social production is simultaneously an act of reproduction. Structure and agency form two sides of the same coin. Hence, the 'instantiation' of structure concurrently draws upon and reproduces structure in a manner akin to the way a speech act draws upon and reproduces the totality of language. Structure is the mode in which the relation between the moment and the totality expresses itself in social reproduction, a process of recursivity:

> The differences that constitute structures, and are constituted structurally, relate 'part' to 'whole' in the sense in which the utterance of a grammatical sentence presupposes the absent corpus of syntactical rules that constitute the language as a totality. The importance of this relation of moment and totality for social theory cannot be exaggerated, since it involves a dialectic of presence and absence which ties the most minor or trivial forms of social action to structural properties of the overall society (and, logically, to the development of mankind as a whole). (ibid., p. 71)

Thirdly, Giddens moves away from a fixed and mechanical conception of 'structure' to one which emphasises fluidity and process and dissolves the dichotomy between statics and dynamics.[4] Having defined the form of structure, Giddens goes on to reveal its content:

> By the term 'structure' I do not refer, as is conventional in functionalism, to the descriptive analysis of the relations of interaction which 'compose' organisations or collectivities, but to systems of generative rules and resources. (Giddens 1976, p. 127)

In a later work on structuration, this conception is broadened, by drawing on Derrida's notions of presence and absence and by tying them to the concepts of space and time:

> As I shall employ it, 'structure' refers to 'structural property', or more exactly, to 'structuring property', structuring properties providing the 'binding' of time and space in social systems. I argue that these properties can be understood as rules and resources, recursively implicated in the reproduction of social systems. Structures exist paradigmatically, as an absent set of differences, temporally 'present' only in their instantiation, in the constituting moments of social systems ... as involving a 'virtual order' of differences. (Giddens 1979, p. 64)

A cluster of related concepts are also introduced, the most important of which is the social system. This is expected to do 'much of the work that "structure" is ordinarily called upon to perform' (Giddens 1984, p. 18). 'Social system' therefore designates what functionalists and Marxists had formerly referred to as patterned social relations. In contrast to structures, social systems have a 'real' existence in time-space and are empirically manifest in 'the situated activities of human agents':

> Social systems, by contrast to structure, exist in time-space, and are constituted by social practices. The concept of social system, understood in its broadest sense, refers to the reproduced interdependence of action: in other words, to 'a relationship in which changes in one or more component parts initiate changes in other component parts, and these changes, in turn, produce changes in the parts in which the original changes occurred'. The smallest type of social system is dyadic. (Giddens 1979, p. 73)

Structure and system relate to each other through social practices:

> Social systems involve regularised relations of interdependence between individuals and groups, that typically can be best analysed as *recurrent social practices*. Social systems are systems of interaction; as such they involve the situated activities of human subjects, and exist syntagmatically in the flow of time. Systems in this terminology, have structures, or more accurately, have structural properties; they are not structures in themselves. Structures are necessarily (logical) properties of systems or collectivities, and are characterised by the 'absence of a subject'. To study the structuration of a social system is to study the ways in which that system, via the application of general rules and resources, and in the context of unintended outcomes, is produced and reproduced in interaction. (ibid., pp. 65–6)

Structuration refers to the dynamic process whereby structures come into being and are reproduced recursively through social practices via the duality of structure. They are subject-less memory traces, which possess a 'virtual' existence consisting of rules and resources which 'bind' time-space. Social systems, on the other hand, manifest themselves empirically as regularised patterns of interaction constituting the effects of these generative rules and resources.

Seen as rules and resources, structures can be divided into three main categories: signification, domination and legitimation. In the course of interaction, actors draw upon all three categories through various corresponding 'modalities': interpretative scheme, facility and norm, respectively. These modalities mediate between the aforementioned structural categories and interactional categories consisting of communication, power and sanction. This is represented in Table 4.1.

Table 4.1   Modalities of structuration

Interaction	Communication	Power	Sanction
(Modality)	Interpretive scheme	Facility	Norm
Structure	Signification	Domination	Legitimation

Source: Giddens (1979, p. 82).

The concepts on the first line refer to properties of interaction, those on the second to modalities and those on the third to properties of structures. During interaction, actors draw on the modalities of structuration, which in turn simultaneously reconstitute structure. The communication of meaning in interaction involves the use of the structure of signification, interpolated by the modality of interpretative schemes as standardised elements of stocks of knowledge. By contrast, the use of power in interaction involves drawing upon the structure of domination which is mediated through the modality of facility. Finally, morality in interaction draws upon the structure of legitimation mediated by the modality of norms. Although this appears to be a rigid and rather formal scheme, not wholly unlike the Parsonian position that he criticises, Giddens argues that it should be only used analytically and that actual social practice combines all three elements in different ways.

RULES AND RESOURCES

In his earliest, albeit brief, statements concerning rules in the *New Rules of Sociological Method* (1976), Giddens claims that his analysis of rule following can 'generally [be] treated in the manner of Wittgenstein's analysis of rule following':

That is to say, to know a rule is not to be able to provide an abstract formulation of it, but to know how to apply it in novel circumstances, which includes knowing about the contexts of that application. (ibid., p. 124)

He does not, however, adopt Wittgenstein's insights wholesale. Wittgenstein, Giddens argues, had argued that children playing games represented the archetypal example of how rules in social life are generally followed. Giddens questions Wittgenstein's use of game analogies. According to Giddens, game analogies are inappropriate because games contain boundaries which are 'clearly delimited and unquestioned'. By contrast, only a few social practices, such as rituals and ceremonials, possess such a '"closed" character': '... most rule-systems must not be assumed to be like this. They are less unified; subject to chronic ambiguities of "interpretation", so that their application or use is *contested*, a matter of *struggle*' (ibid.). All rules embody struggle and conflict which require an examination of resources as 'vehicles' of power. I will return to this below.

In his next work on structuration, Central Problems in Social Theory (1979), Giddens builds upon his earlier remarks concerning rules. Rules or resources should not be regarded as 'aggregates of isolated precepts or capabilities', such as, for example, those rules governing the queen's move in chess, because

> [t]here is not a singular relation between 'an activity' and 'a rule' ... Activities or practices are brought into being in the context of overlapping and connected sets of rules. Rules cannot be described or analysed in terms of their own content, as prescriptions ... because [they] only exist in conjunction with one another. (ibid., p. 65)

Rather than correlating rules with games which possess fixed boundaries (chess, for example), it is, according to Giddens, more illuminating to look at Wittgenstein's references to children's games as an index of social practices since these lack formal properties. To know a rule, 'as Wittgenstein says, is to know "how to go on", to know how to play according to the rule' (ibid., p. 67). By allowing individuals to 'go on', rules imply 'methodological procedures' of social interaction. Here Garfinkel's conception of interpretative work and accountability is important:

What Garfinkel calls 'ad hoc' considerations – the 'etcetera clause',
'let it pass', etc [sic] – are chronically involved in the instantiation of rules, and are not separate from what those rules 'are'.
(ibid., p. 68)

In his model, Giddens connects rules with practices, so that rules
generate – or are the medium of the production and reproduction
of – practices. They are not generalisations of what people do but
rather the medium which allows them to act. Rules and practices
remain ontologically distinguishable: 'a routine practice is not a rule'.
(Giddens 1984, p. 19).

Giddens also rejects a distinction derived from Kant, between
'constitutive' and 'regulative' rules, claiming instead that all rules
possess both of these aspects: those relating to the constitution of
meaning, semantic rules; and those relating to the sanctioning of
conduct, moral rules, or norms. However, semantic rules and moral
rules always 'intersect in the actual constitution of social practices'
(Giddens 1979, p. 63).

It is not until *The Constitution of Society* (1984), however, that
Giddens develops his most explicit account of the nature of rules.
Here he outlines the following instances of what it may be to follow
a rule:

1. The rule defining checkmate in chess ...;
2. A formula: $an = n2 + n - 1$;
3. As a rule R gets up at 6.00 every day;
4. It is a rule that all workers must clock in at 8.00 a.m. (ibid., p. 19)

According to Giddens, in example (3) above, rules are regarded as
equivalent to habits or routines. However, although routines
'certainly impinge upon numerous aspects of routine practice',
'routine practice is not as such a rule' (ibid). By contrast, examples
(1) and (4) represent the two aspects of a rule distinguished earlier:
the constitutive and the regulative. Thus, the rule governing
checkmate in chess says something about what goes into the very
making of chess as a game, and is therefore a constitutive rule. The
rule that workers must clock in at a certain hour does not as such
define what work is, but specifies how work is to be carried out, and
is therefore a regulative rule. Finally, he notes that, although example
(2) 'might seem the least promising as a way of conceptualising "rule"
that has any relation to "structure"'', it is in fact 'the most germane

of them all ... I do not mean to say that social life can be reduced to a set of mathematical principles ... [but rather] I mean that it is in the nature of formulae that we can best discover what is the most analytically effective sense of "rule" in social theory' (ibid., p. 20).

The formula $an = n2 + n - 1$, taken from Wittgenstein's example of number games, is the most appropriate illustration of following a rule. Rule-following, according to this example, 'involves one person writing down a sequence of numbers and a second person working out the formula by supplying the numbers which follow'. Giddens further argues that:

> To understand the formula is not to utter it ... Understanding is not a mental process accompanying the solving of the puzzle that the sequence of numbers presents – at least, it is not a mental process in the sense in which the hearing of a tune or a spoken sentence is. It is simply being able to apply the formula in the right context and way in order to continue the series. (ibid.)

According to Giddens a formula is a generalisable procedure since it applies over a range of contexts and occasions and allows for the continuation of an established sequence (ibid. p. 21). Again he echoes Garfinkel:

> procedure, or mastery of the techniques of 'doing' social activities, is by definition methodological. That is to say, such knowledge does not specify all the situations which an actor might meet with, nor could it do so; rather, it provides for the generalised capacity to respond to and influence an indeterminate range of social circumstances. (ibid., p. 22)

Thus, rules in social life are 'techniques or generalisable procedures' understood for the most part on a 'tacit' unformulated basis, which can be applied in the enactment and the reproduction of social practices.[5] The types of rules which are of most significance for social theory are those which concern institutions, that is, practices which are most deeply 'sedimented in time-space'. These can be analysed in terms of the schema shown in Figure 4.1.

Intensive rules refer to procedures that are constantly invoked in the course of day-to-day activities, and are exemplified by, for instance, rules relating to language or the procedures used by agents taking turns in conversations. These differ from shallow rules which,

[handwritten margin note: A lot of this focused on letting us go on]

intensive	tacit	informal	weakly sanctioned
:	:	:	:
shallow	discursive	formalised	strongly sanctioned

Figure 4.1   Types of rules

Source: Giddens (1984, p. 22)

although broader in scope, have a diminished impact on the day-to-day texture of social life. Tacit rules, which refer to the majority of rules implicated within social practices, are only known practically and may be contrasted with discursive rules. Such rules imply a prior interpretation of a rule, which therefore may alter the application of them. Formal rules are best exemplified by laws and are generally the most strongly sanctioned types of social rules in modern societies, whilst informal rules refer to those rules which remain outside the ambit of laws. Although social analysts commonly assume that it is the more abstract rules, such as codified law, which are the most influential in structuring social activity, it is in fact the trivial procedures of daily life which have the most profound effects. It is for this reason that Giddens privileges intensive, tacit and informal forms of rule over shallow, formal and discursive ones.

POWER ⟹ linked to interaction

Both the constitution and communication of meaning, as well as the role of normative sanctions, have to be linked to power transactions by the concept of resources. Giddens employs the concept of power in both a broad and narrow sense. In its broad denotation, power is tied to agency and refers to the transformative capacity of agents to make a difference in the social world. In its narrower designation, it exists as a subcategory of the transformative capacity of agents and refers to domination. With reference to the latter:

> Power, in this relational sense, concerns the capabilities of actors to secure outcomes where the realisation of these outcomes depends upon the agency of others ... Power within social systems can thus be treated as involving reproduced relations of autonomy and dependence in social interaction. (Giddens 1979, p. 93)

The use of power is contingent upon the employment of resources. Power is not itself a resource; rather, resources constitute the 'bases' or 'vehicles' through which power can be exercised. Just as there is an ontological distinction to be made between rules and practices, so too a distinction is to be made between power and resources. During interaction, agents draw upon power through what Giddens terms 'facilities' in order to achieve certain outcomes. Here power 'is expressed in the capabilities of actors to make certain "accounts count"', and to enact or resist sanctioning processes which 'draw upon modes of domination structured in social systems' (ibid., p. 83).

There are two distinct types of resource which constitute the structures of domination: those based on subject–subject relations or 'authorative' resources; and those embodying subject–object relations or 'allocative' resources. As Giddens explains,'[by] "authorisation" I refer to capabilities which generate command over persons, and by "allocation" I refer to capabilities which generate command over objects or other material phenomena' (ibid., p. 100).[6] The relationship between rules and resources is one of mutual interconnection: the communication of meaning in interaction cannot take place independently of normative sanctions which in turn presuppose relations of power. These are analytical, not substantive, distinctions. All social practices involve each of these three elements. Such practices can, however, be examined from two different standpoints: either in relation to social interaction or by focusing on structure. In order to examine either standpoint, Giddens introduces the notion of a 'methodological epoché'.

EVALUATION

As noted in Chapter 3, Giddens's central sociological/political preoccupation has been the recovery of the subject as a knowledgeable, autonomous, reasoning and capable actor. Rather than remaining an appendage to social structures, such actors actively create or produce them. Essential to his enterprise has been the attempt to construct a less constraining and more enabling conception of structure, through the notion of a 'duality of structure'. For Giddens, structure refers to the structuring of action rather than to the patterning of social relations – it is 'what gives form and shape to social life but it is not itself that form or shape' (Giddens 1989, p. 256). Patterned social relations are instead regarded as the effect of structure and designated as the 'social system'.

Giddens's intervention into the agency/structure debate has furnished an account, which prima facie, strikes a delicate balance between agency and structure. Agency is acknowledged without reverting to the voluntarism characteristic of symbolic interactionism and phenomenology, and structure emphasised without relapsing into determinism or into the reification of Marxism and structuralism. However, on closer scrutiny, his reconceptualisation of structure is marred by difficulties in three main areas: (a) ontology, (b) conceptualisation, and (c) rules and resources.

Ontology

With regard to ontology, Giddens argues that structure has a virtual existence and 'exists paradigmatically, as an absent set of differences, temporally 'present' only in [its] instantiation, in the constituting moments of social systems' (Giddens 1979, pp. 63–4); here, although rules 'bind' 'time-space' they do not actually exist in time or space, but rather as an 'absent set of differences': as such, they possess a 'virtual existence'. It remains unclear, however, what the term 'virtual existence' means and why Giddens wishes to use it. Giddens mentions its use by Ricoeur with reference to speech but not only fails to provide a reference for its location in his work but also tears it out of the context within which it was developed. If it is used by Ricoeur it would probably be used in relation to a number of other concepts which draw upon and presuppose the work of a number of thinkers including Saussure (*langue*) Husserl ('irreal essences') and Aristotle (for whom 'virtual' refers to a state between actuality and potentiality). Giddens wants to extend the term 'virtual' from its designation of speech to refer to structures as rules and resources – however, one has to wonder whether it is equally applicable. Rules, as I will argue later, are *post festum* rationalisations of action, not sources for action in the same way that Ricoeur believes that language is for speech. More importantly, to be able to assert that structures as rules and resources have a 'virtual existence', one must already have an interpretation of non-existent or 'real existence'. In Giddens's usage, the 'virtual existence' of structure appears to be derived from its 'existence' outside of time and space. This accords with his view that social systems, which exist in time and space, possess a 'real existence'. However, the basis for such a distinction remains unclear. Since Giddens plainly regards structures as 'knowable', this would imply that he is aiming at an empirical contrast, between what is visible in time and space and what is not. Such an interpretation accords with his claim that structures exist as mutual knowledge or what Husserl refers to as 'memory traces'. But if Giddens's differentiation is only an empirical one, then does it really make sense to designate non-empirical objects as having a 'virtual existence'? Given that non-empirical criteria such as ideas and beliefs constitute a core component in social life, there seems to be little reason to invoke a decontextualised notion of 'virtual existence'.[7]

Further, as noted above, if structures only have an invisible 'virtual existence', how can we know them? There is no way of discerning empirically their existence independently of their manifestation as patterned social systems (see also Urry, 1982). That is, there is no empirical fact of the matter in virtue of which a distinction can be drawn between Giddens's hypothetical notion of structures and the visible social system of social relations through which they are claimed to manifest themselves as human actions. The elaborate distinctions which Giddens makes – between interaction as communication, power and morality, and social structure as signification, domination and legitimation, mediated by various 'modalities' – have therefore little empirical warrant but remain elaborate metaphysical assumptions.

Conceptualisation

By emending the definition of structure from its previous designation as patterned social relations to the concept of generative rules and resources, Giddens has in fact initiated less of a terminological revolution than appears to be the case at first sight. In order to illustrate this, it may again be helpful to contrast his approach with that of Talcott Parsons. In *The Structure of Social Action* (1937), Parsons regards the social system (here synonymous with structure) as composed of institutions, which in turn consist of roles and statuses. These roles and statuses embody expectations in the form of norms and values which are internalised during socialisation. These internalised norms exist in a state of mutual tension with the actor's egoistic interests.

According to Giddens, the Parsonian account is the paradigmatic example of a dualistic sociological approach: structure (as social system) appears as external to, and determinant upon, a free agent. In his attempt to distance himself from such a dualistic conception, however, Giddens merely shifts the concept of social structure onto what Parsons had previously referred to as 'norms and values'. Such a reconceptualisation, however, brings with it an array of complications. Although Parsons's concepts of social structure/social system were perhaps rigid and highly deterministic, they nevertheless carried considerable explanatory weight in accounting for the persistent patterning of action. However, by decoupling the concept of structure from patterned social relationships, Giddens renders the latter explanatorily redundant: social relations simply appear as the effects of generative rules and resources, possessing no explanatory weight of their own. Despite Giddens's protestations to the contrary, it is evident that his own characterisation of social relations as a 'social system' serves solely as a descriptive label for the empirical manifestation of unintended human actions, and is not to be construed as denoting social relationships which themselves have causal implications.

Many of Giddens's critics have consequently focused precisely on the absence of the concept of causality from his characterisation of social relations. Clegg (1989), Callinicos (1989), Porpora (1989), Layder (1981), Archer (1982) and Thompson (1989) all regard Giddens's theory of structuration as seriously flawed because of its failure to accord any causal value to patterned social relationships. Porpora encapsulates this apprehension:

> Although rules and relationships go together, they are different. The question is which has analytical priority, rules or relationships. Giddens gives analytical priority to rules and in fact denies that the relationships of a social system have any causal properties independent of the rule-following activities of human actors ... I will argue that relationships do have such independent causal properties and, moreover, that such relationships, once established, are analytically prior to the subsequent rule-following behaviour of actors. (Porpora 1989, p. 206)

The call for a reinstatement of social relations as causally, and analytically, prior to rules and resources is a move echoed by the majority of Giddens's critics. They share the belief that rules and resources provide an inadequate basis for the conceptualisation of 'structure' and argue that a conventional conceptualisation as social relations should be maintained. In so arguing, their rationale issues from the assumption that structure, construed as rules and resources, precludes any feasible analysis of constraint. As Clegg (1989, p. 144) argues, 'notions of structural shaping, selectivity and constraint end up being too facile'. The concept of rules and resources reduces the differential capacities of agents and the unequal power characteristic of social life to effects of instantiation. This is not only too voluntaristic but also excessively idealistic or subjectivistic (Callinicos 1989, Clegg 1989, Porpora 1989, Thompson 1989). Giddens's account of structure fails to acknowledge the prior differential distribution of varying forms of constraint within a given system or collectivity. Instead, power and differential structuring capacity are conceived of as an effect of social practices rather than as shaping those social practices in the first place. If rules and resources are regarded as 'structuring' action and creating patterned social relations, what in turn structures the rules and resources and gives them what Althusser (1968) calls various 'indices of effectivity'?

Giddens's response to this sustained criticism has been one of bewilderment. In a reply to Bauman and Thompson, he writes:

> In the course of their contributions, Bauman and Thompson place a good deal of emphasis upon the point that ... some rules are more important than others; a criterion of importance cannot be derived from rules alone. But although they clearly regard this observation as a damaging one, I do not feel in any way uncomfortable with it. The phenomena involved here are to do with relationships of differential power, and I have consistently stressed that power is an elemental characteristic of all systems ... The fact that some actors are more able, as Bauman puts it, to 'structure' their social environments than others is also a matter of power, and has no direct bearing upon either the concept of 'structure' or that of 'system'. (Giddens 1989, pp. 256–7)

Giddens, however, seems here to have missed the central point raised by these critics. Structuration fails to explain why some actors have access to more power than others in the first place. Actors need to be construed as embedded in social relations *prior* to the instantiation of rules and resources in order to account for these power differences. Layder expresses this position well:

> Contrary to Giddens' formulation, the notion of reproduced relations must convey the idea that not only are actors in specific encounters actively engaged in the reproduction of social relations (structural contexts in my terms), but that these relations have already been produced in an historical sense, in order that agents are able to reproduce them. The idea of reproduced relations must

refer to historical 'objective' (in the sense prior to), relatively enduring social facts. (Layder 1985, p. 144)

The conflict between 'structure' construed as structuring action through generative rules and resources via agency and 'structure' as patterned social relations which causally constrain agency, has come to constitute *the* central point of disagreement in the agency/structure debate. Those sociologists who support Giddens's standpoint, including Cohen (1989), Outhwaite (1990), New (1994), Sewell (1992), Manicas (1980) and Hayes (1993), can be contrasted with those who reject such a conception in favour of one that prioritises social structure. The latter group includes Archer (1982), Craib (1992), Thompson (1989), Callinicos (1989), Layder (1985) and Porpora (1993). The debate between these two camps may be regarded as expressing the agency/structure problematic, though in a condensed and modified form. In place of the question of whether to prioritise agency or structure, is the problem whether to regard structure as generative rules and resources on the one hand or as a set of causally efficacious, patterned social relationships on the other. The former variant is seen by one set of critics to result in an exaggerated voluntarism, whereas the latter is regarded by others as a form of dualistic determinism. As I will later argue, whichever standpoint is accepted, intractable difficulties remain. The agency/structure conundrum persists as long as the debate is cast in these misleading terms. Or to put it another way, as long as the initial framework incorporates terms proceeding from a dichotomous relation – between agents and structures or individuals and society or subjects and objects – it matters little whether the next step is to marry the two concepts through duality or to maintain a theoretical dualism. The real problem is twofold: the dehistoricised origin of these discourses and the concepts they use and, as I will now show, their problematic interpretation of rule-following.

Rule-Following

There are two major components in Giddens's analysis of rule-following. First, to 'know' a rule does not presuppose the ability to enunciate it discursively, but rather to 'know' it tacitly, as practical consciousness. This allows an emphasis on the practical nature of rule-following, in contrast to a conception which envisages rules as straightforwardly conscious and discursive. Second, to know a rule is to know 'how to apply it in novel circumstances' or, as Giddens later paraphrases himself, to know 'how to go on' in social life. Here, following Garfinkel, rules are considered to be 'generalisable procedures', which can be applied on a case to case and context to context basis. Rules permit *ad hoc* considerations. It is the second aspect of rule-following that will be discussed here, since the first has been criticised elsewhere (Pleasants 1999, ch. 4). The second criterion gives rise to the fundamental question, how do actors 'go on' or follow rules in an indeterminate range of circumstances? In his sceptical reading of Wittgenstein, Kripke (1982) argues that this is *the* central problem vitiating the account of rule-following in the *Philosophical Investigations*. According to Kripke, Wittgenstein poses this problem by invoking the following 'sceptical paradox': 'no course of action could be determined by a rule, because every course of action can be made out to accord with the rule' (Wittgenstein 1953, p. 81).

Kripke's discussion provides one interpretation of this paradox, although there are others. There are essentially two fundamentally opposed positions in relation to rule-following: an individualist and a collectivist approach (Bloor 1997). An individualist position incorporates a conception of what Bloor (ibid.) calls 'meaning determinism'.[8] This entails the claim that 'the compelling and infinite character of rules derives from the property called "meaning", the meaning of the rule itself and what is meant and intended by the rule follower' (Bloor 1997, p. 11). For an individualist, the meaning of the rule appears as a pre-given and transparent formula. Therefore, the extent to which individuals are capable of deciphering and formulating the meaning of this formula, is the extent to which they can follow the rule. On this interpretation, the meaning of the rule guides and regulates the individual's behaviour in accordance with its precepts. A rule is regarded as something which is independent of the individual, but which is implanted within the individual's mind as an instructional device. Wittgenstein characterises this position as analogous to following rails whereby the meanings of words are already clearly delimited, and therefore in a sense the rule has already been followed:

> Whence comes the idea that the beginning of a series is a visible section of rails invisibly laid to infinity? Well, we might instead imagine rails instead of a rule. And infinitely long rails corresponding to the unlimited application of a rule. (Wittgenstein 1958, p. 85)

Consequently:

> 'All the steps are already taken' means: I do no longer have any choice. The rule, once stamped with a particular meaning, traces the lines along which it is to be followed through the whole of space. (ibid.)

Giddens appears to have distanced himself from such an individualistic and rationalist rendition of rule-following in two major respects. First, he employs a practical, non-discursive conception of rule-following, rather than a conception in which agents are fully aware of their actions. This implies that the meaning of the rule may not be readily or discursively transparent to the individual. Rule-following involves what Ryle (1954) refers to as 'know how', rather than simply 'knowing that'. Secondly, Giddens does not regard rules as delimited and pre-given; instead, he argues that they have to be continuously 'brought off'.[9] Both of these arguments are encapsulated by his statement that:

> Knowledge of procedure, or mastery of the techniques of 'doing' social activities, is by definition methodological. That is to say, such knowledge does not specify all the situations which an actor might meet with, nor could it do so; rather it provides for the generalised capacity to respond to and influence an indeterminate range of social circumstances. (Giddens 1984, p. 22)

Nevertheless, Giddens' arguments on rule-following still contain a high degree of individualism and rationalism. This is especially apparent in his discussion of how rules generate action, how actors 'generalise' rules from situation to situation and how they know they are following a rule correctly.[10] These difficulties once again invoke Wittgenstein's conundrum, posed here in a different manner:

> How is it decided what is the right step to take at any particular stage – 'The right step is the one that accords with the order – as it was *meant*' … But that is just what is the question: what at any stage we are to call 'being in accord' with that sentence (and with the meaning you then put into the sentence – whatever that may have consisted in). It would almost be more correct to say, not that an intuition was needed at every stage, but that a new decision was needed at every stage. (Wittgenstein 1958, p. 82)[11]

Wittgenstein argues that the meaning of the rule cannot be found 'within' the rule itself or according to its meaning, as asserted by meaning determinists, because the search for meaning leads to an infinite regression. He circumvents this possibility by arguing that following a rule is not simply a matter of interpretation, but is habitual, automatic and conventional. Rule-following for the most part is neither a conscious interpretive activity nor a tacit activity, but in strikingly behaviourist terms, is an unthinking, automatic and conventional exercise: 'When I obey a rule, I do not choose. I obey the rule blindly.' For Wittgenstein, most forms of rule-following presuppose instances of action which involve little or no 'thought', let alone rational justification: 'If I have exhausted the justifications I have reached bedrock, and my spade is turned. Then I am inclined to say: "This is simply what I do"' (Wittgenstein 1958, p. 85).[12]

Moreover, rule-following is not an individual matter. According to Wittgenstein, the 'correct' next step in rule-following can only be gauged through the responses of the rule-following community.[13] Individual action which deviates from this collectively ratified consensus is sanctioned by the other rule-following members. 'The prophecy does not run, that a man will get this result when he follows this rule ... but that he will get this result, when *we* say that he is following the rule' (Wittgenstein 1978, s. II, p. 66).

Rule-following is not an inner mental activity – something hidden, something an individual can do by reflecting on his/her action – but a *public* matter which manifests itself in agreed collective practice.[14] What constitutes a rule and its correct application is its collective conventional use, so that to follow a rule correctly is a social phenomenon. For Wittgenstein, rule-following is premised upon agreement based in a form of life.[15] Through social interaction humans collectively (re)create rules upon the basis of social agreement. Rules are ultimately an expression of ongoing social interactions. They are not independent of individuals, nor do they guide them, but they persist as social institutions, customs or conventions. To follow a rule is to participate within these institutions and conventions. Therefore, in addition to consensus and agreement, Wittgenstein's arguments concerning rule-following also emphasise custom, habit and training as a basis for learning conventions.[16] Wittgenstein's 'collectivist' rendition of rule-following undoubtedly entails a number of normative implications. His thought-style is in many ways emblematic of the 'conservative' world-view outlined earlier.[17] Hence his stress on agreement and community, drill, the importance of authority in ostenstion, learning and rule-following, habit, form of life, the contextual and particular, anti-rationalism and a scepticism concerning autonomous individuality.[18]

For this reason it is unlikely that Giddens would adopt such a trenchantly collectivist position on rule-following, since it not only cedes or dissolves individuals into larger consensual collectives, but also downplays the faculty of reason and abrogates the search for rational foundations and first principles. The overall effect of such a position would be a characterisation of actors as 'unthinking dupes', a position that Giddens has persistenly aimed to avoid.[19] It therefore comes as no surprise that Giddens seeks to retain elements of individualism, reasoning and conflict in his own analysis of rule-following. Thus, although he acknowledges the importance of the practical and *ad hoc* element in rule-following, Giddens shies away from the next logical (collectivist) step of dissolving rules into collective practices. This, to some extent, is evident in the ontological separation he retains between rules and social practices (Giddens 1984, p. 19; see also Pleasants 1999, p. 62) as well as in the general implications of his broader assertion that 'rules generate practices'. Giddens claims that he is pursuing a Wittgensteinian approach,[20] yet for normative reasons he also attempts to modify this approach by emphasising the role of the individual and conflict in social life.[21] The effect of this, however, is that his analysis remains suspended between an individualist and a collectivist interpretation, resulting in a number of theoretical inconsistencies and anomalies in his analysis. For instance, the analytical separation between the constitution of meaning and the normativity of interaction and power that Giddens makes when defining structure cannot represent equal aspects of rule-following, whether conceived in analytical terms or otherwise. If one is to remain within the broad compass of Wittgenstein's writings, as Giddens wants to, normative sanctions must hold causal precedence. Rules cannot be followed through interpretive schemes by interpreting and ascribing meaning to them since, as noted above, the search for meaning leads to an infinite regression; interpretation and meaning depend upon a form of rule-following. As Wittgenstein notes:

> 'But how can a rule show me what I have to do at *this* point? Whatever I do is, on some interpretation, in accord with the rule.'
> – That is not what we ought to say, but rather: any interpretation

still hangs in the air along with what it interprets, and cannot give it any support. Interpretations by themselves do not determine meaning. (Wittgenstein 1958, p. 80)

Meaning itself can only issue from what Wittgenstein calls an 'agreement of ratifications' or social sanctioning which forms the condition of possibility for following a rule. *Mutatis mutandis* this applies equally to Giddens's attempt to incorporate power into his analysis. Power, as the capacity of certain agents to make accounts count, also involves recourse to an 'agreement of ratifications' or to a form of rule-following. If one is to begin with Wittgenstein's theory of rule-following, as Giddens does, and social theory must, then the normative sanctions of interacting social actors in collective agreement must be given causal and ontological priority. The sanctioning process of social interactions permit the constitution of meaning and the generation of power to exist.[22] Moreover, such an agreement of ratification does not preclude social conflict. It is merely the condition of possibility for a difference of opinion. For Wittgenstein, although consensus and agreement are required for social practice, this refers to agreement in the form of life or at the level of cognitive order. It does not preclude differences of opinion or conflicts of interest. Rather, the agreement needed for cognitive order is the basis upon which these substantive differences can unfold:

> 'So you are saying that human agreement decides what is true and false?' – It is what human beings say that is true and false; and they agree in the language they use. This is not agreement in opinions but in a form of life. (Wittgenstein 1958, p. 88)

Thus Giddens begins his analysis of rule-following by drawing on Wittgenstein's account. But recognising its social and political implications, he attempts to develop his own conception of rule-following in which individuality, conflict and struggle are conceived as integral co-equal moments. Although this may initially seems an attractive position, as did his epistemological position, it is, unfortunately, untenable. Giddens, as he does with numerous other theorists, adopts Wittgenstein's ideas eclectically and out of context. The insistence on individualism, the privileging of an autonomous choosing actor and the construction of a tripartite account of rules and resources are logically incompatible with Wittgenstein's collectivist conception of rule-following, in which social sanctioning holds causal precedence.

Contrary to Giddens, rules do not generate practices nor can they be separated from the social practices or social relations in which they are embedded. But at the same time, rules do not derive from social relations as an adjunct, as many of Giddens's critics have maintained. These standpoints – some of which emphasise the duality of structure and others of which aim to retain a dualism between structure and agency – involve a fallacious separation of the material and the ideal. Rules collapse into social relations: they are an expression of these social relations. As a result, it is not rules or norms which tell individuals how to 'go on' in social life – a fetishisation of rules – but rather social 'individuals' in determinate relations who collectively carry rules forward, usually by proceeding on the basis of existing practice. Rules are produced and reproduced continually and collectively in all forms of social life by interacting social individuals. Their new applications have to be collectively 'decided' on an ongoing basis. According to this finitist approach to rules, the past application of a rule can guide the future application through analogy, but cannot determine it (see Barnes 1995).

5 Time, Space and Historical Sociology

Giddens's writings in historical sociology emerged at a time when Marxist theories of history were prominent in the field. These analyses often, however, incorporated telelogical, evolutionary and functionalist assumptions within their arguments. Throughout his substantive and methodological writings, Giddens challenged functionalism as a valid approach in sociology, both in relation to Parson's writings but also as a methodological position in Marxist writings as well (see Giddens 1977b). In terms of the latter, both Habermas and thinkers influenced by Althusser, Giddens believed, incorporated functionalist analyses in their writings. Moreover, during the early 1980s, time geography also began to emerge as an influential discipline in the social sciences. Both of these theoretical frameworks need to be borne in mind when examining Giddens's work on structuration generally and his historical sociology specifically.

TIME AND SPACE

Although they later became core elements in Giddens's theory of structuration, the concepts of time and space were absent from its inception in the *New Rules of Sociological Method* (1976). They first emerged in Giddens's next major work on structuration, *Central Problems in Social Theory* (1979). In the introduction he states:

> I regard it as a fundamental theme of this paper, and of the whole of this book, that social theory must acknowledge, as it has not done previously, time-space intersections as essentially involved in all social existence. (ibid., p. 54)

For Giddens, an adequate incorporation of time and space (or what he calls time-space) within social theory can be achieved only by fundamentally reconceiving both terms. Formerly, time and space had both been defined as boundaries or environments within which social life was enacted; correspondingly they became associated with separate disciplines: time with history, and space with geography.[1]

Moreover, in functionalism, time became associated with dynamics or change and was often contrasted with stability or statics.[2] It therefore became necessary to replace such a 'parametric' view of time and space, frequently associated with the Kantian notion of time and space as subjective forms of human sensibility, through which the manifold of sense is given to the mind, that is, as empty concepts or as containers for experiential events, with a standpoint which conceived of them as essentially constitutive features of the social world.

To effect such a meta-theoretical transformation, Giddens draws on Heidegger's notion of Being as constituted through the 'primordial horizon' of time. For Heidegger, time and space represent expressions of the relations between things and events, so that they are constituted through the modes in which the relations between objects and events are articulated:

> If Being is to be conceived in terms of time, and if indeed its various modes and derivatives are to become intelligible in their respective modifications and derivations by taking time into consideration, then Being itself (and not merely entities, let us say, as entities 'in time') is thus made visible in its temporal character. (Heidegger 1978, p. 41)

For Heidegger, furthermore, the concept of 'presence' replaces that of 'a present':

> time-space no longer means merely the distance between two now-points of calculated time, such as we have in mind when we note, for instance: this or that occurred within a time-span of fifty years. Time-space is the name for the openness which opens up in the mutual extending of futural approach, past and present. The self-extending, the opening up, of future, past and present is itself pre-spatial; only thus can it make room, that is, provide space ... prior to all calculation of time and independent of all such calculation, what is germane to the time-space of true time consists in the mutual reaching out and opening up of future, past and present. (ibid., p. 14)

Without entering into the intricacies of Heidegger's philosophy, 'presencing' is to be taken neither as a given object nor as an object in time, but as that which gives form to an empty content, like hours on a clock, or centimetres on a ruler, through structured difference. 'Presencing', through structured difference, holds the past, present and future together, as well as simultaneously apart.

Drawing on these arguments, Giddens asserts that, 'All social interaction, like any other type of event, occurs across time and space. All social interaction intermingles presence and absence' (Giddens 1981a, p. 38). Such a viewpoint has extensive ramifications for structuration theory, not least in terms of indicating the importance of contextuality and situatedness for the understanding of social interactions. All human interaction has to be placed in time and space and an understanding of its form, its context and its immediate outcome must include reference not only to what objects and persons were present, but also to those that were absent when such action took place.[3] For Giddens, 'presencing' and 'absencing', as expressed through the duality of structure, relate the smallest aspect of day-to-day life to the wider attributes of social systems, so that, as agents draw upon structure (as rules and resources), they recursively reproduce sets of spatially and temporally specific practices or social systems. These, in conjunction, contribute to the constitution and reproduction of the 'wider society'. Thus the smallest practices of daily life relate to the widest social forms through a moment–totality relation.

These abstract formulations are made more concrete by drawing upon the substantive views of time-geographers, most importantly Hagerstrand. According to Hagerstrand, a person's daily routine of activities can be charted as a path through time-space, so that social interaction can be understood as the 'coupling' of time-paths in social encounters or as 'activity bundles'. Developing these ideas, Giddens argues that the time-space paths taken by agents can be examined in three intersecting ways: first, in terms of the temporality of their immediate experience of everyday life; second, according to the temporality of their lifecycle or *Dasein*; third, in terms of their experience of institutional time. These three moments, though analytically separate, 'interpenetrate' within an agent's 'time-space paths', so that every moment of social interaction is likewise implicated in the passing of the human organism (or its Being towards death), and in turn, implicated in the *longue durée* of institutions.[4] The binding or intersection of these forms of temporal and spatial positioning constitutes an agent's overall framework of social positioning.

Giddens supplements this notion of activity bundles by introducing two further concepts: 'locale' and 'regionalisation'. The concept of locale is preferable to the concept of place,[5] and refers to encounters which employ space to provide the settings and context for interaction. Such settings include a variety of spaces: 'a room in a house, a street corner, the shop floor of a factory, towns and cities, to the territorially demarcated areas occupied by nation-states' (Giddens 1984, p. 118). Regionalisation, on the other hand, refers to the 'zoning of time-space in relation to routinised social practices' (ibid., p. 119), or, more precisely, to the time-space differentiation between or within locales. In addition, regionalisation 'encloses' time-space and allows actors to exercise the use of 'front' and 'back' regions.[6] Thus a house, construed as a locale, may be regionalised into floors, halls and rooms which are zoned differently in time-space; for example, the rooms downstairs may be employed during the daytime and those upstairs during the night.

Giddens also introduces a methodological distinction between 'micro-' and 'macro-sociological' analysis, by drawing upon and modifying Lockwood's differentiation between social integration and system integration.[7] The distinction between social and system integration is, however, preferable to the 'micro-'/'macro-' distinction for two major reasons. Firstly, the micro/macro approach was frequently conceived of in terms of an opposition in which each side often attempted to outbid the other. Secondly, and relatedly, a division of labour often developed, in which micro-sociology became associated with 'free individual agents' and macro-sociology with collective 'structural constraints'.

Social integration, which refers to 'systemness' in circumstances of 'co-presence' or 'face-to-face' interaction, not only emphasises the spatial significance of presence but also attempts to convey the importance of the 'positioning' of the body within social space. Drawing on Goffman, Giddens argues that the body in relationships of co-presence is positioned both in terms of face-work and bodily gestures.[8] These are both rooted in and motivated by the maintenance of ontological security.[9] By contrast, system integration refers to the reciprocity which exists between actors or collectivities across extended time-space or in relation to absent others outside of the conditions of co-presence. This involves a process of 'time-space distanciation': the 'stretching' of social systems across time and space.[10] The use of time-space distanciation in structuration is crucial for three major reasons. In the first place, as we noted above, it highlights the

connection between social and system integration, by accounting for the stretch of social systems across time-space.[11] Second, it provides the basis upon which Giddens distinguishes various forms of society. Third, it is integral to the generation of power. Social systems, then, consist of 'regularised social practices, sustained in encounters dispersed across time-space' (Giddens 1984, p. 75).

HISTORICAL SOCIOLOGY

During the early 1980s, Giddens also began to develop his own historical sociology which he developed concurrently with his theory of structuration. This was conceived within the context of a planned three-volume critique of Marxism. In the first volume, *A Contemporary Critique of Historical Materialism* (1981a), which alludes to Weber both in title and in substance, Giddens restates a number of criticisms of Marx which he had previously outlined in *The Class Structure of the Advanced Societies* (1973). These include the recognition that (a) there is a need for a distinction between capitalism and industrialism; (b) political factors have played a far more significant role in the latter-day development of advanced societies than Marx had envisaged; (c) the pre-eminence of 'traditional' elements in the capitalist societies is tied to the rise of nationalism; (d) the study of the nation-state within its international context is crucial; (e) there is a need for a move away from evolutionary and endogenous models of social change; and (f) Marxism fails to recognise the influence of military factors in social change.

In *The Class Structure of the Advanced Societies*, Giddens also puts forward a number of challenges to Marx's theory of class and revolution. Not only is revolution not inevitable,[12] but Marx is mistaken in identifying the heyday of capitalist society with early nineteenth-century British capitalism. Such a claim was

> at best misleading, and at worst false. But virtually everyone has accepted such a view, which carries the logical implication that any movement towards state 'intervention' in economic life and, as many non-Marxist writers have suggested, the acceptance of the legitimacy of collective bargaining in industry and the enfranchisement of the working class, represent some sort of partial supersession of capitalist Society. The opposite is the case; capitalist society only becomes fully developed when these processes occur (Giddens 1973, p. 22)

Instead, twentieth-century British society should be taken as paradigmatic of capitalism. In Britain during the twentieth century there existed an institutional separation between industrial and political conflict, developed systems of collective bargaining, rights of citizenship, an enfranchised working class, reformist trade unions and a social democratic government.

In *A Contemporary Critique of Historical Materialism*, Giddens also uses the concepts of social and system integration and time-space distanciation as the basis for a new typology of societal forms. His central aim is to supplant both evolutionary and functionalist accounts of social change, including historical materialism, with the view that history can be understood and explained in terms of the progressive unfolding of the forces of production. Historical materialism is not only dependent on evolutionist and functionalist explanatory frameworks, but is economically reductive. By drawing partly upon anthropological evidence from, *inter alia*, Sahlins, together with Weber's historical sociology, Giddens attempts to replace historical materialism with a non-evolutionary, non-teleological, non-functionalist, multidimensional and historically contingent model of social change. Such a model would incorporate a tripartite societal typology involving tribal, class-divided and class societies.

No Depth ⇒ methodology implied

A TYPOLOGY OF SOCIAL FORMS

Tribal societies, such as hunter-gatherer or small agricultural communities, possess two connected features of social organisation, both of which are anchored in religion: legitimation through tradition and kinship relations. These societal forms are characterised by a 'high presence-availability' and 'low time-space distanciation'. Social interaction with absent others is extremely rare and a distinction between social and system does not exist. In order to connect his concept of time-space distanciation with power, Giddens introduces the notion of 'storage capacity' of which two types exist. These correspond to the two resources of domination: allocative and authoritative. In traditional or tribal societies, storage takes the form of a knowledge of tradition and is maintained through oral storytelling and myth. The principal storage container in these societies is the human memory, which 'brackets' time and space. Power is generally exercised through the flow of information so that

those who possess such resources, for example, oracles and myth-tellers, are also the most powerful.

As a result of the confluence of a number of factors, primarily the development of writing, there is an increase in the degree of time-space distanciation. The emergence of writing permits the development of non-oral communication with the past, the present, and with others who are physically absent. This temporal and spatial extension forms the basis for the emergence of a new form of class-divided society. Class-divided society generically refers to agrarian peasant societies which embody a limited degree of class formation.[13] The low level of state penetration into the everyday life of the local community – which, when it occurs, is usually in the form of military intervention – means that tradition and kinship continue to play a major role in social integration. The development of writing as a storage capacity creates a separation between social integration and system integration. This is expressed through a spatial division between the city and the countryside, in which the former becomes the religious, commercial and administrative centre. City-states use surveillance as a storage container for the generation of power.[14]

Although capitalism is only 400 or 500 years old, the massive social and material transformations it inaugurated, in contrast to those of previous civilisations, means that even Marx underestimated its profound impact. These transformations provide the basis for what Giddens calls a 'discontinuist' view of history. They include the 'insulation' of the state from the economy, a process which involves tying economic power to the harnessing of allocative resources, whilst state activity expands in terms of authoritative resources which take the form of surveillance and administration.[15] The latter process involves the development of the nation-state[16] within an increasingly global state system. The nation-state as a power container is able to penetrate into the minutiae of everyday social life and increasingly to dissolve traditional social practices.

In the economy, free wage-labour develops as a result of a forced expropriation of land. In contrast to the dominance of authoritative resources which characterised class-divided society, class relations tied to allocative resources become the primary medium for the generation of power.[17] In class society social struggle relates to commodified labour-time geared to the mechanisms of capitalism. This, coupled with industrialism, results in commodified time becoming increasingly cut off from commodified space and forming a 'created environment' severed from nature. As the result of the development of electronic communications – for example, Morse's invention of the telegraph system[18] – social and system integration become increasingly separate: interaction with co-present actors becomes replaced by forms of communication between absent others through system integration.

The nation-state and violence

In the second volume of his critique of historical materialism, *The Nation-State and Violence* (1985), Giddens expands and modifies some of his earlier postulates. He now insists that capitalism, industrialism and the nation-state coterminously and historically shape each other in a complex symbiotic relationship. These three spheres provide the basis of four irreducible, though connected, 'institutional clusterings' which characterise modern society: capitalistic enterprise, industrial production, heightened surveillance, and the centralised control of the means of violence. As part of this conceptual quartet, Giddens replaces 'class society' with the concept of 'modernity'.

Repeating caveats he made earlier in *A Contemporary Critique of Historical Materialism*, Giddens argues that the emergence of all three forms of state – traditional, absolutist, and the modern nation-state[19] – did not occur in a successive, inevitable or evolutionary fashion, but according to a Weberian viewpoint which regards 'all social life [a]s contingent, all social change [a]s conjunctural' (Giddens 1984, p. 254). Thus, for example, the emergence of the absolutist state, for Giddens, is wholly contingent upon the confluence of three sets of military developments: technological changes in armaments, the emergence of modern military discipline, and the development of naval strength. This contingency applies with equal force to the character of the nation-state in Europe:

> If the course of events in the Great War, including the participa-
> tion of the USA in the hostilities and the peace settlement, had
> not taken the shape they did, the nation-state in its current form
> might not have become the dominant political entity in the world
> system. (Giddens 1985, pp. 234–5)

Giddens also invokes a number of Eliasian arguments in his analysis of historical change. These include not only a reference to the importance of violence for sociological analysis and how increasing pacification within nation-states is matched by a corresponding potential for violence between them, but also the fact that sociologists have often unwittingly presupposed the nation-state when they refer to society.

ANALYSING SOCIAL CHANGE

As well as putting forward a contingent view of history, Giddens develops a number of methodological precepts for the analysis of aspects of social systems, construed as distinct societies.[20] These include the concepts of 'intersocietal systems', 'time-space edges', 'episodic characterisations' (or 'episodes') and 'world-time' (Giddens 1981a, p. 24). He also makes an important methodological distinction between 'strategic' and 'institutional analysis':

> I want to introduce a distinction ... between institutional analysis and the analysis of strategic conduct. This does not correspond to the distinction between social and system integration because I intend it to be methodological rather than substantive. The point of the distinction is to indicate two principal ways in which the study of system properties may be approached in the social sciences. (Giddens 1979, p. 80)

For Giddens, this differentiation allows sociologists who undertake empirical analysis to concentrate either on agency or on structure as a starting point for their analysis. 'Institutional analysis' permits the sociologist to focus on 'the mode in which actors draw upon structural elements – rules and resources – in their social relations' and by means of this to examine the constitution of social systems as 'institutions' (ibid.). The main feature of institutional analysis is not concrete agents in conditions of co-presence, but the systemic reproduction of rules and resources:

> all the structural relations indicated above, at whatever level, have to be examined as conditions of system reproduction. They help to pick out basic features of the circuits of reproduction[21] implicated in the 'stretching' of institutions across space and time. (Giddens 1984, p. 190)

By contrast, 'strategic analysis' involves bracketing 'institutional analysis'. During strategic analysis, the modalities of structuration drawn upon by skilled and knowledgeable agents during the course of interaction are treated as stocks of knowledge, such that the reflexive monitoring of action in concrete situations of co-presence is regarded as the main feature of social integration.[22] Conversely, the analysis of structures according to the methods of 'institutional analysis' entails that theory remains within the ambit of the 'virtual time-space' of rules and resources. The move to 'strategic analysis', by contrast, allows social analysis to 're-enter' concrete history by focusing upon the reflexive monitoring of action and its reverberations.

LEVELS OF ABSTRACTION   *⟹ In terms of Structure*

In addition to the methodological distinction between social and institutional analysis, it is also possible to analyse structure at three different levels of abstraction. These different levels of abstraction are separed by 'no definite cut-off point', but instead 'shade off' into one another (Giddens 1981a, pp. 55–6). The first level of abstraction examines 'structural elements' or 'axes' which refer to the most concrete level of analysis. The second level examines 'structural sets' or structures which operate at a lower level of abstraction and refer to the isolated 'clusterings' of transformation/mediation relations.[23] It is in terms of structural sets that structures can be analytically distinguished in terms of signification, legitimation and domination.[24] Thirdly, 'structural principles' exist at the highest level of abstraction and represent the mode of societal differentiation and articulation across the 'deepest' reaches of time-space.[25] These principles delineate the basic organisational features of a society, that is, the overall institutional alignment possessed by a society. It is according to structural principles that Giddens distinguishes the three major forms of society.[26]

In addition to the above, Giddens develops a conceptual distinction between 'associations', 'organisations' and 'social movements' which corresponds to the tripartite typology of societal forms. In 'associations', which predominate in tribal societies, little attempt is made by agents to control or alter the circumstances of social reproduction. Instead, there exists a close connection between the prevalence of associations and traditional modes of legitimation. 'Organisations', which predominate in class-divided societies, emerge as a result of the use of writing as information storage. Here, by contrast, the reflexive self-regulation of society becomes possible. Finally, in modern class society, the development of media of mass communication provides a platform for the formation and constitution of fully reflexive 'social movements'. According to

Giddens, individuals in 'associations', 'organisations' and 'social movements' create history on the basis of different degrees of awareness. This awareness depends upon the context and form of information available, which in turn is contingent upon the extent of social and system integration in time-space.[27]

CONTRADICTION

Giddens also discusses the notion of contradiction in relation to structural principles. Contradiction takes two forms: 'existential contradiction' and 'structural contradiction'.[28] The former refers to 'an elemental aspect of human existence in relation to nature or the material world. There is, one might say, an antagonism of opposites at the very heart of the human condition, in the sense that life is predicated upon nature, yet is not of nature and is set off against it. Human beings emerge from the "nothingness" of inorganic nature and disappear back into that alien state of the inorganic' (Giddens 1984, p. 193). For Giddens, the contradictory relation between human beings and nature is mediated through society: through society human beings acquire a 'second nature'. In tribal societies, human beings live in a close, symbiotic relationship with nature, not only in terms of co-presence, but also in terms of 'existing in harmony' with 'the rhythms of nature'. As a result, they 'integrate the natural world cognitively with their activities' (ibid., p. 194). In these societies, existential contradiction is ubiquitous and is expressed through the institutions of kinship and tradition.

By contrast, 'structural contradiction' refers to the constitutive features of human societies and to structural principles which operate in terms of one another 'yet also contravene each other'. Structural contradictions can be differentiated into two basic types, primary and secondary:

> By primary contradictions I refer to those which enter into the constitution of societal totalities; by secondary contradictions I mean those which are dependent upon, or are brought into being by, primary contradictions ... I do not intend by these simply an abstract series of distinctions; they have to be related to the study of the societal types described above. The concept of structural contradiction has reference to a specific characterisation of the state. (ibid., p. 193)

Although existential contradiction persists in all forms of society, it becomes 'externalised' in class-divided society as a result of the emergence of the state. In this society, existential contradiction expresses itself through a structural contradiction between the city and the countryside. By contrast, in modern class societies in which the nation-state replaces the city as the 'power container', the primary contradiction is between the private sphere of civil society and the public sphere of the state. As the state becomes increasingly dissociated from both nature and human social life, the connection between the social and nature is broken. Instead, nature exists as a 'created environment' in which human beings as commodities are reduced to a means for the expansion of production. This is reflected in a secondary contradiction between what Marx calls 'socialised production' and 'private appropriation'.[29]

EMPIRICAL RESEARCH

Since the Enlightenment, empirical research has rightly been regarded as a crucial component of sociology if it is to provide a explanatorily relevant science of society. In contrast to philosophy, which has tended to eschew the systematic gathering of data, the greatest insights of sociology have, more often than not, come from work which has combined theoretical insight with empirical analysis. One only needs to think of Weber's *Protestant Ethic*, Durkheim's *Elementary Forms of Religious Life*, and Marx's *Eighteenth Brumaire* to be reminded of this. It is with this point in mind that we also need to look at Giddens's arguments concerning empirical work. As Giddens notes, '[s]tructuration theory will not be of much value if it does not help to illuminate problems of empirical research' (Giddens 1984, p. xxx). Fittingly, he provides some basic guidelines for the orientation of empirical research. In the first place, he argues that 'all research has a necessarily cultural, ethnographic or "anthropological" aspect to it' (ibid., p. 284). In Giddens's view, since social life is meaningfully constituted, the task of the sociologist is to construct 'second-order' concepts which are based upon the 'first-order' constructs of lay agents. Second, research has to be 'sensitive to the complex skills actors have in co-ordinating the contexts of their day-to-day behaviour' (ibid., p. 285). For Giddens, agents are knowledgeable, not only in the sphere of discursive consciousness, but, more importantly, in regard to their practical consciousness. The role of the sociologist is also to shed light upon the unintended consequences and unacknowledged conditions of action, with the proviso that these have to be conceived as the result of intentional conduct and not in functionalist terms. Third, the social analyst 'must be sensitive to the time-space constitution of social life' (ibid., p. 286). From Giddens's viewpoint, the contextualisation of social activities, both in terms of their locales and regionalisation and in relation to their stretching away through time-space distanciation, is a crucial component in sociological analysis.[30] Giddens highlights the implications of these guidelines by examining four pieces of empirical work, each of which is connected with a distinct tenet of structuration theory.

The first and most extensive example is Paul Willis's 'Learning to Labour' (1977), an ethnographic study of conformity and rebellion in a working-class school in the Midlands.

EVALUATION

For Giddens, the need to stress the importance of time and space as essential components of social theory was a result of the previous theoretical indifference to them and the maintenance, by both functionalism and structuralism, of a distinction between statics and dynamics or synchrony and diachrony. Although '[a]t first sight nothing seems so banal and uninstructive than to assert that social activity occurs in time and space' (Giddens 1979, p. 202), the task of effecting a shift away from conceiving time and space as 'environments' of action to a view which regards them as embedded in the very constitution of action is a complex one.[31] Giddens's use of time and space in sociological analysis provides for brilliant and complex insights into a dimension of social practice which is often taken for granted by many sociologists. In addition, his historical sociology offers a synoptic vision rarely equalled, combining broad historical material with penetrating theoretical analysis. Yet, it was in a sense inevitable that certain theoretical quandaries would arise from his attempt to incorporate time and space into the already elaborate theoretical structure constituting structuration theory. This applies equally to his attempt to remedy the gaps and aporias in historical materialism with arguments drawn from Weber and Freud. The magnitude of these difficulties, however, was less foreseeable.

The first major difficulty in Giddens's work concerns his attempt to move away from a conception of time and space as containers for events. Despite explicit efforts to the contrary, he continues to treat time and space as givens, rather than as constituted in and through human actions. In terms of space, for example, when Giddens talks of locales and regions, he does not look at their generation or production, but, rather, accepts them as already established settings. Hence, locales such as a room in a house or a street corner are drawn upon as contexts for action rather than as the products of social action. They are antecedently established and taken for granted contexts *for* action which are drawn upon to allow the interpretation of action.[32] This applies equally to Giddens's use of time. As Urry notes:

> Giddens seems to regard the organisation of time as given, somehow embedded within the structuring of rules and resources that characterise modern societies in general. The organisation of time is not seen to vary greatly between modern societies or to stem from the particular powers of social forces concerned to 'produce' different ways in which time may be zoned. (Urry 1991, p. 168)

Thus, contrary to his repeated call for an analysis in which time and space are integral features of social life, Giddens unwittingly continues to treat them as pre-established contexts for action. The dualism mentioned in Chapter 4 between structure as verb or noun (that is, as 'structuring' or 'structured') and between rules and practices, reappears; this time, however, it refers to time and space. As was the case with the unresolved dualism between rules and resources, on the one hand and patterned social relationships, on the other, his writings on time and space also evince a dualism between the structured pre-givenness of time and space and the constitution of time and space. Such a dualism becomes reinforced in the substantive methodological distinctions which Giddens draws. In the methodological distinction he makes between 'strategic' and 'institutional' analysis, capable and knowledgeable agents completely disappear in the large swathes of history discussed in his historical sociology.[33] Moreover, this distinction implies the possibility of distinguishing accounts which focus on agency from those that concentrate on structure, allowing a distinction which sits rather uneasily with his view that the two are ontologically inseparable terms.

A second problematic feature concerning the attempt to reconceptualise time-space as a central component of social analysis involves the concept of time-space distanciation. In the first place, by conceiving increasing time-space distanciation as the overriding criterion for the delimitation of one type of society from another, Giddens covertly smuggles in a form of developmental evolutionism. As Wright notes, there is little difference between the evolutionism implicit in Giddens's notion of time-space distanciation and the productivist evolutionism for which he criticises Marx. Moreover, even if this misleading interpretation of Marx is accepted, it is unlikely that Gidden's account of social change is historically or empirically more adequate or more fruitful in explanatory terms (see Callinicos 1989, Wright 1989). Instead, his spatial evolutionism remains wedded to a crude technological determinism. He explicitly credits factors such as transport, writing or electronic media for increasing time-space distanciation and hence for transforming one society into another. Class-divided societies require the development of writing and transport (such as railways, shipping, and so on) in order to shift away from traditional social forms; and class societies, in turn, require the development of electronic communication and media.

Like his theory of structuration, furthermore, Giddens's historical sociology also covertly embodies a number of value assumptions. For example, he argues that routine, continuity and tradition are sustained in day-to-day life as a consequence of an agent's need to maintain ontological security.[34] 'Continuity', he argues, 'persists even through the most abrupt and radical forms of social change.'[35] As he states elsewhere:

> In analysing the conditions of social reproduction, and therefore of stability and change in society, I attempt to show the essential importance of tradition and routinisation in social life. We should not cede tradition to the conservatives! The sedimentation of institutional forms in long-term processes of social development is an inescapable feature of all types of society, however rapid the changes they may undergo. (Giddens 1979, p. 7)

This viewpoint, however, contradicts the majority of Giddens's other claims, not least his discontinuist view of history. It implies a natural-law thought-style or a crude Enlightenment approach in which tradition is simply identified with unreflective dogma. In the majority of his writings, which lean heavily on Weber, routine is correlated with traditional society and social change with post-traditional social forms. Routine and tradition are 'founded in custom and habit'[36] which prevail in tribal or pre-modern societies, in contrast to capitalist society which involves reflexivity and social change.[37] These views are reflected in Giddens's discussion of the relation between non-capitalist and capitalist societies and their relation to ontological security:

> In non-capitalist societies daily life is geared to tradition, and time is experienced as part of the re-enactment of traditional practices. Tradition is the basis of routinisation. In the capitalistic urban milieu, however, the routinisation of day-to-day life is stripped away from tradition. In the 'everyday life' of capitalist urbanism large tracts of activity are denuded of moral meaning; they become matters of habit or of 'dull compulsion'. In such circumstances the level of what Laing calls 'ontological security' in the routines of daily activities is low.[38] This is a phenomenon of some significance.[39]

Notwithstanding the lack of empirical grounding for these claims, Giddens covertly presupposes a contrast between the triad traditional society/routine/ontological security, on the one hand, and the triad capitalism/social change/lack of ontological security, on the other. By identifying change with capitalism, Giddens underestimates the importance of tradition as an essential component within all forms of social life, including the modern. Thus, as demonstrated by a number of thinkers whose work is characterised by a more conservative thought-style – from Heidegger and Wittgenstein to Mannheim and Elias – social forms depend upon tradition to continue. Tradition is essential and ubiquitous. As Mannheim notes:

> strictly speaking it is incorrect to say that the single individual thinks. Rather it is more correct to insist that he participates in thinking further what other men have thought before him. He finds himself in an inherited situation with patterns of thought which are appropriate to the situation and attempts to elaborate further the inherited modes of response or to substitute for them in order to deal more adequately with the new challenges which have arisen out of the shifts and changes in his situation. (Mannheim 1960, p. 3)

To emphasise the importance of tradition is to reaffirm the fact that social life depends upon extending previous forms of knowledge and experience as a basis for future knowledge.

These value-laden contrasts are extended in Giddens's discussion of the relations between reflexivity and social groups, in which various collectivities, including associations, organisations and social movements, are differentiated according to their relationship to social reproduction. Associations, which predominate in traditional societies, are characterised by little attempt to control or alter the circumstances of social reproduction and therefore these result in homeostasis. The existence of organisations presupposes a class-divided society in which the reflexive self-regulation of agents permits some selective 'information feedback', resulting in minor directional change. Finally, social movements involve a fully reflexive self-regulation within class societies, which allows them to undertake major directional social change. We can distinguish between non-reflexivity/stability/homeostasis, on the one hand, and reflexivity/directional change/self-regulation, on the other. It may, however, be asked why should reflexivity result in social change. Is it not feasible that reflexive actors will choose to continue to act in accord with previous practices? Reflexivity and tradition are not mutually exclusive concepts. I will return to this in the next chapter.

Other value-laden assumptions emerge in Giddens's discussion of existential contradiction. Although one may readily accept that capitalism has had profound effects in shaping both the social environment and the relationship between human beings and 'nature', his notion of a 'created environment' is questionable. Giddens here counterposes a brute 'authentic' nature with its own specific 'impulses' or 'rhythms' to the 'artificial milieu' of society. The concept of 'created environment', however, tends to lack any purchase or reference. It is hard to unpack this notion since it is difficult to know what its negation would be. What is an 'uncreated' environment? Giddens probably has some pristine unmediated notion of 'nature' in mind, but as Durkheim rightly showed in *The Elementary Forms of Religious Life* (1976), nature, like society, always requires representation through socially and historically constructed categories. Nature is always and everywhere mediated by human beings, who are also a part of it. Giddens thus tends to employ a romantic contrast between nature and culture, failing to look at the socio-genesis of the terms. Further, he proposes a partial, restricted representation of nature. Nature does not just consist of authentic impulses and natural rhythms but also of failed harvests, savage weather and fatal disease, all of which have remained recalcitrant features of nature in the history of the human struggle for survival.

Hence whether ontological security is only threatened in the created modern environment while remaining intact in tribal societies remains questionable given the precariousness, violence and limited human lifespan which characterised these societies (see also Saunders 1989). These binary oppositions which covertly underlie the dualisms in Giddens's work are represented in Table 5.1.

Table 5.1   Dualisms in Giddens's historical sociology

Tribal society (traditional social forms)	Class society (capitalism)
Homeostasis, routine, stability	Self-regulation, change
Ontological security	Lack of Ontological security
Undeveloped reflexivity	Reflexivity
Nature	Society ('created environment')
Life with meaning	Meaningless existence

Giddens's methodology is also in some ways highly problematic. In his attempt to move away from positivist evolutionary and functional analyses, Giddens follows Weber in regarding all social life and change as contingent. History is the outcome of chance events, in which things could have always 'been otherwise'. Such a view sits well with Giddens's liberalism, in which each moment of social reproduction exists potentially as a moment of transformation where, 'stripped of historical guarantees critical theory re-enters the universe of contingency' (Giddens 1985, p. 335). Nevertheless, such an emphasis often results in a disjointed descriptive analysis. By jettisoning a causal deterministic analysis his historical sociology loses much of its explanatory force. To argue that history is open is not the same as arguing that it is purely contingent. There is pattern and order in social life which calls for explanation in both sociological and historical terms, and this cannot be accounted for by relying on the notion of contingency. In order to avoid such a pitfall, Weber himself adopted a flexible multicausal approach (which he termed 'singular causal analysis') in which particular events or historical outcomes are traced back to their causally-relevant antecedents on the basis of probabilistic and counter-factual reasoning. This, as Fritz Ringer (1998) notes, was conjoined with an empirical analytical practice. However, such auxillary criteria for historical analysis are missing from Giddens's approach.

Perhaps the most serious failure of Giddens's sociology relates to his writings on empirical work, both in the degree to which his theory is capable of illuminating empirical work and in the amount of empirical evidence he adduces to support his arguments. In his view:

> social theory has the task of providing conceptions of the nature of human social activity which can be placed in the service of empirical work. The main concern of social theory is the same as that of social science in general: the illumination of concrete processes of social life. (Giddens 1984, p. xvii)

This assertion indicates the sociological division of labour with which Giddens wants to work. This general division of tasks is, I think, unjustifiable, reflecting his peripheral concern with empirical matters. Hence, when Giddens relates structuration to four pieces of research, this is not undertaken to develop any proximate alliance between his theory and empirical work or to reveal the adequacy of that work in respect of empirical data, but rather to justify the internal coherence and explanatory power of his theory. However, an imposition of this kind, of theoretical principles upon a discrete body of empirical work, is not particularly difficult to accomplish. As E.P. Thompson remarks in a different context:

> Nothing is more easy than to take a model to the proliferating growth of actuality, and to select from it only such evidence as is in conformity with the principles of selection ... In the end, with some splitting at the seams, the job is done: it always can be. (Thompson 1979, pp. 287–8)

The result of this shortcoming is that Giddens's interpretations of these empirical pieces of research are not only strained, but, occasionally, even misleading (see Gregson 1989).[40] Moreover, why, if many of the empirical works to which Giddens refers were developed independently of his structuration theory, is his work necessary in sociology? On occasion, Giddens himself acknowledges such a consideration: 'Why bother with cumbersome notions like "structuration" and the rest if first-rate social research can be done without them?' He provides a Weberian answer:

> There is, of course, no obligation for anyone doing detailed empirical research, in a given localised setting, to take on board an array of abstract notions that would merely clutter up what would otherwise be described with economy and in ordinary language.

The concepts of structuration theory, as with any competing theoretical perspective, should for many research purposes be regarded as sensitising devices, nothing more. That is to say, they may be useful for thinking about research problems and the interpretations of research results. (Giddens 1984, p. 326)

In Giddens's view, then, the methodological status of structuration theory is simply that of a 'sensitising device'. This standpoint constitutes, however, a considerable disclaimer in relation to the general thrust and tenor of his other rather grander theoretical and substantive claims.[41]

That Giddens continues to treat the theoretical and empirical as separate though loosely connected moments is evident in a number of ways. First, it is implicit in his attempt to apply structuration theory to independently formulated empirical work. Second, it is demonstrated by the fact that it was not until Giddens's third major work on structuration theory, *The Constitution of Society* (1984), that he introduced any claims concerning empirical analysis. Consequently, his first two works on structuration, in which his ideas regarding structuration were developed more or less completely, made little attempt to consider any empirical work or analyses (Gregson 1989). Thirdly, it is indicated in the distinction Giddens makes between social theory and sociology:

I use the term 'social theory' to encompass issues that I hold to be the concern of all the social sciences. These issues are to do with the nature of human action and the acting self; with how interaction should be conceptualised and its relations to institutions; and with grasping the practical connotations of social analysis. I understand 'sociology', by contrast, to be not a generic discipline to do with the study of human societies as a whole, but the branch of social science which focuses particularly upon the 'advanced' or modern societies. Such a disciplinary characterisation implies an intellectual division of labour, nothing more. While there are theorems and concepts which belong distinctively to the industrialised world, there is no way in which something called 'sociological theory' can be clearly distinguished from the more general concepts and concerns of social theory. 'Sociological theory', in other words, can if one likes be regarded as a branch of social theory more generally, but it cannot sustain a wholly separate identity. (Giddens 1984, p. xvii)

For Giddens, then, this distinction represents nothing more than an intellectual division of labour, in which those working in social theory 'should be concerned first and foremost with reworking conceptions of human being and human doing, social reproduction and social transformation'. This involves 'the analysis of issues which spill over into philosophy', since '[t]he social sciences are lost if they are not directly related to philosophical problems by those who practice them' (ibid.).

   The self-proclaimed anchorage in ontological and abstract philosophical issues is a good indicator of the distance kept by Giddens between his social theory and empirical work. Giddens generally maintains a cavalier attitude toward empirical facts and assumes, in effect, that his theory is self-validating. In some important respects, as Bauman points out, Giddens's writings parallel those of Husserl (see Bauman 1989). The similarities concern not only their shared rationalism but, more broadly, their style of thought, specifically their respective attempts to seek transcendental features of social life, untainted by empirical particulars. In his early work, Husserl's central aim was to establish a philosophical schema that transcended empirical knowledge. The result was the establishment of a distinction between the ideal universal and the concrete particular. According to Husserl, all empirical particulars should be 'bracketed off' in order to facilitate a 'penetration' to the essence of consciousness and to permit the observation of the process of 'ideation'. Thus, Husserl's 'transcendental phenomenology' involved placing the ordinary assumptions that individuals make about the physical 'lived in-world' – their 'natural attitude' – within a 'methodological epoche' in order to provide an examination of pure subjectivity isolated from empirical particularity. On the basis of this examination of subjectivity, Husserl then aimed to reconstitute the real historical world. However, as he found, the empirical world refused to be reconstituted from this foundation of pure, essential subjectivity.

   This quest for certainty, for knowledge free from presuppositions, also characterises Giddens's work. By focusing on ontology, which provides a conception of the nature of human activity, he cannot but fail to descend to the mundane empirical world, which, however, has already been separated from theory through the imposition of an intellectual division of labour. Hence to analyse the empirical world is always *post festum*. As a result, Giddens can only apply general concepts to the unique features of the lived-in world with great difficulty and at a high level of generality.[42] As Sayer (1990, p. 244) notes, by employing concepts at such a high level of abstraction – as, for example, in describing tribal societies or class-divided societies – he ends up categorising together Greek city-states, Moghul India and the Roman Empire. On the basis of such a level of generality, very little is actually explained about these particular societies. Again, as E.P. Thompson (1979, p. 290) writes, 'A psychology which reduces the infinite variety of sexual expression, from platonic love to a rape in the Romney Marshes, to "sex" tells us everything and nothing.'[43]

Both Giddens's reluctance to undertake empirical work and his tendency to see it as a secondary concern mean that his sociology ultimately remains a weak sociological resource.[44] Although what constitutes important work in sociology will always remain a contested matter, there is little doubt that the endurance and explanatory power of Marx, Weber, Durkheim, Simmel, Mannheim, Elias and, more recently, Bourdieu is in no small way related to their integration of theory with empirical work. It was in large part their ability to mediate the universal with the particular, the transhistorical with the historical, which made such sociological work valuable. The relationship between theory and empirical analysis is not, for Giddens, a two-way symbiotic one, but rather one that presupposes their prior division, resulting in the foisting of theoretical concepts onto a distinct empirical world. A philosophical bias of this kind detracts greatly from the sociological utility of Giddens's work. As a result of this bias, we can extend the earlier table of dualisms constitutive of Giddens's historical sociology to incorporate the distinction between the theoretical and the empirical.

6   Modernity

Giddens's work on modernity represents a new phase in the *NB* development of his writings. Building on the 'discontinuist' and multidimensional characterisation of modern social development which he developed in *A Contemporary Critique of Historical Materialism* and *The Nation-State and Violence*, Giddens states in *The Consequences of Modernity* that modernity refers to 'modes of social life or organisation which emerged in Europe from about the seventeenth century onwards and which subsequently became more or less worldwide in their influence' (Giddens 1990a, p. 1). Rather than talking of postmodernity, which had become fashionable during the late 1980s, Giddens continues to insist on the importance of referring to contemporary society in terms of modernity, though he makes a sharp distinction between 'early' and 'late' modernity in his writings.

RISK, TRUST AND GLOBALISATION

According to Giddens, modernity represents a sharp qualitative break from previous traditional social orders. This break involves a profound transformation that is both extensional and intensional. In terms of extensionality, globalising influences of interconnection span the globe, so that individuals now live in a global world; in terms of intensionality, the intimate and personal features of day-to-day existence become fundamentally altered. After reaffirming his view that modernity has four major institutions – capitalism, industrialism, the capacity for surveillance and military power – he points to three distinct yet interconnected sources which underlie the *NB* dynamism of modernity – the separation of time and space, the development of disembedding mechanisms and the continual reflexive appropriation of knowledge.

It was noted in the last chapter that the separation and recombination of space and time allow a 'zoning' of social life to take place.[1] The zoning of space and time not only allows the development of modern rationalised organisations to take place, but also permits the emergence of a radical historicity in which the past can be appropriated with the aim of shaping the future. More importantly, it allows the 'disembedding' of social systems. Disembedding refers to 'the 'lifting out' of social relations from their local contexts of interaction and permits their restructuring across indefinite spans of time-space' (Giddens 1990a, p. 21).[2] There are two major types of disembedding mechanism, both of which are intrinsically involved in the constitution of modernity. The first mechanism consists of symbolic tokens, of which money is paradigmatic, and refers to media which can be exchanged regardless of who uses them. The second type of disembedding mechanism consists of expert systems: 'By expert systems I mean systems of technical accomplishment of professional expertise that organise large areas of the material and social environments in which we live today' (Giddens 1990a, p. 21). Examples of experts are doctors, lawyers, architects and, most importantly, scientists. Like symbolic tokens, expert systems permit the removal of social relations from their immediate context and their transferral across space and time. Fundamental to both forms of disembedding mechanism, as well as to the reflexivity definitive of modernity, is the concept of trust. Trust refers to a form of 'faith', or, more precisely, it derives from faith in the fact that certain outcomes will arise, or in the reliability of a person or a system. The interface between individuals and abstract systems occurs at 'access points' which take the form of 'faceless commitments' in relation to abstract systems, and 'facework commitments' in relation to persons.

For Giddens, a sense of trust in processes, people and things is a crucial factor in maintaining a sense of ontological security in the modern world: the absence of trust results in existential angst or dread. Ontological security in premodern societies has to be understood in relation to contexts of trust and forms of risk and danger which were anchored in the local circumstances of place. Four localised contexts of trust existed: kinship, local community, religious cosmology and tradition itself. In premodern societies, risk predominantly reflected the hazards of the physical world and violence in social life. Temporally, these societies operated in terms of what Lévi-Strauss calls 'reversible' time, such that tradition as expressed through routine was intrinsically meaningful. By contrast, modernity offers a new 'risk profile'. Modernity is pervaded by risk. In fact the latter becomes the defining parameter of modern culture and life, replacing the preoccupation with wealth.

> Modernity is a risk culture. I do not mean by this that social life is inherently more risky than it used to be; for most people that is not the case. Rather, the concept of risk becomes fundamental to

the way both lay actors and technical specialists organise the social world. Modernity reduces the overall riskiness of certain areas and modes of life, yet at the same time introduces new risk parameters largely or completely unknown in previous eras. (ibid., pp. 3–4)

Here, Giddens draws heavily upon the work of Beck (1998; see also Beck et al. 1994), asserting the impossibility of opting out of trust in the abstract systems of modern social life. In modern social life, trust no longer derives primarily from the world of nature, but instead from socially organised knowledge in the form of abstract systems. This 'manufactured risk' takes on a new and menacing appearance in various forms of risk:

> The possibility of nuclear war, ecological calamity, uncontainable population explosion, the collapse of global economic exchange, and other potential global catastrophes provide an unnerving horizon of dangers for everyone ... [These globalised risks] do not respect divisions between rich and poor or between regions of the world ... The global intensity of certain kinds of risk transcends all social and economic differentials. (Giddens 1990a, p. 125)

Because of the coexistence of manufactured risk and globalisation, individuals are forced to maintain a sense of trust in distant events over which no single person has any direct control. Consequently, a fatalistic view, akin to that which characterised the premodern era, develops, bringing with it repressed anxiety. For Giddens, the two classic constructions of what it feels like to live in modernity – the world of alienation for Marx and the 'iron cage' of bureaucracy for Weber – must be replaced by a new image of modernity, one that is analogous to riding a careering juggernaut. In his view, this juggernaut and the experience it conveys are not of one piece, but are contradictory and tensive. Giddens describes modernity as:

> a runaway engine of enormous power which, collectively as human beings, we can drive to some extent but which also threatens to rush out of control and which could rend itself asunder. The juggernaut crushes those who resist it, and while it sometimes seems to have a steady path, there are times when it veers away erratically in directions we cannot foresee. The ride is by no means wholly unpleasant or unrewarding; it can often be exhilarating and charged with hopeful anticipation. But, so long

as the institutions of modernity endure, we shall never be able to control completely either the path or the pace of the journey. In turn, we shall never be able to be entirely secure, because the terrain across which it runs is fraught with risks of high consequence. (ibid., p. 139)

Giddens's new emphasis on modernity indicates a shift in his theoretical position which is evident in a number of areas. We will now look at two of these: agency and epistemology.

AGENCY

It was noted above that the intensional dimension of the change represented by the advent of modernity implied an alteration of the dialectical relation between the globalising tendencies of modernity and the localised events of day-to-day life. According to Giddens, the transformation of day-to-day life involves a move toward the construction of individual identities as part of a reflexive project, according to which the choices made by individuals are made in the context of an array of strategies and options provided by abstract systems.[3]

The more tradition loses its hold, and the more daily life is reconstituted in terms of the dialectic interplay of the local and the global, the more individuals are forced to negotiate lifestyle choices among a diversity of options. (Giddens 1991, p. 5)

Not only is there a transformation of lifestyle, but also a 'transformation of intimacy' (Giddens 1992). In modernity, the self becomes a reflexive project and a drive towards self-actualisation ensues, founded upon basic trust, in which one individual self 'opens out' to another. This mutuality of self-disclosure results in the formation of personal and erotic ties in the form of 'pure relationships'. According to Giddens, 'pure relationships' involve 'commitment' and demands for intimacy, such that trust develops through mutual disclosure alone, rather than through criteria which exist outside of the relationship itself – such as kinship ties, social duty or traditional obligations.

Just as personal ties are transformed in modernity, so too are lifestyles. Thus, in modern social life, the notion of lifestyle begins to take on a particular significance. In Giddens's view, the plurality of choices which confronts the individual in late modernity derives from several influences. In the first place, in the post-traditional world, the signposts established by tradition now are blank. Second, there exists what Giddens, following Berger, calls a 'pluralisation of lifeworlds'. The diversity and segmentation characteristic of modernity results in the formation of a multiplicity of environments for action, or 'lifestyle sectors', each of which concerns a time-space 'slice' of an individual's activities. Third, post-traditional societies mean that agents live not only in a situation of greater choice, but in one of methodological doubt in which even the most reliable authorities can only be trusted 'until further notice'. Finally, modernity is marked by the mediation of experience through a globalised media which also provides further new choices. As a result of the increasing 'openness' of social life, the pluralisation of contexts of action and the diversification of 'authorities', lifestyle choice becomes increasingly important in the constitution of self-identity and daily activity. All of these factors mean that modernity creates a greater degree of choice than did traditional culture:

> Obviously, no culture eliminates choice altogether in day-to-day affairs, and all traditions are effectively choices among an indefinite range of possible behaviour patterns. Yet, by definition, tradition or established habit orders life within relatively set channels. Modernity confronts the individual with a complex diversity of choices and, because it is non-foundational, offers little help with which options should be selected. (Giddens 1991, p. 81)

Consequently, 'choice within a plurality of possible options ... is "adopted" rather than "handed down"'. Here routines are reflexively open to change in the 'light of the mobile nature of self-identity' (ibid.). Giddens argues that such choice is not optional but, paradoxically, constrained: 'we all not only follow lifestyles, but in an important sense are forced to do so – we have no choice but to choose' (ibid., p. 8).

In such a world of choice and lifestyle options, strategic life-planning becomes important. Here, individuals prepare a course of future actions in terms of a 'self-biography' or 'lifeplan calendar':[4]

> Each of the small decisions a person makes everyday – what to wear, what to eat, how to conduct himself at work, whom to meet with later in the evening – contributes to such routines. All such choices

(as well as larger and more consequential ones) are decisions not only about how to act but who to be. (Giddens 1991, p. 81).

In modernity, moreover, choice transcends all class differentiation, so that its 'influence is more or less universal, no matter how limiting the social situations of particular individuals and groups may be'. He gives the example of a poor, black single mother:

> Consider the position of a black woman, the head of a single-parent family of several children, living in conditions of poverty in the inner city. It might be assumed that such a person could only look on with bitter envy at the options available to the more privileged. (ibid., p. 86)

Echoing his earlier claims that a person can 'always do otherwise', Giddens adds:

> Of course, for all individuals and groups, life chances condition lifestyle choices ... Emancipation from situations of oppression is the necessary means of expanding the scope of some sorts of lifestyle option. Yet even the most underprivileged today live in situations permeated by institutional components of modernity ... In such situations, the reflexive constitution of self-identity may be every bit as important as among more affluent strata, and as strongly affected by globalising influences. A black woman heading a single-parent household, however constricted and arduous her life, will nevertheless know about factors altering the position of women in general, and her own activities will almost certainly be modified by that knowledge. Given the inchoate nature of her social circumstances, she is virtually obliged to explore novel modes of activity, with regard to her children, sexual relations and friendships. Such an exploration, although it might not be discursively articulated as such, implies a reflexive shaping of self-identity. The deprivations to which she is subject, however, might make these tasks become an almost insupportable burden, a source of despair rather than self-enrichment. (ibid.)

For Giddens, life-planning as an activity constitutes an example of the 'colonisation of the future'. He continues his discourse on 'futurology' by emphasising the malleability, intrinsic openness and profusion of choice in the social world:

The 'openness' of things comes to express the malleability of the social world and the capability of human beings to shape the physical settings of our existence. While the future is recognised to be intrinsically unknowable, and as it is increasingly severed from the past, that future becomes a new terrain – a territory of counterfactual possibility. (ibid., p. 11)

The inevitable side-effect of a proliferation of choice, conjoined with a wholesale reflexivity which questions everything, including itself, is a society in which day-to-day moral questions remain unanswered. Meaninglessness becomes a fundamental psychic problem. In addressing the latter problem, Giddens implicitly refers to his earlier developed philosophical anthropology,[5] in which meaninglessness in modern social life is seen as the result of the sequestration of individual experience from existential and moral questions concerning madness, criminality, sickness and death, sexuality and nature.

EPISTEMOLOGY

In relation to knowledge and epistemology, Giddens's later work continues to affirm the fundamental ontological distinction between knowledge of society and knowledge of nature. In the *Consequences of Modernity*, he develops a more critical stance towards the Enlightenment:

> the thesis that more knowledge about social life (even if that knowledge is as well buttressed empirically as it could be) equals greater control over our fate is false. It is (arguably) true about the physical world, but not about the universe of social events. Expanding our understanding of the social world might produce a progressively more illuminating grasp of social institutions and, hence, increasing 'technological' control over them , if it were the case that social life were entirely separate from human knowledge about it or that knowledge could be filtered continually into reasons for social action, producing step by step increases in the 'rationality' of behaviour in relation to specific needs. (Giddens 1990a, p. 43)

Although Giddens had previously argued that reflexivity was a defining characteristic of all human beings, in his theory of modernity he develops a conceptual distinction between a reflexivity which is characteristic of traditional social orders and a reflexivity which characterises modern social orders. In traditional social orders, reflexivity exists in terms of a reinterpretation and clarification of tradition:

> in pre-modern civilisations reflexivity is still largely limited to the reinterpretation and clarification of tradition, such that in the scales of time the side of the 'past' is much more heavily weighed down than that of the 'future'. (ibid., pp. 37–8)

In contrast, reflexivity in modern social orders has little or no intrinsic connections with the past, so that 'social practices become routinely altered in the light of incoming information'. In such a situation, social practices can no longer be defended by simply appealing to tradition. Thus, although traditions may continue, they can only do so in recognition of incoming information and not merely for the sake of tradition.[6] Giddens calls this 'wholesale reflexivity'. Here, in contrast to the Enlightenment, reason subverts reason in terms of establishing foundational knowledge. Knowledge in modernity is continually revisable, such that it holds 'until further notice'.[7] The result is 'futurology', whereby the future constantly remains open to possible alternatives. These social circumstances should not be characterised as postmodernity, but rather as a radicalising of modernity, or as 'late modernity':

> The break with providential views of history, the dissolution of foundationalism, together with the emergence of counterfactual future orientated thought and the 'emptying out' of progress by continuous change, are so different from the core perspectives of the Enlightenment as to warrant the view that far-reaching changes have occurred ... The disjunctions which have taken place should be seen as resulting from the self-clarification of modern thought, as the remnants of providential and traditional outlooks are cleared away. We have not moved beyond modernity but are living through a phase of its radicalisation. (Giddens 1990a, p. 51)

This sense of uncertainty and the lack of grounding available for knowledge is particularly acute for Giddens in the social sciences and sociology. In *The Consequences of Modernity*, he restates the double hermeneutic:

The discourse of sociology and the concepts, theories and findings of other social sciences continually 'circulate in and out' of what it is they are about. In doing so they reflexively restructure their subject matter. (ibid., p. 43)   *Not this much!*

The expansion of social reflexivity severs knowledge from societal control, but also creates a world of 'clever people' (Giddens 1994a, p. 7) who continually filter vast amounts of information relevant to their life situations. This knowledge is filtered by four sets of factors: differential power, the role of values, the impact of unintended consequences, and the circulation of social knowledge through the double hermeneutic. As a result, the 'point is not that there is no stable social world to know, but that knowledge of that world contributes to its unstable or mutable character' (Giddens 1990a, p. 45).

Although Giddens continues to remain reticent on epistemological issues, his work on modernity seems to point towards an epistemological relativism:

One of the most characteristic features of modernity is the discovery that the development of empirical knowledge does not in itself allow us to decide between different value positions ... (ibid., p. 154)

[w]e must now deal with an irredeemably pluralistic universe of values, and indeed the suspension of all value judgments, save for contextual or local ones. (Giddens 1994a, p. 20)   *What does it now stand?*

However, Giddens attempts to sustain his notion of a critical social science by reasserting the notion of a double hermeneutic and, in addition, by emphasising the homogenisation of values in modernity. *On* The latter permits the possibility of collective agreement on the major *Hegel!* problems in society: 'this is probably the first time in history that we can speak of the emergence of universal values – values shared by almost everyone, and which are in no sense the enemy of cosmopolitanism' (ibid.).

These values result from what Giddens, following Hans Jonas, calls a 'heuristics of fear'. They are the result of high-consequence *Massively dialogical ideology* risk which 'transcends all values and all exclusionary divisions of power' (Giddens 1990a, p. 154). They include a belief in the sanctity of human life, universal human rights, the preservation of the species, and a care for the future, and they imply an ethics of individual and collective responsibility which overrides individual divisions of interest.

EVALUATION

Giddens's discussion of modernity, like his theory of structuration and historical sociology, contains both original and brilliant insights into the fundamental changes that characterise modernity without relinquishing to the permissiveness of postmodern theory or to Marxist dogmatism. Risk and reflexivity offer a profoundly unique conceptual framework with which to discern the contours of the late modern world. *Prima facie* Giddens's later substantive writings on modernity indicate a shift in his thought-style towards a more concrete, relativist, dynamic account of the social world which is highly critical of Enlightenment thinking. This conclusion would, however, be both simplistic and misleading. In fact, Giddens retains his underlying ontological perspective and in some ways exaggerates it, particularly in respect of his conception of the individual as an autonomous, free, choosing actor. This may be explained by two factors. The first factor is biographical and concerns the psychological counselling he undertook during 1988 (see Bryant and Jary 2001a, p. 8). The second, and more important, factor is political. Giddens's later work on modernity, although it originated before 1990, really only developed after the 1990s, following the collapse of the Eastern European socialist states.[8] This, as noted above, constituted one half of the original contextual socio-political dualism which provided the basis for and impetus towards, his work. It was argued above that this political dualism was translated onto the sociological field and became expressed in a number of dualisms, some of which are indicated in Table 6.1.

Table 6.1   Political and sociological dualisms in Giddens's work

Liberal aspects	Socialist aspects
Liberalism	Socialism
Freedom	Equality
Agency	Structure

The demise of this political dualism resulted in the development of a number of aspects in Giddens's own theory which had previously been associated with the liberal moment of this political dualism, that is, those concepts which figure on the left-hand side of Table 6.1: capitalism, liberalism, individual freedom, agency.

As noted in Chapter 3, Giddens views the agent in standard liberal terms, as an individual who is an embodied unit and who possesses a range of causal powers which he/she may employ through his/her intervention in the ongoing sequence of events in the world. He also highlighted three major types of constraints on the agent: (a) material constraints which derive from the limits imposed by the physical capacity of the body and by features of the physical environment,[9] (b) constraints deriving from sanctions which are related to power, and (c) structural constraints. Although this conception of the individual and social constraint in Giddens's theory of structuration was highly problematic and contradictory, it did at least make reference to the restrictions on social action. Although Giddens's later work involves a shift from ontology to more substantive issues, his theory of modernity seems to lack any systematic notion of constraint. That is, structural constraint seems generally to disappear from his work on modernity. Modernity involves the construction of individual identities as part of a reflexive project, according to the choices individuals have made in the context of an array of strategies and options provided by abstract systems. The only form of constraint on agents in social life is that choice is inevitable: 'we all not only follow lifestyles, but in an important sense are forced to do so – we have no choice but to choose' (Giddens 1991, p. 8). Consequently, a strong focus on individual self-determination through consumption pervades Giddens's writings on modernity. Thus from what is already a liberal standpoint Giddens moves further towards an atomistic individualism. Yet the position is not so clear-cut. Giddens does speak of constraint, but this refers to collective constraint imposed by modernity as a juggernaut that crushes those who resist it. This emphasis on the capacity of individual choice to produce an unintended outcome which affects the collectivity is by no means new in the social sciences but is exemplified, for instance, by Mandeville's 'private vices, public virtues', Smith's 'hidden hand', Hegel's 'Cunning of Reason' and Engels's 'paralellogram of forces'. All of these concepts nevertheless furnished inadequate accounts of human society, not least because of their inability to explain the problem of order. Giddens's substantive account of modernity has to be viewed in relation to his earlier writings on ontology and as such this account similarly fails to provide an adequate characterisation of the relationship between agency and structure.

Furthermore, in Giddens's early work on structuration and historical sociology, modern society was regrded as problematic and negatively evaluated. This followed the tradition of earlier sociology in which 'society' was characterised as 'alienated' (Marx), as moving away from value-rational action (Weber), or as juxtaposed to 'community' (Tonnies). In Giddens's later work, by contrast, modern capitalist social relations are seen to require radicalisation rather than critique. Thus, as will be discussed in the next chapter, he no longer challenges capitalism on the basis of socialist values but instead calls for an augmentation or radicalisation of the political liberalism inherent in modernity (see Giddens 1996). In addition, Giddens makes a number of sweeping claims in his writings on modernity which both overstate and misrepresent ideas and events. For instance, he is influenced by a number of postmodern writers who, despite emphasising diversity and difference within contemporary discourse, portray the Enlightenment as a one-dimensional Olympian philosophy in which the will to knowledge is linked umbilically to the will to control. His rehabilitation of philosophical conservatism is largely a response to this monochrome conception of the Enlightenment as instrumental rationalisation. However, as argued in Chapter 1, the Enlightenment was a far more complex and self-critical phenomenon than Giddens would allow us to believe.

PROBLEMATIC ASSUMPTIONS OF REFLEXIVITY

A major problem bedevilling Giddens's sociology of modernity springs from his individualistic and instrumentalist conception of reflexivity. By regarding reflexivity as providing a rational basis for freedom and choice in modern society, Giddens simultaneously politicises reflexivity and the relationship between life politics and institutional power. Yet, the distinction he makes between a reflexivity characteristic of all human beings and the 'wholesale reflexivity' of modernity remains unclear (Mouzelis 1999, Pleasants 1999). Hence whether Giddens is talking of an increase in individual reflexivity or in institutional reflexivity is not fully spelled out in his work. Both interpretations of his position are possible. In the first instance, within his stratification model of the actor, reflexivity is regarded as a central feature of all human beings, along with processes of rationalisation and motivation. By contrast, it is argued that there is a dramatic increase in reflexivity in modernity. However, Giddens simply assumes that the increase in reflexivity is an implication of rapid and continued societal change. As noted in Chapter 5, such a conception is based on a covert identification of stability and tradition with non-reflexivity, and reflexivity with social change, as in his earlier writing in *NSV*. But why should this be so? Reflexivity is required both in order to reproduce existing relations along what Giddens calls 'traditional lines', as well as to 'modernise' traditional practices. Giddens does acknowledge that people continue with tradition in 'the traditional way', but refers to this continuation as fundamentalism, a form of non-negotiable, unreflexive action. The ultimate implication of Giddens's viewpoint is that traditional societies – which are implicitly non-Western – were and are simply unreflexive. This not only contradicts other assertions he makes in *The Nation-State and Violence* but also runs counter to most historical evidence. To imply, for example, that ancient Greece, ancient Egypt or the various Chinese dynasties were 'unreflexive' is both theoretically and empirically spurious.

The question therefore arises of the vantage-point from which Giddens conceives and constructs his conception of late modernity. As Anthias (1999) rightly notes, Giddens's writings on modernity express the position of a privileged academic. His undifferentiated account of the experience of modernity is based on a universalisation of the Western experience. He therefore fails, despite his continual emphasis on reflexivity, to actually engage in what Bourdieu calls a 'reflexive sociology': a sociology that examines the institutional presuppositions of its own standpoint (Bourdieu and Wacquant 1992). Because Giddens's liberal vision of autonomous individual actors does not begin with a notion of the agent as an embedded social being, or, as a more conservative thought-style might express it, being-in-the-world, it fails to explain shifts or changes in human action. Individuals do not alter patterns of actions away from traditional practices simply because of an abstract notion of 'heightened reflexivity'; rather, this shift in behaviour stems from the fact that human reflexivity is socially grounded or concretely embedded within determinate contexts of social/material interests. It is these interests which help to account for the struggles in the social world. Thus what Giddens refers to as 'fundamentalism' does not necessarily refer to unthinking or uncritical action, or to a refusal to engage in dialogue for the sake of it. On the contrary, 'fundamentalism' refers to the pursuit by individuals of both habitual and conscious normative orientations within determinate power contexts, both social and material.[10]

If the distinction between 'reflexivity' and 'wholesale reflexivity' is regarded as a *non sequitur*, then, *mutatis mutandis*, his basis for distinguishing modernity from traditional societies also becomes problematic. If, however, Giddens's notion of wholesale reflexivity is taken instead to refer to institutional reflexivity, or to the relation of individuals to bodies of 'expert knowledge', this leads to a further series of problems. According to this interpretation, Giddens wants to argue that knowledge is not just 'referential' or about distinct objects, but rather is constitutive of social relations – for example, in cases in which expert knowledge feeds into, and conditions, individuals' actions and self-identity. In reflexive modernity, then, knowledge increasingly feeds into the constitution of social life and forms the basis upon which an increasing number of situations in which 'clever' people make conscious choices between alternatives. Giddens fails, however, to acknowledge that such reflexivity will be both hierarchically distributed and ideologically loaded. Due to differential access to various forms of knowledge and to the political economy of media broadcasting and the information highway, not all citizens are empowered equally (Rustin 1995). Again in this context, Giddens refers to communications and information in abstract liberal terms which presuppose a democracy of signifying practices (see Williams 1977). He provides no critical analysis of the importance of the media in constructing and relaying information and in constituting peoples' experiences of modernity (Thompson 1995, Bourdieu 2000).

Again this failure to acknowledge the power of the media to define the world, what Goodman (1978) calls 'worldmaking', issues from the represention of individuals as free agents capable of choosing in relation to abstract knowledge, rather than as embedded within determinate and unequal power relations. Here Giddens echoes some interpretations of the Enlightenment in which knowledge is equated with freedom. Consequently the politically repressive uses of abstract knowledges as forms of moral regulation are ignored by Giddens, as are questions concerning state power and moral regulation.

7 Rationality and Reflexivity

Giddens's discussion of rationality in terms of freedom and bondage is emblematic of the political as well as the sociological dimension of his theoretical work. This chapter examines what Giddens refers to as the 'paradox of socialism', which expresses his world-view in a condensed form, and discloses the dilemma concerning the relationship between liberty and equality which runs throughout his work and provides a crucial rationale for his thinking.

BETWEEN CAPITALISM AND SOCIALISM

In *Capitalism and Modern Social Theory* (1971a), Giddens undertakes what he describes as an analysis of the relationship between 'bourgeois sociology' and Marxism. Importantly, this sociological analysis mirrors the political synthesis towards which he aims in terms of liberalism and socialism.[1] For Giddens, such a synthesis is possible, since capitalist and state socialist societies are converging in a number of ways. As he notes:

> It is no exaggeration to say that a major process of theoretical re-thinking is taking place today within both Marxism and in academic sociology. In large degree, this has been stimulated by the same circumstance: the apparent 'convergence' in the social structure of capitalist and socialist societies (Giddens 1971a, p. 245).

He adds:

> But, just as the western countries have changed in considerable degree over the past three or four decades, so have Russia and the European countries which followed it in experiencing socialist revolutions. In these countries, Marx's anticipations of an order in which class domination would be replaced by a rational order 'in which the free development of each is the condition of the free development of all' appears as far from attainment as in the western liberal democracies. Rather, an epistemologically distorted form of Marxism has been employed to legitimate a commitment

129

to industrialisation, in which the 'overtaking' of the economic level of the western countries has become the primary goal. (ibid.)

Not only have defenders of state socialism interpreted Marx's theory in a misleading way, but Marxism as a theory has served as an ideological cloak for state socialism. The result has been a failure, on the part of both Marxism and sociology in general, to analyse adequately the changing contours of modern society (ibid., pp. 244, 246).

In his next major work, *The Class Structure of the Advanced Societies*, published two years later in 1973, Giddens highlights once again the conflict between the political field and the field of sociological analysis:

> We are told that modern sociology is in a condition of crisis ... The 'crisis' – a trite and unsatisfactory term in itself – in contemporary sociology is symptomatic of the fact that we stand at an important phase of transition in social theory. In broad outline ... [t]wo connected sets of factors are involved. One is to be found in the events which, in the past few years, have disrupted the pattern of 'consensus politics' in the capitalist societies: the increase in strike levels in certain countries, the struggles in France in 1968, and the eruption of student protest movements. To these may be added the conflicts which have arisen within the socialist world, culminating in the Soviet invasion of Czechoslovakia. The second factor is the manifest poverty of the dominant forms of theory in sociology in accounting for these events. In academic sociology, structural-functionalism and its main interpretative support, theories of 'the end of ideology', appear blank and barren in the face of a new upsurge of social and political conflict in the West. But Marxism, especially as transmuted into the official ideology of state socialism, seems equally inept when confronted with the events of the recent past (Giddens 1973, p. 13).[2]

Giddens outlines what he perceives to be the failures of Marxism:

> The crisis of sociology is also a crisis of Marxism, in its two major forms, Marxism and social democracy. While I shall not discuss the merits of these, in any direct sense, as forms of political philosophy, I believe that the analyses given in this book are of immediate relevance to their claims as normative guides to political action. (Giddens 1973, p. 19)

He adds: 'I make no bones about declaring that new departures are needed in contemporary social theory' (ibid).

In a discussion of an 'inherent connection between capitalism and liberal democracy',[3] Giddens draws upon T.H. Marshall's *Citizen and Social Class* (1973), which examines the unfolding of three major types of citizenship rights in Britain: civil, social and political. According to Marshall, the development of citizenship rights between the eighteenth and twentieth centuries took place against a background of feudal hierarchy, market inequality and the social injustice of the state.[4] However, political reform meant that the worst aspects of each of these domains had been palliated, so that the modern capitalist system and liberal polity formed a sphere in which the sovereignty of the free individual, as bearer of political and social rights, was institutionally protected. The implication of these changes, according to Marshall, is that a greater degree of equality and justice develops incrementally in modern society without the need for political revolution. For Giddens, Marshall's liberal position serves as a crucial foil to Marx's (nineteenth-century) analysis of capitalism; in particular, the former's emphasis on the importance of a sovereign and free individual whose rights are guarenteed. Marshall's insights therefore constitute a core aspect of the libertarian component of Giddens's world-view.

This preoccupation with the development of free and sovereign individuality within an egalitarian social order also forms the basis of Giddens's analysis of the problems of rationality and bureaucracy within socialism. For Giddens, the problem of reconciling the free subject of capitalism with the egalitarian tendencies of socialism is particularly acute in relation to the communist aim of constructing a rational social order. The length of the following quotation from *The Class Structure of the Advanced Societies* is warranted by its importance:

> I have suggested that there are two strands in socialist theory, which give it a paradoxical aspect. These can readily be related to the conditions which originally generated socialism (and sociology) as a coherent body of thought – the tug of war between post-feudalism and emerging industrial capitalism. The vision of an escape from the exploitation of man by man, the prospective entry into a new realm of human liberty, is one which was stimulated by the sloughing-off of the constricting social, economic and moral bounds of the traditional order ... The advent of 'simple market society' and its imminent transcendence by

capitalism, produced a series of genuine social and economic freedoms, when viewed in the perspective of the preceding order, which stimulated both a perception of the potential malleability of human society and the idea that future transformations could complete the emancipation already apparently begun by the emergence of new social forms. In this regard, socialism is aptly viewed as a radicalisation of bourgeois ideology, and has to be seen as part of a reaction to a feudal past. In its other aspect, socialism comprises a quest to complete the rationalisation of human society by making possible the application ... of technical rationality to social life itself ... However, the search for the elimination of exploitation comes into blunt opposition to the endeavour to rationalise social organisation through the conscious direction of social and economic life. The dilemmas inherent in this antagonism are not resolved in Marxian theory, nor have they been resolved by the practical development of the advanced societies since the close of the nineteenth century. The contradiction which Marx identified in capitalism is itself contradictory! The present-day confrontation of capitalist and state socialist society has in effect given concrete shape to the issues involved. In capitalist society, the class system continues to constitute the fundamental axis of the social structure, and remains the main channel of relationships of exploitative domination. The state socialist societies, on the other hand, have genuinely succeeded in moving towards a classless order, but only at the cost of creating a system of political domination which has altered the character of social exploitation rather than necessarily diminishing it. The challenge to socialist thought today, or rather to those forms of political philosophy which seek to advance beyond the traditional confines of socialist ideas without abandoning them altogether, is to explore the limits of the opposition between rationalisation in each of its aspects, and then to attempt to build a new reconciliation between them. (Giddens 1973, p. 294)

This socialist agenda, which involves a move to a more equal and rational social order while retaining individual freedom, is termed the 'paradox of socialism' by Giddens:

The contrast between capitalist and state socialist society[5] is the living manifestation of what I shall refer to as the 'paradox of socialism': a dilemma resulting from two constituent elements in socialist theory, a clash between the principle of the regulation of production according to human need, and the principle of the elimination or reduction of the exploitative domination of man over man. This is, if one likes, a modern expression of the classical dilemma of freedom versus equality, but manifest in a very specific form. (Giddens 1973, p. 22)

Echoing Hayek, Giddens asserts that the advent of a new type of society founded on the socialisation of the means of production has arisen at the expense of human freedom and liberties.[6] The threat to individual liberty issuing from the social ownership of the means of production (based on rational organisation) is not merely a practical conundrum, but runs through the core of Marxist and Weberian theory. According to Giddens, Marxism retains an excessive dependence on an Enlightenment view of rationality: although Marx believed that alienation would end with the transcendence of capitalism, he failed to specify how production involving 'paratechnical relations' – that is, relationships between different individuals with differing distributions of technical knowledge and skills – could coexist without authority relationships to distribute these skills. This failure was part of Marx's broader failure to stipulate exactly what a socialist society would look like, particularly in regard to the role of the state. This failure was in turn rooted in the overly narrow conception of rationality employed by Marx and defined simply in terms of technique and liberation.[7] Occasionally, however, a second, alternative, view of rationality is also implicit in Marx's writings which, while not clearly distinguished from the first, concerns the domination of human beings over one another. Consequently,

the two aspects of rationalisation which I have distinguished ... appear as two interwoven themes within Marxian socialism. One theme involves a call for the overall extension of the rational understanding and control of social life which, according to Marx, is lacking in capitalism ... [which] sweeps away the alienated forms of human consciousness represented by religious belief systems, but substitutes for these the 'hidden god' of the market. The irrationalities traced by Marx in the functioning of the capitalist economy express this. Socialism, based upon the rational control of economic life, provides a mode of completing the process of rationalisation on the plane of the overall organisation of the social activity of man ... The second theme inherent in socialist thought

... bearing upon the other aspect of rationalisation, is concerned with the liberation of men from the coercive imposition of the will of other individuals. Its most characteristic expression is the Saint-Simonian idea, developed by Marx, of the transcendence of the political power of the state in the projected socialist society. (Giddens 1973, p. 279)

By contrast, Weber's analysis of bureaucracy usefully highlights the second view of rationality which is only touched on by Marx. For Weber, rationality of technique was one of the primary factors which distinguished industrialism from all preceding forms of social order. Weber's portrayal of the 'steel-hard cage' with no reprieve in socialist society constitutes the flip-side of Marx's account, in which the rationality of technique has become the rationality of domination. By tying the two conceptions together, Weber, according to Giddens, inevitably reduces socialism to a utopian dream which implies unacceptably 'that there can be no fundamental alternative to capitalism'. Giddens concludes that:

The Marxian interpretation of bureaucracy is weak because it links the existence of bureaucratic domination only to existence of the state as a form of class domination which disappears when class domination ends and not in terms of the administration needed in a complex society and economy. That is to say, it links the state and bureaucracy to the rationality of domination and not to that of technique ... However the Weberian conception of bureaucracy, by contrast, is flawed because, by assimilating the two aspects of rationalisation, it addresses itself almost wholly to the second.[8]

In the works which follow the publication *of The Class Structure of the Advanced Societies*, Giddens includes an examination of elites. These articles continue to discuss in more detail the failure of capitalism to approximate to any liberal notion of meritocracy or equality (see Giddens 1972a, 1972b; see also Stanworth and Giddens 1974, especially pp. 1–21).

THE DEVELOPMENT OF STRUCTURATION THEORY AND HISTORICAL SOCIOLOGY

The period dating from the late 1970s to the late 1980s represents a new phase in Giddens's work and it was during this period that his theory of structuration, as well as his historical sociology became developed. In the Preface to *New Rules of Sociological Method* (1976), Giddens briefly outlines what he had started to call his 'overall project'. This embraced three major concerns, united by an attempt to analyse nineteenth- and twentieth-century social theory in terms of its contemporary relevance.[9] These themes and the continuity of his project were repeated in his introduction to *Central Problems in Social Theory*, written in 1979. During the early 1970s, Giddens made some explicit references to politics but, as noted above, these were usually isolated comments or remarks made peripherally in the introduction or prefaces to his writings. However, during the early 1980s his political views became increasingly explicit. Such views were expressed in a number of articles, many of which were published in *Profiles and Critiques in Social Theory* (1982), as well as in his two-volume critique of historical materialism (Giddens 1981a, 1985). In these later works a more critical stance towards Marx began to be revealed, sometimes more critical in tone than substance. To a certain extent, this shift reflected the social and political changes which took place during the 1970s and 1980s as Marxism came increasingly to be questioned following the rise of a number of social movements which appealed to human interests and which were irreducible to the struggle between capital and labour. While, for example, the women's movement developed discourses on the family and sexuality, the activities of ecological and peace movements increased in response to the growing possibility of a global nuclear war.

Having previously employed Weber as a theoretical counterweight and corrective to Marx in *The Class Structure of the Advanced Societies*, Giddens now draws increasingly on Durkheim. In his article 'Durkheim, Socialism and Marxism' written in 1981 (Giddens 1981b), Giddens uses Durkheim's distinction between 'communist' and 'socialist' doctrines as a reference point for a discussion on socialist governance.[10] Although Durkheim mistakenly downplays the importance of the role of class in modern society, Giddens believes that he correctly focuses 'upon themes which are at best confronted only in a rudimentary way in Marx' (Giddens 1982, p. 125). These themes include individual rights, or what Durkheim calls 'moral individualism', and Marx's assumption that the repressive power of the state will eventually give way to a democratic socialist state concerned only with 'the administration of things'. Reiterating earlier claims from *The Class Structure of the Advanced Societies*, Giddens argues that Marxists are misguided in their dismissive attitude to what they call 'bourgeois rights'. On the contrary, whether they are labelled 'bourgeois freedoms', 'moral individualism' or, following T.H. Marshall, 'citizenship rights', such social freedoms 'have proved to be of great significance' in alleviating the worst effects of modern capitalism. Therefore 'using Marshall against Marx' (Giddens 1982, p. 173) provides a useful corrective to the utopian excesses of Marx and proves that 'Marshall's account has by no means lost its contemporary relevance to the critique of Marx' (ibid., p. 175).

Many of these arguments are restated in other essays written during the same period,[11] particularly in his first critical volume on historical materialism, *A Contemporary Critique of Historical Materialism* (1981a).[12] In the last chapter of this book, entitled 'Between Capitalism and Socialism' – a title which Giddens had originally aimed to give to the last volume in this three-volume project – he continues to show his sympathy for the socialist project by arguing that it exists on two levels: first as a series of ideas which can be critically discussed and developed and secondly as actually existing state societies.[13]

Elsewhere he writes:

> We live in a world for which the traditional sources of social theory have left us unprepared – especially with those forms of social theory associated with liberal or socialist politics ... To someone sympathetic to, yet critical of, Marxist theory and of the libertarian aspects of socialism, it should be clear that my discussion has important implications for normative political thought. (Giddens 1987, p. 180)

The end of the bipolar world

The collapse of the Eastern Bloc and state socialist societies after 1989 represented a massive transformation in the world's social, political and economic landscape. As Giddens notes in a personal aside, the fall of the Berlin Wall constituted one of the most important events shaping his political beliefs (in Brasher 1997, p. 32). The years following 1990 therefore represented not only a fundamental social and political transformation but, in keeping in line with the argument of this book, a sociological transformation in Giddens's work. The writings which post-date 1990 express a new phase in Giddens's work, amply demonstrated in *The Consequences of Modernity*, published in 1990 (Giddens 1990a), and the writings which follow. In *Beyond Left and Right*, written in 1994, Giddens

(1994a) re-emphasises Durkheim's arguments concerning socialism, and points to the increased risk of authoritarianism should the state be abolished and a planned economy introduced:[14]

> For Marx, democratisation in a socialist society is one aspect of the disappearance of the state. A substantive democracy would return power to civil society, but therefore 'abolish' it along with the state itself. The difficulties to which this sort of position gives rise are well known … Well before the Soviet Union had tried to translate it into practice by developing systems of Soviets, its limitations and paradoxes had been indicated by Durkheim. Who is to protect democratic rights or define obligations in a democratic way, Durkheim quite properly asked, if the state is pulled down into civil society? This is a recipe either for a vacillating and impotent populism or – as became the case in the USSR – for authoritarianism. (Giddens 1994a, p. 161)

In addition, socialism mistakenly accepted the Enlightenment correlation between an increase in knowledge and greater control of the social world. This dictum may have had some validity during 'simple modernity', but it becomes increasingly problematic in late modernity, where 'globalisation, increasing social reflexivity and manufactured uncertainty mean, despite our "increase" in knowledge, [that] … we live in a world of dislocation and uncertainty, a "runaway world"' (ibid., p. 3).

Giddens then connects these two arguments by asserting that 'New Right' authors such as Hayek were correct to point to the inherent deficiencies of socialist planning as a major obstacle to democracy. However, for Giddens, authoritarianism does not arise because of the state's tendencies towards social engineering and through its attempts to centralise the tacit knowledge of individuals in order to regulate the market, as Hayek had argued. Giddens's argument is, rather, that economic planning is incompatible with modern wholesale reflexivity. Socialist planning has its origins in, and remains bound to, a cybernetic model of control in societies of low reflexivity.

> Socialism was based on what might be called a 'cybernetic model' of social life … But while this set up might work reasonably effectively for more coherent systems – in this case a society of

low reflexivity, with fairly fixed lifestyle habits – it doesn't do so for highly complex ones. (ibid., p. 8)

Thus, although the possibility of socialist planning may have existed in simple modernity which was characterised by societies with fixed national boundaries, low reflexivity and static lifestyles, it cannot work in modern, global, reflexive, individualised societies. Centralised planning and the socialisation of production cannot keep pace with, or account for, the highly volatile, shifting preference structures of reflexive individuals. Consequently,

> In sum, although not solely for the reasons given by Hayek and the others, the idea that 'irrationalities' of capitalist enterprise can be overcome by the socialising of production can no longer be defended. With its dissolution, the radical hopes for so long carried by socialism are as dead as the Old Conservatism that once opposed them. A modern economy can tolerate, and prosper under, a good deal of central planning only so long as certain conditions hold – so long as it is primarily a national economy; social life is segmentalised rather than penetrated extensively by globalising influences; and the degree of institutional reflexivity is not high. As these circumstances alter, Keynesianism falters and Soviet-type economies stagnate. (ibid., p. 67)

Modern societies – which are distinguished by complex decision-making processes – by contrast require a devolution or decentralisation in decision-making processes. Since social regulation is impossible, such devolution and decentralisation has to form an integral part of a post-scarcity system (see Chapter 8 for a fuller discussion) in which the economic market functions as a signalling device for individuals' wants and needs. It is only through a post-scarcity system that modern society can maintain the freedom of the individual while at the same time catering to social needs: only thus can the dilemma of freedom and equality be resolved.

> A post-scarcity system, however, takes us beyond this dilemma [freedom and equality]. For when the major goods of life are no longer scarce, market criteria can function solely as means of signalling devices, rather than being also the means of sustaining widespread deprivation. (Giddens 1990a, p. 165)

It is the post-scarcity system within a context of heightened institutional reflexivity that provides Giddens with a solution to the 'paradox of socialism'. The rational social control which was implemented through state allocation in socialist societies in order to achieve equality, but was simultaneously the source of social oppression, can only be replaced by a model which looks to the market as a signalling distributive mechanism. In a post-scarcity system, the Enlightenment ideal of merging equality and freedom can be achieved. A rational society does not necessarily mean one which is characterised by instrumental rationality and domination by means of an iron cage, as Weber believed, but is, rather, one of institutional reflexivity and individual choice. Thus rational control in complex societies need not involve the interference of distorting and usually oppressive social mechanisms; rather, in a society of heightened institutional reflexivity, the market can perform such a signalling function while maintining an emphasis on human freedom. Yet this is not a society inspired by the Enlightenment ideas of economic control and regulation in the Marxist sense, but one of reflexive liberation. Here, when the goods of life are no longer scarce, market criteria function as signalling devices for reflexive individuals engaged in 'life politics'. Here, Weber, who was in many respects an heir to the Enlightenment as well as one of its fiercest critics, has his bleak prognosis of the future and his claims concerning the double-edged nature of reason answered.

EVALUATION

Weber's theory of rationality – perhaps more than any other viewpoint – has encapsulated the central dilemmas of the debate concerning reason and rationality in sociology. As MacIntyre notes, 'the present age in its presentation of itself is dominantly Weberian' (cited in Bernstein 1986). The problem of rationality and reason was of course also a central preoccupation of Enlightenment thinking and Weber's use of Nietzschean arguments was in turn employed by Adorno in his discussion of the 'administered world' and by Heidegger in his discussion on humanity's 'forgetfulness of being', and most recently, by Habermas in his discussion of the 'colonisation of the life-world' (see ibid.).

Giddens's discussion of the Marxian and Weberian conceptions of rationality in terms of liberation or domination respectively therefore provides an interesting and insightful discussion of a nexus of fundamental problems which have haunted and continue to haunt socialist thinkers: the question of rational social planning. However, his theoretical reflections on these issues do not do justice to the complexity of the issues involved. A corollary of Giddens's reductive identification of socialism with the Soviet Union is his rejection of Marx's notion of democratic social planning, which argued for the free association of producers regulating production. For Marx, the central feature of a socialist society, which was developed only in sketched form, was the transformation of private property into the social ownership of 'associated producers' or 'free association of producers'. This not only involved the abolition of private property but also the abolition of the market as a transactional medium determined by individual decisions. These arguments were challenged by economists on the political right as part of an attempt to restore the intellectual legitimacy of market liberalism, which had been badly damaged by the rise of socialism. Criticisms of socialist planning have usually taken two related forms: those concerning bureaucracy, management, incentives and related questions of social repression, on the one hand, and those concerning the practical possibility of rational calculation in a planned economy, on the other (Bottomore 1990, p. 52).

In the early 1920s, the Austrian economist Ludwig von Mises argued that in a developed complex economy, economic calculation for what he termed 'higher production' and 'lower consumption' goods was only possible in a free market in which the exchange and value of all goods could be established through a visible price mechanism (ibid., p. 58). In a free market, every individual, whether buyer or seller, producer or consumer, is informed via the price mechanism of which products are available for purchase and which are in demand and therefore need to be produced. A monetary system of priced goods, which serves as a signalling device, makes rational production and the allocation of resources possible. The abolition of the free market with the advent of socialism would mean the abolition of a signalling device: '[w]here there is no free market, there is no pricing mechanism; without a pricing mechanism, there is no economic calculation' (ibid., p. 54). His countryman and student, Ludwig von Hayek, re-emphasises this view concerning the impossibility of central planning, but reconfigures von Mises's argument by proposing that it is not the rational allocation of resources that is impossible, but the practical implementation of a social order without the market as a signalling device. Hayek argues that individual desires and needs are indeterminate, tacitly held, and dispersed among a number of individuals, and, as such, they can only be 'spontaneously' communicated through market transactions. Hayek's later arguments deal more explicitly with the safeguarding of personal and political freedom under socialist governance. Socialist planning, he argues, consistently leads to tyrannical and bureaucratic government (Hayek 2000).

Giddens's discussion of socialist planning reverses the order of Hayek's arguments. Giddens's earlier discussion concerning rational planning is constructed around the idea that social planning, though necessary for an egalitarian society, leads to a concentration of power and to bureaucracy and repression, as was demonstrated by the Soviet Union. Coversely, his later argument emphasises the impossibility of implementing socialist planning on a practical level because of the form that human knowledge takes in modern society. In contrast to Hayek, however, for whom the dispersal of tacit knowledge in society precludes the possibility of socialist planning,[15] it is the heightened reflexivity of individuals which is the principal obstacle to socialist planning (see Chapter 6). Because their wants and desires are in flux and unpredictable, the market alone can allow reflexive individuals to express their spontaneous choices and as such it is therefore also the guarantor of their freedom and choice.

Given the political stakes involved, the arguments concerning rational planning and socialism are highly contested. Whether and to what extent it is possible to institute rational forms of social organisation which are fundamentally different from capitalism is a crucial normative question and ideological claims are frequently woven into the very fabric of responses to it.[16] The central importance of this question for socialist politics has not, however, been reflected in any systematic or widescale attempt to discuss it, although there are some exceptions. In his discussion of democratic planning, however, Giddens tends to ignore the meagre, though nuanced literature on the subject and instead constructs a dualistic standpoint in which there are only two possible mutually exclusive positions: market liberalism or the Soviet model of economic planning. Such a stark polarity is, however, misleading. As the economic historian Karl Polanyi argues in *The Great Transformation* (1944), free market capitalism was a utopian vision based on the erroneous notion of a disembedded market. In reality, all markets are embedded to various degrees, and even socialism, as the attempt to transcend the self-regulating market by consciously subordinating it to a democratic social process will require a role for markets. Such a relational approach implies that markets can be embedded in many different ways, permitting numerous historical possibilities in terms of democracy and efficiency. Other non-Marxist writers such as Schumpeter (1987) and Lange and Taylor (1938) have also challenged Hayek's belief on the possibility of achieving socialist planning in practice, by arguing for the importance of trial and error. More recently, a defence of socialist planning has been put forward by socialist thinkers including Wainright (1994), Devine (1988), Mandel (1986) and Bottomore (1990), whose work Giddens systematically ignores.

In essence, Giddens's epistemological argument against social planning is constructed upon a problematic ontology: his arguments, like Hayek's, presuppose a metaphysics which starts from the grounding assumption of the autonomous sovereign individual of liberalism (Wainwright 1994, p. 50). Individuals, he believes, act autonomously when they reflexively express their choices through the market. This argument begins, however, with a dehistoricised individual agent. The doxic[17] effect of this reifying position is to reverse the explanation for the existence of the market by regarding it as a self-instituting, self-regulating system. In reality, the market is a product of historical and social relations involving power and conflict. As Marx (1976) rightly notes, it is social individuals in determinate relationships who express their interactions through the 'price mechanism', rather than the other way around (see also Lukacs 1971). Furthermore, these social relationships are both expressed through, and orchestrated within, a broader social and cultural environment which involves unequal power. This not only includes powerful media cartels which stimulate consumer desires (Pleasants 1999), but also extends to economic interests which encompass powerful multinationals and international organisations such as the General Agreement on Tariffs and Trade, the North American Free Trade Agreement, the World Trade Organization and the International Monetary Fund (Wainwright 1994, p. 53).

Further, and more importantly, there are problems with Giddens unquestioned use of Weber's notion of rationality and bureaucracy. The concept of rationality is undeniably complex and the ambiguities of the term, as Brubaker (1984) notes, have been reinforced by the related concepts of reason and rationalisation used by Weber. In some ways, Weber's entire *ouevre* can be seen as a world-historical attempt to explain the different modalities of rationality (see Lowith 1982,

Collins 1985, Sayer 1991). Weber famously distinguished between various types of rationality, the most important of which was the opposition between formal and substantive rationality (Kalberg 1979). According to this distinction, formal rationality refers to a relationship between means and ends or to means–ends calculations which have come to characterise all spheres of social life, while substantive rationality refers to rational social action which occurs 'under some criterion of ultimate value'. As Mommsen (1974, p. 57) notes in relation to formal rationality: 'the further advance of capitalism was inevitably tied up with the rise of ever more efficient bureaucracies, and an ever greater degree of formal rational organisation on all levels of social interaction'. However, in Weber's discussion of bureaucracy as an administrative organisation, rationality also generally refers to predictability and regularity. Hence the market is rational rather than irrational when it gives rise to the predictable, regular setting of prices (Collins 1986, p. 63). Underlying the different uses of the term, as Kalberg (1979) notes, are the notions of mastery and control. For Weber, modern rationality is a double-edged sword: while it creates fixed rules which enhance the capacity for social coordination and creativity, at the same time the fixity of these rules thwarts individual creativity and prevents social progress in human societies. This is exemplified by modern rational bureaucracy which creates legal-rational forms of domination. The technical efficiency and administrative superiority of modern burcucracy is offset by the suppression of democracy and individual freedom, by an increase in worldly disenchantment, and by the negation of creativity and substantive rationality.[18] Wellmer (1985) refers to this double-edged process as 'the paradox of rationalisation'. In contrast to Marx, for whom bureacracy is generally tied to private property, Weber argued that the pervasive spread of bureacracy in capitalism and its attendant institutions would be accelerated rather than controlled under socialism (see Weber 1971). Although he was no simple-minded champion of capitalism, Weber nevertheless saw a dynamic 'market economy' as infinitely superior to a 'planned economy' (Mommsen 1974, p. 65).[19]

Significantly, the intellectual relationship between Giddens, Weber and Hayek is complex and interwoven and contains many parallels. In his early comments on state planning, Giddens not only adopts Weber's moral liberalism, though he retains a greater degree of sympathy towards socialism,[20] but also endorses Weber's view of formal rationality as a mode of domination. In addition, Giddens follows the Austrian libertarian school of economics which, as part of the *Methodenstreit*, not only influenced Weber (particularly the writings of von Wiese, Menger and von Mises) but was in turn influenced by him (see Mommsen 1974, Holton and Turner 1989). Moreover, all share a belief in the problems created for economic planning by individual reason and knowledge, a sympathy towards methodological individualism which recognises the importance of the unintended consequences of human actions,[21] and the individual as the sovereign unit of action capable of judging moral and epistemological claims.

Nevertheless, it is difficult to understand Giddens's discussion of rationality independently of a variety of contemporary explorations of Weber's notion of rationality which were prominent at the time at which he was writing – the views of Marcuse, and particularly those of Habermas. Giddens's solution to the pessimistic implications of Weber's notion of *Zweckrational* action is, however, unlike Habermas's in the sense that in contrast to Habermas's (1981) concept of 'communicative rationality', he looks to the radicalisation of the notion of reflexivity as a solution to increasing formal rationality as a form of domination. However, Giddens's discussion of bureaucracy and domination, unlike Habermas's, is extremely terse and leaves one asking exactly which element of Weber's complex and multilayered thinking is being adopted. Though he refers to 'technical' superiority ('paratechnical relations') and bureaucratic domination, Giddens does not relate this more specifically to one or more of the following characteristics of bureaucratic domination: (a) the rigorous mechanisation of codified and impersonal rules, (b) the isolation of the private work of bureaucracy from the outside public world, and (c) the distinction between bureaucratic power as a result of the hierarchical allocation of tasks or as constituting a power in itself. In addition, Giddens fails to address a wide literature which has questioned the overall utility of Weber's approach.[22] That bureaucracy is not technically superior to other forms of social organisation, nor particularly efficient, has long been established in the literature. However, what is particularly problematic in Weber's work, given his liberal individualism and subjectivism, is his failure to conceptualise adequately intersubjectivity as a necessary element in the construction of the social order. Such a lacuna has serious implications for his theory of rule-following as a basis for his notion of instrumental rationality and bureaucratic hierarchy (see Barnes 1995, ch. 8). Weber's notion of impersonal rules presupposes an individualistic and rigid notion of rule-following which ignores the social and contingent nature of rule application. Rather than seeing formal rules as an expression and rationalisation of human actions, Weber fetishises rules by regarding them as generative of action. As noted in Chapter 4, social individuals decide the 'correct application' of a rule, rather than the converse: reified rules constraining individuals. This presupposes a different distribution of power in which individuals follow rules in any one of a number of ways, according to various tactics and forms of subversion (De Certeau 1984). This is not to overstate the extent of volition that an agent has within a bureaucracy but rather to break away from the misleading image of an unstoppable bureaucratic machine or the 'iron cage'.[23]

Moreover, Weber's theory of rationality, though rendered in historical terms, lacks a deeper social and historical grounding for the emergence of rationality in the first place. Socially, it fails to examine what Durkheim calls the 'precontractual basis of contract': historically, it lacks an analysis of what Elias refers to as the changing relationship between drives and effects, on the one hand, and drive and affect control, on the other. It provides too rationalistic and individualistic an image of human beings. There is, then, a definite tension and inconsistency in Giddens's writings on social planning. His sociological focus on the competing bureaucratic rationalities of domination and technique reveals a conundrum in which a central political dilemma for his progressive liberalism is refracted. Such a liberalism champions benevolent state intervention in social life, but is equally concerned with the protection of individual liberties. This political conundrum has definite historical roots in the historical standoff between Eastern European rule and Western capitalism. Sociologically, it is rooted in the distinctive contributions of Marx and Weber to the debate concerning bureaucracy and social planning. Yet the solution to this dilemma was provided by history. The fall of the Soviet Union in 1989 provided a new context for the reaffirmation of the liberal values of individual sovereignty and choice. It was in light of this development that Giddens suggested an increase in individual and institutional reflexivity as a solution to the 'paradox of socialism'. Pervasive institutional reflexivity avoids the pitfalls of bureacratic self-sufficiency and inflexibility which lead to social domination, as evidenced in the Soviet Union. Instead, institutions need to remain open and reflexive to new information flows and to democratic notions of accountability.

The importance of the questions Giddens raises concerning social planning are undeniable: he rightly points to the weaknesses inherent in the Marxist conceptualisation of bureaucracy and social planning and the subsequent failure of Marxist writers to remedy such a deficiency. Yet Giddens's own arguments are equally misjudged. The aporia between rationality as domination and rationality as technique or liberation has for the time being been resolved by leaning toward the latter pole. This emendation, however, contains some substantial weaknesses. The concept of 'reflexivity', which underwrites Giddens's theory of modernity is, as we have noted, deeply problematic: it is based on the central concept of a disembedded and dehistoricised individual. In addition, the 'post-scarcity system' Giddens envisages within a utopian realist framework simply allots the market a central role in regulating the economic order. As a result, issues of equality are bypassed. The 'paradox of socialism' has ultimately been 'resolved' by favouring the liberal aspect of the liberal-socialist continuum. Rather than having a basis in sociological or in logical grounds, such a standpoint is simply a reflection of the current triumph of capitalist hegemony.

As we shall see in the next chapter, institutional reflexivity is not only confined to Giddens's discussion of a 'post-scarcity system', but forms a central guiding principle of New Labour's Third Way politics and its attempt to create a new system of governance. It is to this politics that we now turn.

8   Politics and the Third Way

It has been a central argument of this book that a fundamental connection exists between Giddens's social theory and his liberal standpoint. This liberalism is most clearly visible in Giddens's political sociology and the prescriptions which follow from it. In 1994, Giddens also explicitly attached himself to the Labour Party. His move into the political field and his adoption of a generalised political programme rooted in his theoretical writings occurred within the context of a marked alteration in the social, political and intellectual atmosphere of the time, following the collapse of the Soviet Union. This move was followed, a couple of years later, by a departure from Cambridge to the London School of Economics, of which he became Director in 1997. The Directorship of the LSE has frequently been filled by academics tied to mainstream politics. It has provided many incumbents with a bridge between the academy and the polity.[1] Giddens therefore took on the role of a major high-profile British public intellectual in the tradition of Russell, Webb and Hobhouse among others.

BEYOND LEFT AND RIGHT

Giddens has become not only a central advisor to the Blair government,[2] but also an intellectual spokesman for New Labour's 'Third Way' political manifesto. However, the insulation of academic life has permitted him some critical distance from the right-wing excesses of Blairism. Notwithstanding this distance, the parallels between the writings of Giddens and Blair remain significant, not least in their shared vocabulary. Both have argued that (a) globalisation has led to new forms of individualism, diversity and complexity in modern life, (b) the dissolution of the traditional manual working class has forced the Labour Party to broaden its electoral base and appeal to the voters of Middle England, and (c) the increase in globalisation precludes active Keynesian-style economic management. Yet at the same time both credos have retained a commitment to an inclusive society and emphasise communal, solidaristic values, according to which individuals remain free, yet responsible agents. Giddens's work therefore provides both an impetus toward and a rationalisation of Labour's Third Way policy and its shift from a materialist, economistic and class-based understanding of socialism to an idealistic, individualistic and populist conception (Rustin 1995).

With the elaboration of his theory of modernity, Giddens began to delineate a general political programme. In *Beyond Left and Right* (1994a), but also in a series of articles in the *New Statesman and Society* (Giddens 1994b, 1994c, 1994d), he considers the ways in which radical politics can be rethought, both theoretically and in practice, in the context of a changing modern world. In the Preface to *Beyond Left and Right*, Giddens reflects that his political arguments were originally shaped within the context of the bipolar era and were initially to be expressed in a planned third volume of *A Contemporary Critique of Historical Materialism* (1981a) entitled 'Between Capitalism and Socialism', a volume which was never written because his interests developed in a different direction.[3]

The subsequent theorisation of modernity furnished the baseline for Giddens's political theory. From this point onwards the concepts of globalisation, reflexivity and individualisation became pervasive in his political writings. Although the theorisation of modernity provided an obvious point of departure for what was to become the politics of the Third Way, it is also true that this programme was in important ways prefigured in the individualistic ontology underlying Giddens's earlier work. For Giddens, the dramatic transformations in social relationships in 'late modernity' including reflexivity, detraditionalisation and globalisation have rendered the existing political ideologies either obsolete or defunct. Across the political spectrum, he identifies three dominant political strands:

1. socialism and communism
2. conservatism
3. social democracy.

What he will later refer to as 'third way' politics (Giddens 1998) involves a re-evaluation of these political traditions in the light of the altered social conditions of modernity. We can look at these ideologies in turn.

Socialism and communism

For Giddens, the Soviet-planned economy under the control of a repressive centralised state represents the paradigmatic and singular expression of socialism. As an ideology, the beginnings of socialism can be traced back to the Enlightenment in a number of respects. First, in contrast to conservatism, socialism was represented as standing against tradition and an uncritical reverence for the past. Second, it promoted a greater understanding of the social and natural worlds as a prelude to an increased mastery and control over them. Finally, socialism embodied a sense of 'progressivism' – the idea that history had a direction and purpose which could be controlled through appropriate social and political intervention. All of these Enlightenment ideals were embedded in socialist economics and in the socialist belief that an unsupervised and divisive capitalism could be regulated or even replaced by a more rationally coordinated system of production through social intervention.

Conservatism

For Giddens, the disparate tenets that compose conservatism, extolled primarily by Edmund Burke in the eighteenth century, have included the steadfast exaltation of hierarchy, aristocracy, collectivity and state, as well as an acute suspicion of radical forms of change. These various strands, however, have become incompatible with a number of social changes ushered in by late modernity, forcing 'old style' conservatism to reinvent itself. Such a rebirth has embodied two distinct ideological strands. On one side neo-conservatives, such as Oakshott and Freyer, have re-emphasised the importance of authority, allegiance and tradition. In contrast, neo-liberal thinkers such as Hayek and Friedman and politicians such as Thatcher and Reagan, have advocated the unencumbered expansion of market forces, minimal state interference and individual sovereignty. Despite these ideological alterations, both dimensions of conservatism remain problematic. Within post-traditional society, the conserving of tradition for its own sake as pursued by neo-conservatism becomes unfeasible in a society in which all values are deemed questionable.[4] Yet the celebration of rampant market forces by neo-liberalism paradoxically undermines the very unacknowledged traditions upon which it depends.[5] As a feasible political ideology conservatism, like socialism, is also unequipped to deal with modernity.

Social democracy

Giddens understands the notion of social democracy as embracing a variety of diverse parties and other groups of the reformist left, who shared a similar political perspective in the early postwar period. These parties all regarded the unregulated free market as highly problematic. However, rather than transforming capitalism wholesale as in the doctrine of socialism, social democrats instead pursued a reformist policy which attempted to alleviate the inherent torsions within capitalism by strong state intervention. State regulation included the provision of public goods that could not be delivered by the market, allied to a policy of progressive taxation geared toward fiscal redistribution through Keynesian economic management. In common with Marxism, social democracy advanced an internationalist orientation. The social democratic world-view also incorporated a linear model of modernisation which conceived of socialism as an eventual replacement for capitalism.

Yet just as it problematised conservatism, late modernity has also rendered Fabianism and 'old-style social democracy' redundant. A number of key social and economic prerequisites for Keynesianism have been undermined or eliminated, including (a) the structure of industrial work associated with notions of a male breadwinner, (b) a homogeneous labour market, (c) the dominance of mass production, (d) a blue-collar workforce, (e) an elitist state, and (f) a national economy within sovereign fixed boundaries.

For Giddens, all three political ideologies were inoperable in modernity: socialism because it was based on a cybernetic model which could only work in a society of low reflexivity, conservatism because it was self-contradictory, and social democracy because it was conditional upon a homogeneous nation-state and bounded national economy. In high modernity social reflexivity compels individuals to demand greater access to decision-making, to challenge traditional modes of authority, and to try to cope with the effects of rapid change and uncertainty.

BETWEEN AND BEYOND CAPITALISM AND SOCIALISM

It has been the argument of this book that Giddens's original ambition had been nothing less than the steering of a political position 'between' capitalism and socialism. This relied upon retaining the positive aspects of both credos whilst shedding their negative residues. However, the collapse of socialism at the end of the 1980s rendered any such transcendence impossible. The new political context was widely interpreted as a triumph for liberal democracy and was characterised by a robust capitalist hegemony. In light of these changes, Giddens shifted his intellectual and political trajectory to the right by attempting to rethink and renew social democratic politics at both a theoretical and practical level. The defining premise of this political project was the collapse of state socialism, which for many on the left signalled the impossibility of any alternative to capitalism.

> No one any longer has any alternatives to capitalism – the arguments that remain concern how far, and in what ways, capitalism should be governed and regulated. These arguments are certainly significant, but they fall short of the more fundamental disagreements of the past. (Giddens 1998, 43–4)

He came to refer to this altered political trajectory as 'third way' politics, which he describes as:

> a framework of thinking and policy making that seeks to adapt social democrats to a world which has changed fundamentally over the past two or three decades. It is a third way in the sense that it is an attempt to transcend both old-style social democratism and neo-liberalism. (ibid., p. 26)[6]

The aim of Third Way politics is 'to help citizens pilot their way through the major revolutions of our time: globalisation, transformations in personal life and our relationship to nature' (Giddens 1998, p. 64).

A logical corollary of Third Way politics is that the collapse of communism has made the distinction between the political 'left' and 'right' superfluous. Such a semantic effacement has been compounded by the emergence of a gamut of social issues which evade the imposition of a left–right political binary. These include ecological questions as well as issues relating to the nature of the family, work and personal identity. In addition, individualisation and social reflexivity engender political processes and engagements outside the arenas of traditional party politics. What Beck refers to as 'sub-politics' has meant that knowledgeable active citizens who no longer pursue values relating to scarce material resources, but post-materialist values, must be recognised. One index of this has been the delinking of voting behaviour and social class.

In this way an increasing number of social and economic issues are seen to circumvent the left's steadfast preoccupation with social justice and emancipation. Consequently, the idea of a fixed left–right binary therefore needs to be supplanted by the notion of a radical centre or active middle:

> The idea of the 'active middle', or the 'radical centre', discussed quite widely among social democrats recently, should be taken seriously. It implies that 'centre-left' isn't inevitably the same as 'moderate-left'. Nearly all the questions of life politics mentioned above require radical solutions or suggest radical policies, on different levels of government. All are potentially divisive, but the conditions and alliances required to cope with them don't necessarily follow those based upon divisions of economic interest (ibid., pp. 44–5)

In *Beyond Left and Right* (1994a), Giddens develops this conception of radical politics in terms of the four institutional dimensions of modernity which he outlined in *The Nation-State and Violence* (1985) and *The Consequences of Modernity* (1990a). Each of these dimensions incorporates high-consequence global risks; namely the impact of social development on the world's ecological system, the development of poverty on a global scale, the widespread existence of weapons of mass destruction, the use of collective violence and the large-scale repression of democratic rights. The compound result of these risk-laden processes is 'the inability of increasing numbers of people to develop even a small part of their human potential' (Giddens 1994a, p. 99).

Notwithstanding the oppressive weight of these manufactured risks, Giddens argues that attempts to 'steer' the juggernaut of modernity should not be abandoned. Rather, the openness of the future and the absence of any privileged agents or teleology permit alternative scenarios to be envisaged. Such prospective futures necessitate both utopianism and realism – utopian realism:

> Utopian realism, such as I advocate it, is the characteristic outlook of a critical theory without guarantees. 'Realism' because such a critical theory, such a radical politics, has to grasp actual social processes to suggest ideas and strategies which have some purchase; 'utopianism' because in a social universe more and more pervaded by social reflexivity, in which possible futures are constantly not just balanced against the present but actively help constitute it, models of what could be the case can directly affect what comes to be the case. (ibid., pp. 249–50)

In relation to these four institutions of modernity, utopian realism sets out to combat poverty, redress the degradation of the environment, reduce the role of force and violence in social life and contest the arbitrary use of power. However, such a project requires a radically transformed framework for politics that selectively utilises principles from both socialist and conservative traditions. Thus both 'philosophic conservatism' – a philosophy of conservation, protection and solidarity embodying the conservative principle of living with imperfection – and a number of socialist values are conjoined.[7]

In his book *The Third Way* (1998) Giddens develops a manifesto of these themes. A renewed form of social democracy should include a number of Third Way values:

1. equality
2. protection of the vulnerable
3. freedom as autonomy
4. no rights without responsibilities
5. no authority without democracy
6. cosmopolitan pluralism
7. philosophic conservatism.

Giddens develops these values by establishing an integrated political programme which we can examine in relation to civil society, the state, ecology and violence and the economy.

Civil society

According to Giddens, the rising participation of individuals in social movements, single-issue groups and self-help groups demonstrates the increasingly reflexive nature of citizenry in late modernity. Consequently Habermas's (1975) notion of a 'legitimation crisis' should not be seen as an indication of political apathy but rather as a symptom of a frustration with the existing modes for expressing democratic participation. In such a context the fostering of an active civil society becomes a central focus for Third Way politics. This involves the state and civil society acting in partnership with one another by providing material and social support to local groups in order for them to engage in 'generative politics' orientated towards empowerment. Third Way politics aims to link reflexive individuals and groups to the state by maintaining a public domain in which beliefs and interests can be expressed freely (see Giddens 1994a, p. 93).

Absolute Rubbish

One consequence of late modernity has been the emergence of new forms of individualism. Such individualisation provides the possibility for both social disintegration and the generation of new solidarities. Giddens distinguishes sharply between the newly emerging 'individualism' of modernity and a neo-liberal understanding of individualism as self-seeking, profit-maximising behaviour. The core modality of this new individualism, which has its origins in the work of Durkheim, is autonomy. Modern individualism is less about 'egoism' or moral decline and more an expression of autonomy and moral transition, which is reflected in the post-materialist values (ecological values, human rights and sexual freedom) of the people who express it.[8] Refusing to accept tradition or authority for its own sake, institutional autonomy is seen to express the active, reflexive life choices of actors on an ongoing and contingent basis. In such a context the active generation of trust and a renewal of personal and social responsibility for others in the form of obligations also becomes paramount in personal and social relationships where the 'pure relationship' is emblematic. For Giddens, changes in personal relationships have had important implications for public roles. He argues that the individuals 'who have a good understanding of their own emotional make-up, and who are able to communicate effectively with others on a personal basis, are likely to be well prepared for the wider tasks and responsibilities of citizenship' (Giddens 1998, p. 16).

By dissolving the liberal separation between the public and the private sphere, Giddens hopes that 'pure relationships' based on trust, equality, responsibility, dialogue and openness in the private sphere will replace the blindness of tradition-bound fundamentalism in the public sphere. Accountability in the public sphere needs to be made paramount: 'One might suggest as a prime motto for the new politics, no rights without responsibilities' (Giddens 1998, p. 65).

Increasing individualisation and reflexivity have also led to new forms of democratisation or 'dialogic democracy'. This democratisation of democracy presupposes uncoerced discussion as a basis for agreement. Giddens's reflexive understanding of democracy differs from Habermas's (1981) 'ideal speech situation' in a number of ways. Specifically, it is not a transcendental theorem, and it implies not consensus but merely mutual tolerance.

A further consequence of this process of reflexive individualisation is the need for the re-evaluation of the traditional left-wing understanding of emancipation that was invariably connected to the notions of life chances and freedom. According to Giddens, 'Emancipation means freedom, or rather, freedoms of various kinds: freedom from the arbitrary hold of tradition, from arbitrary power and from the constraints of material deprivation' (Giddens 1994a, p. 14).

However, emancipatory politics must be supplemented with 'life politics': lifestyle, leisure, consumption, identity. Conversely, emancipatory politics relates to how individuals should live in a world which was previously 'fixed' either by nature or tradition but has now become subject to human decision and volition. Life politics breaks out of the restrictive cast of class politics: it concerns rich and poor groups alike by addressing issues such as global warming which affect everyone.

The state

Globalisation is central to Giddens's account of late modernity and refers to more than the economic geography of corporate capitalism: it turns on a transformation of space within people's lives. This understanding of globalisation has a number of implications for the notion of a sovereign nation-state. Firstly, it 'pulls away' some of the power of the nation-state and thereby limits the state's ability to implement various interventionist measures, including economic management schemes.[9] Secondly, it 'squeezes sideways', creating new transnational systems and organisations which cut across the boundaries of nation-states. Thirdly, by 'pushing down', globalisation provides 'democratic' possibilities for individuals to generate new identities by drawing upon and reinventing traditions.

Despite these effects, globalisation is not an inexorable force of nature that is progressively corroding the power of nation-states. On the contrary, Giddens argues that the power of the nation-state is actually increasing in terms of governmental, economic and cultural power over citizens. Giddens calls for a reconstruction – rather than abolition or augmentation – of the state in response to these changes, in order to widen democracy. Such a reconstruction involves the move towards decentralisation, or what he calls 'double democratisation': balancing the downward movements resulting from globalisation with upward movements. Such democratisation also involves additional alterations in state practices including a greater transparency of government and constitutional and electoral reform.

In addition, in a reflexive society political legitimacy can no longer depend solely upon tradition as its basis and instead the possibility for more radical forms of dialogic democracy emerges. Rather than referring to the extension of social and civil rights, dialogic democracy points towards a 'deliberative democracy' where forms of social interchange, social solidarity and cultural cosmopolitanism can be established. 'Liberal democracy is a set of representative institutions, guided by certain values; deliberative democracy is a way of getting, or trying to get, agreement about policies in the political arena' (Giddens 1998, p. 113).

The Social Investment State

Giddens argues that the welfare state has to be fundamentally rethought in late modernity. Although originally introduced by Bismark in order to placate working-class agitation, since the Second World War the welfare state has become championed by the left and the working classes as a mechanism for securing social and economic equality. However, Giddens believes that a number of long-standing criticisms of the welfare state by the right must be accepted. These include:

*hardly of right!
orginal # right*

1. the failure to counteract poverty or produce large-scale redistribution of wealth
2. the implicit acceptance of the traditional family and gender roles
3. the fostering of welfare dependency as a culture as well as an economic condition
4. the bureaucratic, inflexible and impersonal nature of state institutions
5. the undemocratic, top-down dispensation of benefits
6. the failure to adapt to social changes particularly in relation to patterns of class stratification, demographic changes, shifts in family structure (for example, increasing divorce rates and single-parent families) and the transformation of the labour market (for example, the rise of part-time and female employment and the decline in blue-collar work)
7. the failure to reach beyond the economic sphere and engage with wider emotional, moral and cultural concerns
8. the wasteful use of financial and human resources.

For Giddens, the failure of the welfare state must be understood in terms of risk and a societal shift from external to manufactured risk.

Risk refers to the dangers we seek actively to confront and assess. In a society such as ours, orientated towards the future and saturated with information, the theme of risk unites many otherwise disparate areas of politics: welfare state reform, engagement with world financial markets, responses to technological change, ecological problems and geopolitical transformations. We all need protection against risk, but also the capability to confront and take risks in a productive fashion. (Giddens 1998, p. 64)

As a system of social insurance, the welfare state was organised on the basis of an Enlightenment conception in which risk could be quantified through the application of reason, and controlled and countered by deliberate social intervention. Such a conception involved the management of external risk and only dealt with social 'problems' once they had arisen. In contrast, Giddens argues that manufactured risk – that is, 'risk actively confronted within frames of action organised in a reflexive way' – escapes human evaluation and control and implies a 'treatment at source' rather than after events have taken place (Giddens 1994a, p. 152).[10] In addition, it retains a positive side which can be harnessed and channelled in a fruitful manner by individuals and social groups. In place of an anachronistic and inefficient welfare state he advocates a 'social investment state' operating in the context of a positive welfare society. Positive welfare involves a greater emphasis on personal liberty and collective responsibility, in a context in which life politics has replaced emancipatory politics. Here welfare is not only concerned with economic well-being, but also with psychic well-being: welfare institutions should not just provide economic benefits, but also psychological ones, such as counselling. Positive welfare would look towards private-sector organisational practices to roll back the pervasive inertia which characterises welfare institutions.

[It]would replace each of Beveridge's negatives with a positive: in place of Want, autonomy; not Disease but active health; instead of Ignorance, education, as a continuing part of life; rather than Squalor, well-being; and in place of Idleness, initiative. (Giddens 1998, p. 128)

Ecology and violence

As well as addressing issues relating to the state and civil society, utopian realism sets out to confront the deterioration of the environment and the increasing use of violence in social and political life. According to Giddens, two different sources for the ecological crisis exist. On the one hand, there are wealthy societies which create environmental disasters by promoting wasteful patterns of production and consumption; on the other hand, there are poor societies whose harmful practices are secondary and defensive. For Giddens, sustainable development and ecological modernisation are required to combat both of these deleterious practices. Such modernisation involves the pooling of social and economic resources between governments, capitalists and environmental groups and the formation of an environmental compact. On this point he quotes Dryzek:

> Ecological modernisation implies a partnership in which governments, businesses, moderate environmentalists, and scientists co-operate in the restructuring of capitalist political economy along more environmentally defensible lines (Giddens 1998, p. 57).

According to Giddens, ecological issues must also be examined at another level, namely in our relation to scientific advance and our response to risk. The progress of science has broken down any boundaries between the natural world and the social world. Humanly contrived science and technology have transformed, for instance, both the natural world of climate and the world of the human body. Moreover, questions relating to risk as both a negative and positive phenomenon in terms of ecology need to be collectively answered. This cannot occur by looking only to experts but must also involve the public and government in a further collective pact.

Giddens argues that there are only two major ways in which a clash of values in human affairs can be dealt with in society: through dialogue or violence. He adds that the extension of autonomy and solidarity in modernity has made the use of dialogue into a counter to violence and fundamentalism, a realistic possibility in everyday life. Here nationalism is exemplary. Nationalism is a Janus-faced phenomenon: on the one hand, providing an integrative mechanism towards citizenship, yet serving as a basis for nationalist conflicts and wars, on the other. Although the latter aspect cannot be eradicated fully, Giddens believes that it can be checked by a more cosmopolitan version of nationalism in which dialogue is held at a premium.

Moreover, state borders are dissipating and instead becoming frontiers due to the growth of regional ties and transnational connections. Hence, in contrast to the conservative nationalism of a unitary nation and the cultural pluralism and extreme multiculturalism of the left, Giddens posits the cosmopolitan nation in which open and reflexive identities are constructed not in antagonism to others but with their collaboration. In addition, the end of the Cold War means that a cosmopolitan outlook becomes increasingly possible on an international as well as national basis, since states no longer have any 'clear-cut enemies'. Giddens asks: 'Is benign, cosmopolitan nationalism actually possible? ... As with other notions discussed earlier, it is an ideal, but given the changing nature of the global order, one not so distant from reality' (ibid., p. 137).

Such a cosmopolitan nation, for Giddens, implies a cosmopolitan democracy operating on a global scale. The end of the bipolar world also means that global governance becomes a realistic possibility. The precedent for such global governance, according to Giddens, is the EU which, he argues, is already responsible for 75 per cent of economic legislation and 50 per cent of all domestic legislation across its member-states (ibid., p. 142). Without global governance, the problems of inequality and ecological risk remain recondite.

The economy

In addition to establishing a social investment state and fostering a dialogical civil society, Giddens calls for the creation of a 'new mixed economy'. In *Beyond Left and Right* (1994a) he argues that such an economy would form part of a 'post-scarcity society'. In his view, 'the new mixed economy' involves 'a synergy between public and private sectors, utilising the dynamics of market but with the public interest in mind' (Giddens 1998, p. 100). Such a balance of markets and public services requires the intervention of 'big battalions – states, businesses and international organisations' (ibid., p. 162).

Although the Marxist ideal of subjecting economic life to centralised control has lost any purchase in late modernity, the notion of a post-scarcity economy can nevertheless be approached within a framework of utopian realism. In a post-scarcity economy personal growth is not sacrificed to economic growth or productivism. Here values relating to productivism are replaced by ideals of self-actualisation. Through this substitution, happiness is introduced as the defining parameter of equality. Giddens reintroduces his notion, first discussed in *The Class Structure of the Advanced Societies* (1973), that the fundamental defining characteristic of humans is that they are meaning-seeking creatures. For Giddens, then, the definition of equality in terms of wealth – made not only by those on the right, but also by many on the left – is highly misleading: 'Living a happy and satisfying life is one thing, wealth creation is another' (Giddens 1998, p. 174). Instead of wealth one must look to security, self-respect and self-actualisation as a basis for happiness and governments must be regarded as institutions which ensure the latter:

> the aim of good government should be to promote the pursuit of happiness, and that both individual and social 'welfare' should be defined in such a way. Let us also accept that happiness is promoted by security (of mind and body), self-respect and the opportunity for self-actualisation plus the ability to love. (ibid., p. 180)

Consequently, '"Happiness", it has been said by one of the most prominent contemporary students on the subject, "is not something that happens". Happiness "does not depend on outside events, but rather on how we interpret them"; it is "a condition that must be prepared for, cultivated". It depends less on controlling the outer world than on controlling the inner one. "People who learn to control inner experience will be able to determine the quality of their lives, which is as close as any of us can come to being happy"' (Giddens 1994a, citing Csikszentmihalyi 1992, p. 2).

The move away from productivism towards a conception of equality can help to foster an autotelic self. The autotelic self is a self which has

> an inner confidence which comes from self respect, and one where a sense of ontological security, originating in basic trust, allows for the positive appreciation of social difference. It refers to a person able to translate potential threats into rewarding challenges … The autotelic self does not neutralise risk … risk is confronted as the active challenge which generates self-actualisation (Giddens 1998, p. 192).

This switch in emphasis from issues of material distribution to questions of self-actualisation, or what Giddens calls a 'generative model of equality', could then provide the basis for a new compact between the rich and the poor and furnish the basis for an attack on global poverty. In this view, the rich and the poor have a common interest in moving lifestyles away from productivism to those that prioritise happiness. Generative rather than distributional equality provides the basis for a global convergence around a series of post-industrial values. These common interests include 'environmental protection, the protection of traditions and local solidarities, the advocacy of democratic rights and the avoidance of violence' as well as 'the fostering of the autotelic self' (ibid., p. 194).

Such a compact would constitute an 'effort bargain' founded on 'mutual responsibility for tackling the "bads" which development has brought in its train' (Giddens 1994a, p. 194). Could such a lifestyle position really provide the basis for global social justice?

> The question remains whether a lifestyle pact such as here suggested for the wealthy countries could also apply when applied to the divisions between North and South. Empirically, one certainly could not answer this question positively with any degree of assurance. Analytically speaking, however, one could ask, what other possibility is there? (ibid., p. 197)

The issue of equality needs to be rethought for Giddens not only in terms of its correspondence with wealth, but concomitantly in terms of a redistribution of possibilities rather than a *post festum* redistribution of wealth. As he notes, 'The cultivation of human potentials should as far as possible replace "after the event" redistribution' (Giddens 1998, p. 101).

> The contemporary left needs to develop a dynamic, life-chances approach to equality, placing the prime stress on equality of opportunity. Modernising social democrats also have to find an approach that reconciles equality with pluralism and lifestyle diversity, recognising that the clashes between freedom and equality to which classical liberals have always pointed are real. Equality of opportunity, of course, has long been a theme of the left and has been widely enshrined in policy ... Yet many on the left have found it difficult to accept its correlates – that incentives are necessary to encourage those of talent to progress and that equality of opportunity typically creates higher rather than lower inequalities of income. Equality of opportunity also tends to produce high levels of social and cultural diversity since individuals and groups have the chance to develop their lives as they see fit. (Giddens 2000, p. 86)

In a rather confused discussion, Giddens asserts that equality of opportunity should not be correlated with meritocracy – which is unrealisable anyway – but should instead be seen in terms of inclusion[11] and inequality. Equality thereby refers to social inclusion or exclusion from the opportunity of achieving happiness in one's life.

Giddens identifies two forms of social exclusion which urgently need to be tackled: the forced exclusion of those at the bottom of the social order and the voluntary 'revolt of the elites' at the top of society. As part of the solution to this problem he points again to the creation of a number of social pacts between various groups of 'committed' individuals. The spirit of the cosmopolitan nation is invoked to counter the passive disengagement of the professional middle classes. Such valorisation can aid in the binding of various strata, because 'people who feel themselves members of a national community of elites, through a common morality of citizenship, are likely to acknowledge a commitment to others within it'.[12]

In terms of social exclusion at the bottom, since previous attempts at redistributing wealth through fiscal measures have failed, a new approach to poverty based on life politics and generative politics is required. Such an approach would entail a strong emphasis on the generation of wealth through competitiveness, which has traditionally been anathema to the left. Hence, rather than encouraging regulation and continuous governmental intervention, social democrats need instead to strike a delicate balance between regulation and deregulation and between the transnational, national and local levels of society. By investing in human resources and developing an entrepreneurial culture, Third Way politics helps to foster the development of 'responsible risk-takers' in government and in business. Governments need to support entrepreneurial initiatives concerned with small business start-ups and technological innovation and to encourage public project partnerships where private enterprise is geared to public interest. Despite the fact that the gap between the highest paid and lowest paid in the UK is now greater than it has been for the past 50 years, Giddens asserts, rather glibly, that this may change.

For that to happen a new economic climate must be developed. The modern economy has witnessed a dramatic shift in the nature of work and in class composition: less than 20 per cent of the workforce in the most developed countries are now employed in manufacturing. In its place a knowledge economy based on information and technology has emerged. Since new economic exigencies require a skilled and adaptable workforce, labour must continually be flexible in a competitive economy. In relation to employment, welfare expenditure should be switched to human capital investment through education policies, particularly within the changed context of a knowledge-based economy.[13] Such education policies should emphasise lifelong education and enhance the mobility of workers through common standards of education. For Giddens, investment in education and the labour force is a crucial basis for the redistribution of possibilities. This can be supplemented by employee stock ownership schemes. He summarises his vision thus:

> Old-style social democracy concentrated on industrial policy and Keynesian demand measures, while the neo-liberals focused on deregulation and market liberalisation. Third way economic policy needs to concern itself with different priorities – with education, incentives, entrepreneurial culture, flexibility, devolution and the cultivation of social capital ... The aim of macroeconomic policy is to keep inflation low, limit government borrowing, and use active supply side measures to foster growth and high levels of employment. (Giddens 2000, p. 73)

Agency

The question of who or what can bring about these desired changes remains crucial. A consequence of the rejection of providentialism – the view that history has some great metaphysical purpose or direction – is that there is no privileged historical agent that can initiate change. No individual or group has a monopoly on radical thought in the post-traditional order. Instead, a broad variety of groups such as feminists, environmental groups and peace groups, as well as a multiplicity of other social movements and 'self-help' groups, can all participate in political engagement. Although it appears that increasing globalisation, heightened reflexivity and growing individualisation have created a postmodern universe of plural, local, fragmented values, it is in fact the first time in history that there exists a set of universal values, that is, 'values shared by almost everyone'. These arise, paradoxically, from global interdependence and, though many of these values are created negatively, under a 'heuristics of fear' – the collective threats or high-consequence risks which humanity has created for itself – they also have a positive aspect. Such values include a recognition of the sanctity of human life, universal human rights including the right to happiness and self-actualisation, and the preservation of the species. They also comprise the care of the future and of present generations of children. These values require an ethics of individual and collective responsibility that transcend social divisions of interest. Moreover, they can be achieved only through responsible dialogue and discursive justification rather than through fundamentalism.

EVALUATION

The death of socialism

The evanescence of the state socialist system, which spanned a third of the global order between 1989 and 1991, had enormous repercussions for the traditional stalemate between left and right politics. The global hegemonic ascendancy of right-wing politics, which began at the turn of the 1980s, reached its apogee by the early 1990s, establishing neo-liberalism as the only feasible political ideology.[14] The result was an uncontested consolidation of American right-wing politics manifested in economic, political and cultural dominance of the New World Order. Such total ideological domination further precipitated an 'organic crisis' of the left. Its upshot was the comprehensive and rapid shift of European social democracy and socialist ideology towards the right, with American capitalism providing the gravitational pull.

In Britain, a political lurch to the right had begun earlier following the oil crisis and IMF bailout of the mid-1970s. With gathering pace from 1979, the Thatcherite neo-liberal government had implemented a deregulatory agenda informed by a neo-liberal ideology. The introduction of radical right-wing economic policies inspired by Friedman's monetarist doctrines looked to fiscal prudence as a solution to economic decline.[15] Supply-side economics was soon to replace Keynesian demand management, which had held sway from the 1940s up to the early 1970s and whose pursuit of full employment and growth had made it synonymous with social democracy. The naked power of the state was further used to defeat the miners when they went on strike and to introduce numerous forms of reactionary legislation. It was within this dominant hegemonic conjuncture that post-Thatcherite social, political and economic reorganisation became adopted in Labour's new policies following a number of successive General Election defeats (Shaw 1994, Hay 1999). This policy shift towards the right included a rejection of unilateral disarmament, the acceptance of privatisation, restrictive trade union laws and a conversion to free market capitalism (Roberts 1995). Hence Blair's project to modernise the Labour Party following his appointment in 1994 was already based on transforming a party hitherto bereft of a number of left-wing policies. One of Blair's most far-reaching initial gestures was the shedding of Clause Four of the party's 1918 constitution, which had argued for the common ownership of the means of production. More broadly, it was signalled discursively by a shift from 'Old Labour's quasi-corporatism, collectivism, egalitarianism and expansive welfarism' to 'New Labour's language of individualism, responsibility, fiscal prudence and moralism'. The net effect of this repositioning was to diminish the differences between the parties.

In addition, the collapse of the Soviet Union altered not only the already right-tilting Western political landscape but also the intellectual landscape. The disintegration of the Eastern Bloc resulted in an exaggerated view of capitalism as inevitable, expressed most apocalyptically in Fukuyama's notion of 'the end of history', a leitmotif which came to stand for the global intellectual shift to the right. Giddens did not remain unaffected by this conjuncture and followed suit. In his view, the collapse of communism signalled both the end of the possibility of any alternative society to capitalism and a loss of meaning from the term 'left politics':

> Does being on the left retain any meaning now that communism has foundered completely in the West, and socialism more generally has been dissolved? (Giddens 1998, p. 24)

> No one has any alternatives to capitalism, the arguments that remain concern how far, and in what ways, capitalism should be governed and regulated. (ibid., pp. 43–4)

Stemming from his interpretation of Weber's critique of bureaucratic rationality and Durkheim's discussions of socialism, Giddens had always been sceptical concerning the possibility of rationally coordinating economic production. The demise of state socialism intensified these misgivings which became evident in his wholehearted acceptance of Hayek's views (see Chapter 7).

As well as refracting a broader political shift, there are also significant problems in Giddens's political sociology which are expressed throughout his arguments.

At the outset of his discussion, Giddens reductively equates socialism and Marxism with the Soviet Union. Such definitional fiat occludes an examination of the multiple definitions and diverse interpretations and conceptions of socialism which have existed and which currently exist. Thus, rather than speaking of socialism we need instead to speak of the reality of a number of socialisms. These include numerous political traditions that have been critical of the Soviet Union, such as, for example, the New Left and Western Marxism. The effect of reducing socialism to the Soviet model also precludes any attempt to distinguish socialism as a theory or set of values from socialism as a practice.[16] There is also an acute failure here by Giddens to engage with a vast literature (such as Cliff, Deutscher, Trotsky and Mandel) which argues that such a distinction is necessary. Ironically, in his evaluation of Marx in *Capitalism and Modern Social Theory* (1971a) written admittedly in a more sympathetic political climate, Giddens had made exactly this criticism of other writers. Such a *petitio principii* is therefore perhaps not merely a logical or semantic failure on his part. On the contrary, such an ideological conceptual compression is probably based on a political rationale.

The purported semantic exhaustion of the terms 'left' and 'right', and their substitution by a 'radical centre', is likewise problematic. Giddens is not the first to repudiate their use. As Bobbio (1996) argues, the notion of an 'included third' or 'transverse third' which synthesises and supersedes this dyad has been repeatedly asserted by political parties; specifically, in modern times, the Green Party.

Giddens's definition of conservatism and neo-liberalism allows him to argue that the distinction between the three major political positions is no longer clear-cut. Such an argument is, however, based on an extremely narrow and suspect definition of the ideologies. For example, he rightly asserts that certain views of conservatives and Marxists do overlap, such as their emphasis on the social nature of humans and criticism of capitalism. However, as Benton (1999) rightly notes, they also differ profoundly in other ways. The conservative emphasis on deference, paternalism, status, hierarchy patriarchy, patriotism and militarism is largely absent from the Marxist conceptual register.

Moreover, as Bobbio rightly states, the division between the terms 'left' and 'right' is relational.[17] The left–right dyad therefore continues to play an important role in delineating political life, for example, in identifying the Christian Right in the US, the National Front in

France and fascism in Austria, or, in marked political contrast, the anti-capitalist movement and the support for Nader in the US. In fact, the logical consistency of the metaphor of left and right has always been compromised by libertarianism, which straddles both poles. The identification of the left with socialism was equally problematic given the historical significance of the anarchist movements, as well as of contemporary liberation movements which often associated themselves with the left without necessarily identifying with socialism.[18] So, like all metaphors, the language of left and right has inherent limitations, but these are not new and did little to undermine the common-sense utility of the terms which have been used to express programmatic polarities in political life for over 200 years.[19] The notion of a radical centre therefore does not alter the contrast, and nor does it cancel them out.

The shift in meaning of these concepts is an empirical consequence of the dramatic shift in power relations between the left and right following the collapse of state socialism. The result has been the rejection of this very distinction by a number of thinkers of the left who, as Anderson (1998, p. 74) notes, compensate 'for an experience of defeat with a rhetoric of supersession'.

Lack of acknowledgement of political interests

Although the issue of power is discussed in his theory of structuration and historical sociology, Giddens's political sociology fails to situate power as a central feature of political experience and defining concept for political structures. Giddens ignores issues of power, for example, in terms of all three of the dimensions of power relations famously discussed by Lukes (1974). Firstly, one set of interests prevails over another so that political decisions are made to the benefit of the more powerful party. Secondly, policy issues are framed and formulated in the interests of the dominant group, so as to set the agenda. In such circumstances, according to Lukes, a failure to act is just as important as how you act. Finally, the dominant group shapes the perceptions, cognitions and consciousness of others for its own benefit. His analysis fails to address how power enforces relations of domination, subordination and inequality.

The abstract, voluntaristic conception of the individual agent devoid of interests characterising his ontology is attenuated by a move away from any materialist grounding in his substantive political writings. Problems concerning material scarcity, unless they refer to the environment, are pushed to the background or submerged under a discussion of lifestyle, consumption, reflexivity, risk and ethical choice. By substituting the notions of interest and power for that of risk, which applies equally to everyone, Giddens fails to examine how power differentiates within social formations or how it dominates groups by shaping social processes so that they only benefit some groups.

The inadequate acknowledgement of power and interests is overwhelmingly evident in Giddens's call for the construction of 'consensual' pacts between, for example, the sexes or different ethnicities as a means to resolve conflicts within the social world. In relation to ethnicities, the notion of 'cosmopolitan pluralism', defined in opposition to xenophobic nationalism or international or interethnic inequality, is simply offered even within the visible context of 'Fortress Europe' and restrictive migration policy (Callinicos 2001). As a rationale for why these pacts should come about, given their prior entrenched conflicts based on material, cultural or ideological grounds, Giddens simply asserts, 'What other possibility is there?' Such an anodyne view of the social world is repeated in his notion of the cosmopolitan nation where 'States have no enemies.' However, wars beginning in the twentieth century, particularly those following the First World War and including the current Israeli–Palestinian conflict, provoke the questioning of such a complacent and idealist viewpoint.

By implicitly prioritising the abstract individual as the basis for his sociology, Giddens's politics fails to acknowledge conflict and contradiction as a pervasive feature of the social world. Such a view of the social world permits him to argue for the importance of dialogue in resolving value choices, where, following Habermas, the force of the better argument is triumphant. In abstract terms individuals may be able to transcend conflicts of interest simply through reason and dialogue, but in actual reality embedded social individuals in material conditions of unequal power have been more successful through the use of violence and force.

It is only by ignoring power, interest and materialism that Giddens can claim to have discovered a middle course between all the existing conceptual and material extremes. The 'Third Way' attempts to be a broad, all-inclusive doctrine without enemies or adversaries. By construing individuals at such a high level of abstraction, Giddens can allege to have captured the 'radical centre' in politics, a substantive as well as etymological oxymoron. A politics which ignores or bypasses considerations tied to power, interest and conflict is unlikely to be realistic or feasible. Essentially, most of the problems in his political sociology stem from his liberalism, whose influence he admits:

> Rather than seeking to suppress these consequences we should accept them. Social democrats should be happy to acknowledge that this position brings them closer to ethical liberalism than many used to think. Alan Ryan is right to point to the affinities between third way politics and the ideas of ethical liberals. (Giddens 2000, p. 86)

This includes liberals such as T.H. Green, Hobhouse and Toynbee, whom Giddens acknowledges took an affirmative attitude towards market mechanisms and saw it as compatible with community cooperation and ethical precepts.[20]

Ignoring the power of capital

Political interests are not only ignored in Giddens's discussion of civil society, but they are also largely absent from his economic analysis. There is no systematic treatment of questions regarding capital as a social relationship and issues relating to the control and ownership of capital and private property in his politics. The role played by international capitalist accumulation and the dynamics of the market in explaining the current crises affecting the modern world became a *fin de non recevoir* for many sociologists in recent times. Recent works by Brenner (1998), Harvey (1990), Hirst and Thompson (1999) and Hardt and Negri (2000) have, however, re-emphasised the continuing explanatory importance of capitalist mechanisms for understanding the local, national and global order in the modern world.

As noted, Giddens retains a distinctive reading of capitalism in his work. In his early writings he drew an institutional distinction between 'capitalism' and 'industrialism'. Later, in his discussion of modernity in *The Nation-State and Violence* (1985), he substitutes capitalism with modernity and adds two further institutions as central foci for understanding society: surveillance and the means of violence. The net effect of this institutional quartet was to increasingly reduce the recognition of the power of capital as a social force in modern society. In its place stands a contingent juxtaposition of institutions, described without reference to any conceptual hierarchy and often devoid of any explanatory power.

Giddens also defines globalisation solely in terms of the transformation of space. Such a definition *a priori* rules out any systematic discussion of the economic aspects of globalisation and the expansionary nature of capital. The result is a thoroughly misleading and restricted analysis of globalisation, leaning heavily on technological discoveries as its impetus and largely bereft of empirical support.

The underestimation of capitalist accumulation is further evidenced in the exaggerated freedom that Giddens allots nation-states in terms of enforcing policies aimed at securing social and economic equality. Thus no attention is given to the dynamics of international capitalism and the limits and obstacles that multinationals place on the actions of nation-states or even to the interaction between them. There is no mention of the role the World Bank, the IMF, GATT, G7 or multinationals have played in shaping global social and economic policies (Callinicos 2001). Notwithstanding various mediations, the increase in poverty, the degradation of the environment, and the human rights abuses Giddens identifies have originated from or been sustained by policies arising from these interest groups in their efforts to direct and distribute capital flows. Capitalism, as generalised commodity production, and capital as production for profit have intrinsically set up structural impediments to nearly all the values that Giddens adumbrates in the Third Way. The only values that matter on the whole for capitalist reproduction are those that are tied to or conditional upon profit-maximisation.[2] In such a context, Giddens's comment that 'the demonising of large corporations, so popular among some sections of the left at one time, does not make much sense now' (Giddens 1994a, p. 197), is acutely misjudged and naive.

Equality

The above contentions particularly apply to Giddens's arguments for the redistribution of wealth:

> A global redistribution of wealth would be called for. Yet the motivation to produce such changes could be forthcoming ... there is some evidence that many people in the economically advanced states experience 'development fatigue', and much evidence of a general awareness that continued economic growth is not worthwhile unless it actively improves the quality of life of the majority. (Giddens 1990a, p. 166)

Giddens's belief that a generative model of equality can provide the basis for a new lifestyle pact between the rich and the poor, North and South, through an 'effort bargain' also depends upon omitting the nexus of global capitalist interests which currently exist. His underestimation of the role played by capitalist relations in maintaining undemocratic and inegalitarian structures and forms of economic dependency between centre and periphery through, for example, the maintenance of Third World debt produces an unrealistic and idealistic view of the persistence of global economic contradictions.

Such an argument equally applies to his belief that there are shared human interests in transforming the current global order created by the emergence of globalised manufactured uncertainties tied to risk and factors relating to inequality.

Although Giddens does recognise the acceleration of social inequality in the world, he fails to adequately account for this in terms of the structural effects of capitalism. Instead he masks over the incidence of poverty through a definitional fiat. Equality, poverty and happiness are all redefined in terms of social exclusion and inclusion to indicate that economic factors are not the only reason why different groups find themselves excluded from mainstream society. Although this reasoning is on one level a truism, by redefining equality as inclusion there is a shift of focus away from material redistribution and the parity of access to resources, towards the pursuit of policies designed to recreate a national sense of belonging for all classes. Giddens's concern is less with material equality than with promoting the idea of community. As a result, equality as it is ordinarily understood becomes difficult to recognise.

The shift away from an emphasis on attaining material equality is again evidenced in Giddens's stress on education and the development of a knowledgeable, flexible workforce. Such narrow policy commitments suggest an agenda driven less by a social democratic aim of opportunities for all than by a post-Thatcherite vision of supplying a flexible workforce to a competitive global labour market (Hall 1998). Rather than intervening to ensure that there are secure, rewarding jobs and a high degree of material equality for all, the Social Investment State makes people more employable by providing education and 'knowledge' skills for jobs that are generated by the private sector.

As Carling notes, his redefinition of equality is further problematised in his terse and unclear discussion of justice. Here he draws equivalences between neo-liberalism, meritocracy and equality of opportunity. However:

> meritocracy does not equate with equal opportunity once the unequal distribution of internal resources is taken into account, since meritocracy allows a moral merit to talent that deep (and arguably true) equal opportunities thinking discounts ... Giddens conflates three of the main four positions on social justice ... [his] view of the distributive policy of the Social Investment State is that 'the cultivation of human potential should as far as possible replace "after the event" redistribution ... the basic point is that you may have to do a great deal of Old Labour redistribution in order to equalise New Labour opportunities. (Carling 1999, pp. 234–5)

It has been argued that Giddens underestimates the power of capital, yet in other contexts he also exaggerates it. Hence in the context of the international hegemony of the right, Giddens regards capitalism as inevitable: 'No one has any alternatives to capitalism. The arguments that remain concern how far, and in what ways, capitalism should be governed and regulated' (Giddens 1998, pp. 43–4).

Although written after the disappearance of Cold War politics, such a generalisation contradicts any view of society as intrinsically open to changing social practices, a view which is pervasive elsewhere in his work. By taking capitalism as a given, whilst on the hegemonic ascendant, Giddens's political sociology reveals the extent to which his assumptions and his overall analysis are essentially framed within the terrain defined by the New Right. Hutton sums up these failures well:

> He is too frequently naïve about the exercise of raw American political power in driving globalisation forward ... As a result he can appear too credulous about business and the US, and too ready to abandon positions that business defines as threatening to its interests – rather as New Labour is prone. He too readily generates a partial insight into a universal theory; for example he is right to argue that the US possesses a powerful egalitarian which has made great gains for women, the disabled, gays, and some ethnic minorities – but wrong to conclude that, as a result, inequalities of income and wealth are yesterday's preoccupation. Both propositions can be true. (Hutton 2001, p. xvii)

In conclusion, given the context of their formation, Giddens's liberal politics fail to account for the interests which accrue to social groups and positioned individuals. As a result his political strictures are not so much a synthesis of utopianism and realism, left and right, as a radical utopianism: they are not 'beyond left and right' but probably beyond realisation.

9 An Alternative Sociology

In this chapter I will provide a sketch of what I believe to be an alternative to Giddens's approach to sociology. Yet it would be both simplistic and misleading to believe that Giddens's contribution to sociology has little utility despite the numerous criticisms outlined in this work. Firstly, although his theory of structuration and historical sociology are deeply problematic, as a critic and a commentator on the work of others, his writings remain unsurpassed. Secondly, although his sociological analyses are unsystematic, lack empirical reference and often applicability, his idiosyncratic insights and synpotic sweep, if used selectively, provide conceptual tools which continue to stoke the sociological imagination. And it is for this reason that his importance and standing as a foremost sociologist remain. Nevertheless, the implicit political and normative presuppositions underlying his writings, as I have tried to show throughout this work, ultimately render them problematic. What is ultimately missing from Giddens's approach is a thoroughgoing historical and social foundation, despite a formal acknowledgement of social practice. A reassertion of the importance of history in addition to a recognition of our profound social nature as human beings renders possible a more fruitful and productive approach to the study of the social world.

A GENEALOGY OF AGENCY AND STRUCTURE

It will be argued here that the replacement of Giddens's question concerning the way in which agency and structure are related, with the anterior question of how the agency/structure debate arose in the first place, provides the beginnings of a possible resolution to the debate. That is to say, a resolution of the agency and structure debate should be sought in a historical sociology rather than in social theory. By investigating the historical genealogy (Foucault 1982, 1991) or socio-genesis of the terms 'agency' and 'structure' – that is, their socially determined conditions of possibility – it is possible to reframe the dualism of agency and structure as a contingent social and historical construction, rather than conceiving it merely in terms of an abstract universal or transhistorical frame of reference. On the former reading, the dualisms of agency and structure, or individual and society, or freedom and determinism, are historical constructs. Philosophically, the terms 'agency' and 'structure' were preceded by the dualism between subject and object and between the 'individual' and 'society'. These earlier versions of the dualism expressed interpretations of a social experience which had gained currency at a particular point in history, and which in time came to be accepted as absolutes through a process of fetishism in which what is social and historical comes to be understood as natural and atemporal.

It was noted in Chapter 1 that the rise of capitalism was concomitant with the rise of the natural-law style of thought and its conservative counterpart. In what follows, that discussion will be extended.

It will be useful, therefore, to provide a brief analysis of the historical emergence of these terms by locating the point at which they enter into social discourse. Of course, such a description will be at best a rough and somewhat crude approximation, since empirical reality and history display a greater degree of unevenness and discord than is allowed for by theory. We have already referred to the Enlightenment as a point of departure for any such understanding. The subject–object split has been at the basis of Western philosophy at least since Descartes.[1] The related dichotomy between the individual and society appears to stem from this Cartesian period as well. As Williams (1976) points out, in its earliest usage in medieval thought, 'individual' meant 'inseparable'. Its use within the Holy Trinity was geared largely to explaining the problem of how a being could be thought simultaneously to exist by virtue of its own nature and as part of an indivisible whole. Notwithstanding the tremendous unevenness of any historical period in terms of social consciousness, it may be argued that medieval thought was characterised by a view of society (construed here as 'society of one's fellows') as a fixed, hierarchical and established order in which everything had its place. This cosmology was not only embodied in the Thomistic idea of community, but also, as Goldmann (1964) argues, in the Aristotelian conception of space.[2]

With the establishment of the bourgeoisie as the ruling economic class in the late sixteenth century, however, social life underwent a series of profound changes. Generally, as Bloch (1965) notes, medieval conceptions of society had characterised people according to their position within the social order – that is, in terms of their membership in a group – in such a way that people identified with the role they played in society. As such, the 'individual' was understood as a courtisan or an artisan, but not an 'individual' who happened to have this role as a courtisan or artisan. As Marx notes, at this point in time, things were understood as particular and concrete: individuality and social identity coincided; 'a nobleman always remains a nobleman, a commoner a commoner, a quality inseparable from his individuality irrespective of his other relations' (Marx 1846a, p. 78, cited in Sayer 1991). However, as mobility increased, people had the capacity to alter their status, to the extent that a person could be conceived of as an 'individual' separable from his or her role in society.[3] Correspondingly there arose, as Sayer (1991, p. 66) notes, a number of ways in which a person's existence could be defined: in terms of nationality, class, occupation, and so on. As a result, a situation in which feudal ties of personal dependence between, for example, lord and serf formed the basis of society and individual identity became replaced by a situation in which

> ties of personal dependence, distinctions of birth, education etc., (all the personal ties that appear as personal relationships), are in fact broken, abolished. The individuals appear to be independent ... appear to collide with one another freely, and to exchange with one another in this freedom. (Marx 1858a, p. 100)

From this point on, the concept of the isolated individual came to supplant that of the collectivity or community. This shift in emphasis from an 'individual' in relationships with others to an 'individual' in *his* own right was a slow and tortuous one, involving a move to a conception of the individual as a subject which is independent of social contexts and social positions, now understood as something 'accidental'. Thus with the triumph of the bourgeoisie came the replacement of the hierarchical society in which every person knew and recognised the value of his/her own place, with a conception of society as composed of free, equal and isolated individuals in which communal interests came to play a lesser role than that played by personal and private interests.

Concommitant with this process of 'individualisation' was the development of an increasingly abstract conception of 'society'. Again the term 'society' had originally referred to an actual relationship between individuals or 'society of one's fellows', but came during the sixteenth century to designate 'the common life'.[4] As Williams notes:

The idea of the 'individual' was not only a reaction to the complex of social, economic and religious changes; it was also a creative interpretation of them, – as a way of living ... the idea of 'society' had to be wrought out, as a creative description, if the problems of human organization were to be considered in terms wider than those set by any particular social system. The later stress on community, and on the social basis of individuality, was again a creative response to practical difficulties which could not be resolved while the idea of the individual as the bare human being remained dominant. (Williams 1961, pp. 111–12)

The emphasis placed by the new ruling social and economic class on the rational production of wealth was reflected not only in epistemology and physics – in which rationalism became the paradigmatic model of knowledge acquisition – but also in the spheres of religion and ethics. Thus religion ceased to play the independent and determining role it had played during the medieval period, with the result, as Dawe (1970) notes, that if 'God was the centre of the medieval world; man is the centre of the post-Medieval world'. This long and protracted process comprised many intermediate stages, which compressed accounts fail to differentiate, but if Protestantism represented a major transitional factor in religion, Spinoza's work on ethics constituted a crucial factor in ethical thought. Since there no longer existed a theistic supra-individual reality by reference to which human action could be carried out, actions could no longer be judged according to the standards of good and evil, but only in relation to those of success and failure.[5] Rationalism, taken to its ultimate conclusion, promoted an understanding of people as isolated, reasonable 'individuals' for whom other individuals existed only as objects. As such, 'the various forms of the social nexus confront the individual as merely a means towards his private purposes, as external necessity' (Marx 1858b, p. 18).

Concommitant with the rise of individualism within ethics was the rise of 'agency'. In the modern-capitalistic social orders human beings were isolated, communally rootless 'individuals', on the one hand, and creative, independent beings performing motivationally opaque, situationally contingent and unpredictable actions on the other. The separation between the conscious subject and the object of his/her action formed the basis for a theoretical standpoint in which a knowledgeable and capable 'individual' confronted an opaque natural and social world which he/she attempted to understand and transform. This dualism of subject and object, individual and society, in turn underpinned the basis for a range of other dualisms: agency and structure, determinism and freedom, thought and action, synchronism and diachronism, and so on. Even at its inception, however, the subject–object dualism had proved difficult to defend. If a subject's consciousness and action were construed as subject to the causal influence of the world in which they occurred, it was very difficult to safeguard the rational character of consciousness and the significance of action directed towards an end. Conversely, if the absolute and free nuture of consciousness and action were retained, the deterministic and ordered character of the universe in which the action of the subject constantly intervened was difficult to defend (Goldmann 1964). This difficulty, as Goldmann notes, afflicted all the major philosophers of the Enlightenment, from Descartes and the major rationalists (Leibniz, Malebranch and Spinoza) to the Encyclopaedists and Diderot – a difficulty which Kant hoped to resolve by effecting a radical separation between the intelligible world and the world of experience (ibid.). Thus the concept of the 'individual' arose from a confluence of changes which are often regarded as either following the Reformation or the beginnings of capitalist economy.[6] This solitary, abstract individual, construed in abstraction from the 'accidental' contingencies of concrete circumstances, thus constituted the moral subject of the modern world and became the theoretical starting point for the major traditions of social and political thought.[7]

It was also against this background that the discipline of sociology emerged during the nineteenth century. Notwithstanding the profound social transformations which took place, the line of development from Descartes and Hobbes to Simmel and Weber, although complex, was continuous. As Sayer (1991, pp. 11–12) notes, nineteenth-century sociology was characterised by its emphasis on the marked distinction between 'past' and 'present' societies: respectively, Durkheim's mechanical and organic solidarity, Tonnies's *Gemeinschaft* and *Gesellschaft*, Spencer's military and industrial societies, Weber's traditionalism and rationalisation, Simmel's non-monetised and monetised economies, and Marx's feudalism and capitalism. These typologies and theories were all grounded in the assumption of a distinction between modern social forms and their previous incarnations.

Thus not only was the relationship between individual and society a social, political and historical construction, but so too was the agency/structure debate, which provided a new gloss upon the former. Although the specific origins of the agency/structure debate in modern sociology are difficult to trace, it appears to have arisen in part as a political and theoretical reaction to the Parsonian 'orthodox consensus'. Its conscription into sociological discourse from the mid-1960s to the present day was undoubtedly influenced by books such as Berger and Luckmann's Schutzian-inspired *The Social Construction of Reality* (1966), as well as by landmark papers such as Dawe's 'The Two Sociologies' (1970).

For modern sociology centers on the opposition between a sociology of social system and a sociology of social action ... The opposition between the two sociologies is central to any discussion of theories of social action ... In a sociology of social system, then, social actors are pictured as being very much at the receiving end of the social system. In terms of their existence and nature as social beings, their social behavior and relationships, and their very sense of personal identity as human beings, they are determined by it. The process is one whereby they are socialized into society's central values and into the norms appropriate to the roles they are to play in the division of labor, the roles which give them both their self-identity and their social place and purpose in meeting the functional needs of the system. They are totally manipulable creatures; *tabulae rasae* upon which can be and are imprinted the values and behavioral stimuli necessary for the fulfillment of the functions and, therefore, the maintenance of what is thus a supra-human, self-generating, and self-maintaining social system, ontologically and methodologically prior to its participants ... In total opposition to this, a sociology of social action conceptualizes the social system as the derivative of social action and interaction, a social world produced by its members, who are thus pictured as active, purposeful, self- and socially-creative beings. The language of social action is thus the language of subjective meaning, in terms of which social actors define their lives, purposes, and situations; of the goals and projects they generate on the basis of their subjective meanings; of the means whereby they attempt to achieve their goals and realize their projects ... Clearly the whole picture especially that of the relationship between social action and social system, is in this perspective the exact opposite of that painted by a sociology of social system. (Dawe 1978, pp. 366–7)

Dawe's question concerning the 'two sociologies' was not merely a commentary on or reflection of the issue of the relationship between agency and structure, it was also recursively constitutive of that discourse. It was in relation to this theoretical context that Giddens began his theoretical work. In his early work Giddens accepted the notion of the 'abstract individual' who, according to T.H. Marshall, was seen to enjoy social, political and civil rights as a crucial counterweight to the authoritarian pretensions of socialism. This individual was later transposed into the context of Giddens's preoccupation with the relationship between agency and structure.[8]

HUMANS AS SOCIAL BEINGS

By providing this short genealogy of the social and historical foundation upon which the respective discourses of individual/ society and agency/structure arose, it has become clear that the classical sociological and philosophical preoccupation with these couplets provides an unsound basis for the construction of a general theory of social life. These are not eternal oppositions between two fixed categories but, rather, specific social and historical constructs which emerged during the course of development of modern social relations. The result of abstracting these definitions from the actual social relations in and through which they are expressed, and the adoption of either pole of the dualism, led to an interminable and irresolvable dualistic debate.[9] In his work on structuration, Giddens moved some way towards a resolution of this debate by introducing the term 'duality'. According to the theory of the duality of structure, 'structure enters simultaneously into the constitution of the agent and social practices, and "exists" in the generating moments of this constitution' (Giddens 1979, p. 5). Giddens's solution, however, continued to operate on the basis of a dualistic Enlightenment framework. As such, his notion of 'duality' still presupposed a prior analytical and ontological separation of agency and structure before any reconciliation could be effected. That these moments were separable is not only implied in Giddens's definition of the duality of structure, but is further evinced by reliance on a strategy of methodological bracketing in terms of 'strategic' and 'institutional analysis', as well as by his distinction between rules and practices. It has been contended that Giddens continued to retain a distinction between agency and structure for political reasons. However, attempts to grasp the properties of social relations on the basis of such dichotomies cannot be sustained.

How is the theoretical conundrum of agency and structure at all resolvable if the agency/structure dualism and the agency/structure duality which seeks to overcome it by means of the theory of structuration are both ultimately flawed? In other words, how is it possible to overcome the conflict between the claim that people 'make' history (structure, society, system, and so on), on the one hand, and the claim that history (structure, society, system, and so on) 'makes' people, on the other, without relapsing into accounts that either give rise to a reified or deterministic structure or advocate a voluntarism of unconstrained formless agency? One possible avenue towards achieving a solution has been provided by the disclosure of the social and historical conditions of possibility for the agency/structure debate, that is, by the provision of an outline of the historical practices which made the debate possible in the first place. By examining the distinction between agents and social structures through a historical, political and social lens, it was possible to acknowledge that the debate itself was historically constructed and did not rest on a universally valid opposition. Although such an examination may clear the ground, however, it does not in itself resolve the debate. In certain respects, it can be argued that a feasible solution to the agency/structure debate could issue from a perspective which embodies a conservative thought-style. Rather than referring to autonomous, sovereign individuals and arguing at a high level of abstraction and generality, such a thought-style would make reference to the social and collective nature of human existence and to empirical and contextual modes of evaluation. Such a view is reinforced when we look, for example, at Heidegger's profound insights. Thus the conservative thought-style finds exemplary expression in Heidegger's emphasis on historicality and *Dasein* as always 'already in the world'; in his recognition of the importance of praxis and 'ready-to-handness' (*Zuhanden*) of equipment; in the emphasis on the concrete, on 'being-in-the-world' and its 'average everydayness', as well as in his attempt to methodologically deconstruct metaphysics, including the subject–object dichotomy. Most importantly, Heidegger's reaction against Cartesian individualism, influenced by St Augustine's emphasis on the sociality of humans and expressed in terms of his own concept of being-with (*Mitsein*) reveals him as a representative of the conservative thought-style. As Rorty (1993, p. 339) notes, '*Dasein* was linguistic through and through just as it was social through and through.' Of course, this thought-style takes an increasingly explicit political tenor in Heidegger's romanticism and in his search for primordiality, in the introduction of the concepts of falling (*Verfallen*) *das Man* and being-among-one-another, in the reaction against reason which 'glorified for centuries, is the most stiff-necked adversary of thought', and, even more explicitly, in his statements referring to the 'will of the German *Volk*' and the 'forces of blood and soil'.[10]

Not all approaches which epitomise this conservative thought-style are as insightful as those of Heidegger or Wittgenstein in their shared emphasis on traditional practices as the basis for future actions, thought and experience:

> How can human behaviour be described? Surely only by showing the actions of a variety of humans, as they are all mixed up together. Not what one man is doing now, but the whole hurly burly, is the background against which we see an action, and it determines our judgement, our concepts, and our reactions. (Wittgenstein 1980b, p. 97)

Although it provides a valuable resource for conceptualising and re-evaluating the agency/structure dualism, the conservative approach is just as flawed as the traditional Enlightenment epistemology it claims to have transcended since it frequently relies upon the same framework of evaluative oppositions. Some conservative thought-styles have therefore aligned themselves too strongly with anti-theoretical tendencies, with a strident emphasis on particularity, with a thoroughgoing relativism, with an unreflective acceptance of tradition, romanticism, and with ungrounded notions of hierarchy. For this reason, the pattern of oppositions adopted by both of these approaches has to be rejected as a foundation for sociological thinking. Thus rather than by challenging rationality *per se*, as representatives of the conservative thought-style have often done, by advocating what Habermas calls 'an Other to Reason' only strong versions of rationalism need to be questioned (see also Taylor 1982, Gellner 1992, Alexander 1995). Rather than collapsing the distinction between the individual and the collective, the human trajectory towards individualisation must be acknowledged. A similar transcendence of the dualisms of Enlightenment and post-Enlightenment was, as noted, the basis for the sociology of Marx, Weber and Durkheim. These thinkers aimed to achieve a balance between these two thought-styles by selectively drawing on elements of both these approaches. While emphasising the inherently social nature of humans (though Weber remains an exception), they recognised at the same time their modern individuation; they acknowledged the importance of theory yet expressed it through empirical work; they were critical of modernity yet also adopted a resolute monism by seeing both the positive and negative aspects of modernism; they looked to contextual historical explanation yet also acknowledged the transhistorical dimensions of the social world. More recently, their ideas have been usefully extended in the work of both Elias and Bourdieu.

The positive argument proposed here, which draws on all the writers mentioned above, is that instead of opposing humans beings to a world which they try to understand and act upon – or, conversely, which acts upon them, as dualistic approaches claim – and instead of regarding individuals as existing through an onto-logically distinct world, as Giddens's theory of duality argues, we should see social humans *as* this world (Goldmann 1977). A more satisfactory approach must therefore begin with an ontology based upon the category of *social* human beings. According to the sociological perspective proposed here, human beings are to be regarded as fundamentally social creatures. On this interpretation, humans are not placed in opposition to or juxtaposed against a reified world or society which they try to understand and influence. On the contrary, it is only within and through this world that they attain 'individuality' in the first place, so that a social being only becomes an 'individual' through historically acquired social forms. Giddens's notion of duality of structure partly recognises this when he argues against sociological dualism. Yet as a result of his world-view, he continues to maintain a separation between the irreducible agent or 'individual' and social forms. However, the approach championed here rejects such a residual or implicit 'individualism'. There is no distinction between the individual and society, nor between the agent and structure. Rather, 'the individual' is an abstraction from *social* relations. The 'individual' is a thoroughly social agent, a microcosm of society. The shift from premodern to modern social orders is a shift in the details of communal social existence: a change from one type of communal social relation to another type of qualitatively different communal social relation. Thus a more satisfactory sociological approach must begin with an ontology based on the category of a social being, a category which falls between the reifications of both individual and society and agency and structure. As Marx (1843, p. 175) notes, 'man [sic] is not an abstract being squatting outside the world. He [sic] is the human world, the state, society.'

The sociality of humans was, of course, a fundamental preoccupation of both Durkheim and Marx, and Giddens himself also mentions interacting individuals and talks of social practices. However, like Weber's individuals, these individuals tend to interact in a formal and superficial way and Giddens fails to push this insight to its theoretical conclusion. Human sociality in terms of a profound mutual susceptibility of interacting non-independent social individuals provides the basis for a more suitable ontology for sociology. The intrinsically social nature of individuals incorporates human social identity as socially bestowed, socially sustained and socially transformed. Humans are social in every aspect of their being. That is, their activity and its enactment *are* social activity and social enactment (see Taylor 1989). Moreover, as Durkheim recognised, the very mental frameworks in accordance with which individuals think are socially and communally constituted:

> The nature of the concept, thus defined, bespeaks its origin. If it is common to all, it is the work of the community ... it is unquestionable that language, and consequently the system of concepts which it translates, is the product of collective elaboration. What it expresses is the manner in which society as a whole represents the facts of experience. (Durkheim 1976, p. 434)

As Elias (1978, 1994) also emphasises, social individuals are deeply interdependent agents, not only in respect of their forms of shared and aligned cognition, language and knowledge, but also in respect of their actions. The ontological interdependence of agents can be highlighted in two major respects. First, agents enter a field of interaction in which they are tied to other participants through their mutual susceptibility to the status evaluations of other socially interacting individuals. What is relevant here is the need to emphasise the importance of social recognition, conferred through esteem or status, as a universal characteristic of all human beings (Collins 1979, 1985). A second factor determining the ontological interdependence of social beings is the acknowledgement that humans are producing beings.[11] Humans require cooperation in order to produce their means of subsistence through their productive activity. As Marx notes (Marx and Engels 1844, p. 299), through their relations of production, social individuals produce their material life. For this reason, Giddens's sharp distinction between the natural world and the social world has to be rejected. The productive activity of human beings is a fundamental condition of all social life. An examination of the way in which people produce their means of subsistence is a crucial component of sociological analysis. The production of material life includes the production of material objects as well as the production of social relations, the latter encompassing family forms and gendered social relations. These two determinations are analytically separated here for theoretical purposes, but can and should be analysed and taken in conjunction with one another. Their relationship is neither fixed nor wholly independent, but changes historically. It falls to empirical research to uncover their historical variation and mediation in terms of psychogenesis and socio-genesis. Analysis of the production of material and mental life-forms in addition to the production of social relations and psychological drives constitutes only the starting point for sociological analysis (Elias 1994).

An alternative to Giddens's sociological approach must also adopt a different sociological methodology in order to conceptualise the complexity of social forms and relations. In order that social life can be characterised in terms of social struggle and conflicting interests, the divergent interests of agents have to be placed at the heart of any sociology. As Marx notes:

> The so-called enquiry from the standpoint of society simply amounts to overlooking the differences which precisely express social relations (the relations of bourgeois society). Society does not consist of individuals but it represents the sum of relations in which these individuals stand to each other, and of the connections between them. As if anyone would ever say: from the standpoint of society there are no slaves and citizens; they are both men. On the contrary, they are men outside society. To be a slave and to be a citizen are determinations, the relations of human beings A and B. Human being A as such is not a slave. He is a slave in and through society. (Marx 1857, p. 265)

A more adequate sociology, as Bourdieu points out, needs to be reflexive – both in terms of the position of the academic in social life and in terms of the concepts used by sociologists.[12] Exemplary historical work which embodies some of these methodological precepts has been carried out by Norbert Elias, E.P. Thompson and Pierre Bourdieu in their various writings, most notably in *The Civilising Process* (Elias 1994), *The Making of the English Working Class* (Thompson 1968) and *Distinction: A Social Critique of the Judgement of Taste* (Bordieu 1984). Their concentration upon what Marx (cited in Sayer 1989, p. 22) refers to as 'real individuals, their activity and the material conditions of their life [which] can be verified in a purely empirical way' is a testimony to the fruitfulness of their insights and their explanatory approach. This critique of Giddens's work is a fundamentally different reading of the sociological triumvirate of Marx, Durkheim and Weber. It employs a reading of Marx which draws on his view of the social character of human beings, his methodology and his notion of material production, broadly conceived. It employs a reading of Durkheim which draws on his emphasis on the social character of human beings, his stress on the social nature of categorisation and his conception of interdependence. Finally, it is based on a reading of Weber which endorses his notion of status as a major factor in social life.

10 Conclusion

Having examined Giddens throughout the course of this book, it is now possible to recapitulate and summarise the most salient issues addressed above. The central conjecture of this book has been that Giddens's sociology can be conceptualised in terms of a world-view. His use of concepts is not solely comprehensible in terms of their theoretical or intellectual value. Nor is the selective principle which underlies his theoretical synthesis an empirical one; rather, since his analysis is undertaken at such a high level of abstraction within the sphere of ontology, it is largely a metaphysical one. Giddens's world-view was that of a left-liberal intellectual, marked by a peculiar combination of tension and dependence in relation to both the Soviet Union and to capitalism. It is in reference to this background that Giddens attempted to marry the divergent intellectual and political traditions of liberalism and socialism within a liberal framework. This political, and subsequently theoretical, concern aimed to unite the greatest degree of individual liberty and freedom of action with the value of social equality.

However, by failing adequately to conjoin these liberal and socialist traditions in any coherent unity or synthesis and instead merely juxtaposing the two, Giddens's world-view remained characterised by an unresolved political dualism. These dualisms, then, some of which were more explicit than others, provided the source for a permanent oscillation in his theorical work and remained unresolved until the eventual disappearance of one side of the original political dualism: the domino-like collapse of the state socialist societies following the '1989 Revolutions'. However, the resulting sociology of 'modernity' and politics remained just as problematic because of their excessive dependence on the notion of the autonomous individual agent.

An alternative to Giddens's sociological position has been sketched. This drew on a tradition of sociology which was espoused originally in the work of Marx and Durkheim and upheld in modern sociology in the work of Goffman and Elias and Bourdieu. This was a sociology in which human beings are regarded as intrinsically *social* agents. It interposed the *social* between the terms of the long-established dualisms between individual and society, agency and structure, in order to dissolve them, embodying a fundamental warning issued by Marx:

> Above all, we must avoid postulating 'society' again as an abstraction vis-a-vis the individual. The individual is the social being. His [sic] manifestations of life – even if they may not appear in the direct form of communal manifestations of life carried out in association with others – are therefore an expression and confirmation of social life. Man's [sic] individual and species life are not different. (Marx 1844, p. 299)

Notes

INTRODUCTION

1. This is by no means the first attempt to look at Giddens' work as a world-view: see in particular Kilminster's brilliant 'Structuration as a World-View' (1991). Another paper which attempts to look at Giddens's work contextually is Clegg's (1992) 'How to Become a Famous British Social Theorist'. To some extent this book attempts to incorporate the valuable insights of both of these papers.

CHAPTER 1

1. According to Mannheim, a world-view is 'a structurally linked set of experiential contextures which makes up the common footing upon which a multiplicity of individuals together learn from life and enter into it. A world-view is then neither the totality of spiritual formations in an age nor the sum of individuals, then present, but the totality of the structurally interconnected experiential sets which can be derived from either side, from the spiritual creations or from the social group formations' (Mannheim 1982, p. 91).
2. For Bourdieu there exists a 'field' in relation to a habitus, consisting of objective, historical relations between positions anchored in various forms of power, or what he calls forms of capital. These fields, which may be subdivided into smaller fields that possess their own intrinsic logic and specific interests, form sites of conflict and competition for various forms of capital: 'In analytic terms, a field may be defined as a network, or a configuration, of objective relations between positions. These positions are objectively defined, in their existence and in the determinations they have upon their occupants, agents or institutions, by their present or potential situation (situs) in the structure of the distribution of species of power (capital) whose possession demands access to the specific profits that are at stake in the field, as well as by their objective relation to other positions (domination, subordination, homology, etc.)' (Bourdieu and Wacquant 1992, p. 97).
3. For a more comprehensive biography see Bryant and Jary (2001a, pp. 5–9) and Pierson (1998, especially ch. 1).
4. The central theme of Giddens's early work is suicide. See Giddens (1964, 1965a, 1965b, 1965c, 1965d, 1966). I have examined this work in another chapter and so will not repeat it here. Further interesting work includes Giddens's two review articles 'Recent Works on the History of Social Thought' (1970b) and 'Recent Works on the Position and Prospects of Contemporary Sociology' (1970c). In the first article, Giddens reviews *inter alia* the works of Nisbet, Aron and Zeitlin, all of whom examine the various writers in sociological canon such as Marx, Weber, Durkheim,

Simmel and Pareto. In the second part of the review Giddens discusses the work of Shils and C.W. Wright-Mills on American sociology and Georges Gurvitch on French sociology. The mention of Gurvitch's work is interesting since the latter uses the notions of structuration and destructuration and may be the source of Giddens's usage of these terms, though they became common currency in France during the early 1970s. A commentary on Simmel's work (Giddens 1968a) as well as a critique of Parsons's theory of power (Giddens 1968b) are also of note.

5. Max Scheler first introduced the term *Wissenssociologie* in the early 1920s and subsequently in his *Problems of a Sociology of Knowledge* (Scheler 1980).

6. The coherence of an author's standpoint may on occasion prove elusive since he/she will simultaneously be involved in a number of interwoven and overlapping groups. In Giddens's case, we may discount certain groups and concentrate on others. Thus his intellectual and socio-political groups are of more importance than his national, religious and familial groups. Moreover, we must bear in mind that the socio-political situation to which the writer and his group are responding is often in flux, as is the writer's consciousness of these changes.

7. The same can be said about undertaking a 'pure chronology' of a writer since the data that comprises this must first be selected and structured from a determinate standpoint before it can acquire any meaning whatsoever. Thus meaning, at any level and in all contexts, is not simply found in the subject of one's inquiry but unfolded from it through the meaning of the searching temporality. It is the author's existence in a particular social situation at a determinate juncture in history, rooted in specific social forces with interests, needs and orientations, which constitutes the necessary principle of selection.

8. 'Strictly speaking it is incorrect to say that the single individual thinks. Rather it is more correct to insist that he participates in thinking further what other men have thought before him. He finds himself in an inherited situation with patterns of thought which are appropriate to the situation and attempts to elaborate further the inherited modes of response or to substitute others for them in order to deal more adequately with the new challenges which have arisen out of the shifts and changes in his situation. Every individual is therefore in a two-fold sense predetermined by the fact of growing up in a society: on the one hand he finds a ready made situation and on the other he finds in that situation pre-formed patterns of thought and conduct' (Mannheim 1960, p. 3).

9. '[C]lassifications were modelled on the closest and most fundamental form of social organisation. This however, is not going far enough. Society was not simply a model which served as divisions for the system of classification. The first logical categories were social categories; the first classes of things were classes of men, into which these things were integrated. It was because men were grouped and thought of themselves in the form of groups, that in their ideas they grouped other things' (Durkheim and Mauss 1963, p. 82).

10. Although Bourdieu moves away from a conception which credits concepts, beliefs and principles with an inherent potency as autonomous

by collapsing them into social practices, he retains a strong structuralist or rigid bias in his use of concept application. Bourdieu is correct in arguing that what is possible to think and to know is to an extent pre-structured and that whatever attains credibility does so through processes involving cognitive commitments, acquired through socialisation and maintained by the application of authority and forms of social control; he does not, however, adequately examine how conceptions of knowledge are communally and *actively* extended on a contingent and finite basis. Here, what Hesse refers to as a finitist theory of classification is required. Since experience is immeasurably more complex and richer in information than language permits, 'it follows that past experience and the past usage of a concept can never suffice to determine a future usage. When an individual confronts a putative new instance of a term, he confronts an array of similarities and differences, between the new and the past instances, and among the past instances. Formally, his assertion that an instance falls under a term is only his contingent judgement to the effect that similarity outweighs difference. Past usage offers precedents for his usage, but is not sufficient to fix it because there is no natural or universal scale for the weighing of similarity against difference' (Barnes 1982a, pp. 28–9). For a more explicit analysis of classifications which looks also at their contingent nature, see Barnes (1982b, 1987).

11. The notion of a world-view employed here is not an empirical fact, but rather a conceptual working hypothesis. It is argued that this conceptual tool is indispensable when attempting to understand the way in which individuals express their ideas. It treats the social individual as an interactive group being who represents a 'we' as well as an 'I'. This social individual is involved in a number of different groups and activities, some of which are more important in understanding his/her work than others. By analysing the writer through group consciousness, it is necessary to move from the text to the writer, and then from the writer and his/her whole work to his/her social group, in order to understand the text. By examining his/her world-view it is possible to elucidate the social, political and moral issues which guide and structure his/her work as causal inputs or determinations. These are often expressed by the 'individual' writer in terms of sets of aspirations, tendencies and desires which not only reflect reality, but attempt to constitute it. The world vision then constitutes a complex of ideas, aspirations and feelings of what reality is and what it should be according to a particular group's standpoint. As Goldmann notes in his study of Kant, 'Social groups and society, which are empirical realities, create the concrete character of the natural world really (by technical action), and, through the mediation of that action on nature, create all economic, social and political structures, psychological structures and mental categories' (Goldmann 1971, p. 15).

12. For example, the French philosophers often looked to Britain as the birthplace of the modern with its constitutional monarchy. As Voltaire noted: 'The English are the only people on earth who have been able to prescribe limits to the power of Kings by resisting them' (Voltaire 1733).

They also turned to the writings of Locke, Bacon and Newton. In terms of time period, Porter (2000) talks of an 'early' or 'first' Enlightenment referring to pre-1750 developments and a 'late' or 'second' enlightenment following that date.

13. It is generally accepted that as a diverse intellectual movement the Enlightenment was rooted in seventeenth-century England in the work of Hobbes and Locke. It subsequently became developed in Scotland in the work of Smith and Ferguson; in France in the work of Voltaire, Bayle, Rousseau, Diderot, d'Alembert and the Encyclopaedists; and later in Germany in the work of Wolff, Lessing, Mendelssohn and Kant.

14. As Adorno rather reductively and misleadingly writes: 'For the Enlightenment, whatever does not conform to the rule of computation and utility is suspect ' (Adorno and Horkheimer 1944, p. 6). And again, 'Men pay for the increase of their power with alienation from that over which they exercise their power. Enlightenment behaves towards things as a dictator toward men. He knows them in so far as he can manipulate them' (ibid., p. 9).

15. As Hampson (1968) points out, the Protestant Church, in Lutheran Germany and Anglican England for example, accommodated to this Enlightenment world-view more readily than Catholic Europe, which was more dogmatic, although in Scotland Calvinism also proved recalcitrant.

16. Examples include Diderot, L'Holbach, Helvetius and, most famously, Kant, who, in his critiques of the logical, practical and the aesthetic, perceptively acknowledged the dual contribution of reason and sense-impressions whilst retaining a strong emphasis on the former.

17. Extending this emphasis on the individual as the *ens realissmus* of the social world, many Enlightenment writers, including Hobbes, Locke, Grotius, Diderot and Rousseau, regarded society as the result of a contract between numbers of autonomous individuals. Contract theory's main aim was to specify universal principles deduced from *a priori* reasoning whereby maximum freedom could be guaranteed to individuals without impinging on the freedom of others.

18. Other radical materialist writers such as Mably and Morrelly went further still by underscoring equality to an even greater extent as the basis of freedom. Hence, although Rousseau accepted limitations to equality in order to safeguard freedom, Mably and Morrelly steadfastly advocated the abolition of private property as the basis for liberty.

19. Condorcet's *Sketch for a Historical Picture of the Progress of the Human Mind*, originally published in 1795, was particularly important in this respect.

20. 'Kant's importance lies in the fact that he not only expressed with the utmost clarity his predecessors' individualist and atomist conceptions of the world taken to their logical conclusions, and thereby encountered their ultimate limits (which become for Kant the limits of human existence as such, of human thought and action in general): he did not stop, as did most of the neo-Kantians, at the recognition of these limits, but took the first steps, faltering no doubt, but nevertheless decisive, towards the integration into philosophy of the second category, that of the whole, the universe' (Goldmann 1971, p. 36).

21. The term came into Britain in the 1830s from Spain and France to describe the Whig party.

22. However, liberalism was never just purely a bourgeois ideology of possessive individualism as C.B. MacPherson (1962) remarks, though it can certainly be characterised partially as such. For example, Britain never experienced a clear-cut conflict between an ascendant middle class and an aristocracy in decline since the landed classes themselves became involved in commerce and industry. Liberalism was a diverse movement which also had a conservative stream. For example, the Whigs, though wishing to check the power of monarchy through Parliament, were also committed to the maintenance of wealth, privilege and property as equally important.

23. Thus, the ideas of Beveridge, Keynes, Hobhouse and T.H. Green played a major role in constructing the post-war social democratic consensus by arguing that the excesses of capitalism could be regulated through a partial management of the economy and adequate social welfare.

24. However, the differences remain, most acutely in relation to the communal ownership of the means of production. As Eccleshall remarks, 'Socialists contend that the liberal objective of an equal right to freedom remains frozen as an unfulfilled potential within capitalism: that a system of Private property necessarily congeals into a class structure in which the rhetoric of freedom masks the privileges of an exploitative minority. It follows that liberal values can only be given substance outside liberal society – in a community which displaces the competitive struggle for scarce resources by a co-operative pursuit of human needs and so resolves the age-old antagonism between capital and labour' (Eccleshall 1986, p. 61).

25. Mannheim writes: 'The central problem for all sociology of knowledge and research into ideology is the linkage between thinking and knowing on the one hand, and existence on the other (*Seinsgebundenheit allen Denkens und Erkennens*)' (Mannheim 1986, p. 31).

26. As Barnes notes, 'Examples of a style share no essence or essential identity, nor is there any essential identity of any of their analysable features or characteristics. Style itself, which is evident only in the examples that represent it, must necessarily vary over time. However, this is not a random variation between unconnected particulars; it is a systematic variation that arises from the mode of connection between one example and another. One work in a given style will serve as a model or inspiration or source of influence for another later work, which, even though it differs from its model, will nonetheless be similar to it – and it will be the similarities between the particulars that allow us to recognise something worth calling a style running through the whole stream of examples' (Barnes 1994, p. 76).

27. Mannheim's analysis is both incomplete and vague. By taking nineteenth-century France as his basis, Mannheim fails to look at the specificity of British, German and American liberalism, which, because of their social and political contexts and different class balances, ensured that there was no singular manifestation or interpretation of what counted as liberalism.

In addition, Mannheim's work is often politically reductive. For Mannheim, thought styles are simply reducible to, or reflective of, class position. What is missing from Mannheim's account is an explanation of the various academic mediations, particularly within the university system, which shape knowledge and provide a site for the assertion and questioning of various theories and perspectives. However, rather than examining these academic mediations and how they shape or inflect social and political determinants from the wider social order, Mannheim instead goes to the opposite extreme by talking of the unfounded notion of 'free-floating intellectuals'. As Eagleton notes: 'The only problem with this approach is that it merely pushes the question of relativism back a stage; for we can always ask about the tendentious standpoint from which this synthesis is actually launched' (Eagleton 1991, p. 108). This is not to argue that intellectuals within the university system cannot have a certain relative autonomy in relation to advocating scientific analyses corresponding to a greater or lesser degree to some notion of 'social scientific truth'. It is merely to state that there are numerous examples of how social and political presuppositions enter and shape much intellectual work. There are of course many other criticisms of Mannheim: see Remmling (1973); for a criticism of his analysis of mathematics, see Bloor (1973).

28. In the political field, conservatism emphasised the collective compared to the individual and looked to ethical values contained in institutions which had grown steadily through trial and error over centuries. By admitting to the fallibility of knowledge which remained largely tacit and unexplicated, conservatives also pointed to the dangers of constructing long-term plans based on reason rather than on experience. They set themselves against rapid reform rather than against reform *per se*. By incorporating the strengths, endurances and wisdom of tested traditions these institutions can adapt to human needs as well as to the provision of identity and culture. The conservative conception of freedom attacks the notion of equality of humans upon which the liberal conception rests. Humans are unequal in their nature, in their innermost being, and freedom consists in the condition in which each and everyone, in accordance with 'his' innermost principle, actualises the laws of development uniquely peculiar to himself.

29. 'Action can only be effective in the immediate particular concrete environment in which one is placed. In contrast to liberalism, which not only sees the actual in terms of it potentialities, but also in terms of the norm ... the conservative ... tries to comprehend the actual in its contingency or attempts to understand the normative in terms of the existent' (Bloor 1993, p. 95).

30. See, for example, the work of De Bonald and De Maistre. However, some Romantics, including Rousseau, also carried pronounced liberal preoccupations.

31. Using Kant's distinction between reason and understanding as a basis for their thinking, the Romantics emphasised the limits of the latter. The German Idealists, most notably Fichte, Schelling and Hegel, all accepted this distinction.

32. They all attempted to transcend a number of dualisms which had emerged in both Enlightenment and post-Enlightenment thought, though each theorist achieved this end in different ways and with more or less different degrees of success. As Seidman (1983) notes, their efforts broadly involved the integration of materialism and idealism, individualism and holism, rationalism and historicism, and science and critique.

33. In the natural sciences, such a framework came under severe criticism in the natural sciences following the writings of Kuhn and Feyerbend in the 1960 and 1970s. These writers reasserted a conservative thought-style as a basis for understanding science which drew heavily on Wittgenstein's *Philosophical Investigations* (1958) and Quine's 'Two Dogmas of Empiricism' (1951). Hence many social constructivist accounts have re-emphasised a conservative thought-style by arguing that science is a collective accomplishment rather than an individual enterprise, an artefactual process rather than revealing a given real world, and based on contingent local forms of consensus rather than logically compelling or rationalist accounts (Barnes 1993).

34. This survey of political context draws heavily from Perry Anderson's (1977, 1983) exemplary work.

35. For an analysis, see Kilminster (1998, ch. 2).

36. As a result, 'it is not political stances which determine people's stances on things academic, but their positions in the academic field which inform the stances that they adopt on political issues in general as well as on academic problems' (Bourdieu 1988, pp. xvii–xviii). Moreover, although a number of the participants within the intellectual field share a similar 'habitus', during periods of crisis, what Collins calls 'structural rivalry' leads to the emergence of differing perspectives that become more explicit and codified through the challenging of orthodoxies (Collins 2000, p. 6). Regarding the social contributions of academics towards the social world, Bourdieu remarks: 'If the agents do indeed contribute to the construction of these structures, they do so at every stage within the limits of the structural constraints which affect their acts of construction both from without, through determinants connected with their position in the objective structures, and from within, through the mental structures – the categories of professorial understanding – which organise their perception and appreciation of the social world. In other words although they are never more than particular angles of vision, taken from points of view which the objective analysis constitutes as such, the partial and partisan view of the agents engaged in the game, and the individual or collective struggles through which they aim to impose these views, are part of the objective truth of this game, playing an active part in sustaining or transforming it, within the limits set by the objective constraints' (Bourdieu 1988, p. xiv). Collins talks more explicitly of symbols: 'Intellectuals have something in common with all social membership. Every local group is attached to its symbols; but the nature of these symbols varies, and so does members' self-consciousness in relation to them' (Collins 2000, p. 24).

37. As Mills states: 'It must be evident that the particular view of society which it is possible to dig out of Parsons' texts is of rather direct

ideological use; traditionally, such views have of course been associated with conservative styles of thinking ... The ideological meaning of grand theory tends strongly to legitimate stable forms of domination' (Mills 1959, p. 59). In relation to Parsons's *Structure of Social Action* (1937) and its emphasis on 'continuity' and 'convergence', Gouldner writes: 'The call to intellectual convergence and cumulation began to crystallise in the United States under certain distinctive social conditions ... In short, the American call to convergence and continuity in social theory had its social foundation in collective sentiments that favoured all kinds of social unity, and which had developed in response to the military and political exigencies of World War II. Correspondingly, however, with the breakdown of national unity after the war as with the later growth of widespread racial conflict and student rebellion, the ideology of convergence and continuity no longer resonated collective sentiment... The ideology of convergence and continuity ... was also congenial to the drive to professionalise sociology that was mounted at the same time ... There is no possible way of transcending the present and the past from which it derives, without a thoroughgoing criticism of it' (Gouldner 1971, p. 18).

38. During the 1960s the widespread development of spontaneous and organised anti-establishment 'movements' appeared to challenge the stability of the prevailing social and political structures, institutions and values. Many of these movements (anti-colonial, liberation, black power, civil rights, worker, student, women's, feminist, socialist, neo-fascist) were unable to change existing ways of behaving and thinking, but some proved more successful. What is important in the present context is that contemporary social theory not only failed to predict these events, but also appeared to be unable to help understand, let alone explain, them. A 'crisis in social theory' was noted by many commentators at the time and was a particularly important starting point for the intellectual development of Giddens.

39. This conjunctural change also formed the basis for the beginnings of a rapprochement between Marxism and sociology, which had previously remained antithetical. It was expressed most obviously through works like Marcuse's *One Dimensional Man* (1964) and Bottomore and Rubels's *Karl Marx: Selected Writings* (1963) London: Penguin, which emphasised Marx's early 'humanist' writings. See Sklair (1980).

40. See the importance Giddens places on the student radicalism and his experience of teaching in Canada and America in Bryant and Jary (2001a, p. 7).

41. As Giddens notes, 'I believe that sociologists must always be conscious of the social context within which theories are formulated' (Giddens 1971a, p. x). Unfortunately, Giddens was to ignore this principle in the remainder of his work and hence offer decontextualised analyses of other writers.

42. Giddens questions Parsons's interpretation of Durkheim as predominantly a functionalist thinker concerned with the group mind and his interpretation of Weber as a sociologist concerned largely with social action. 'Apart from Marx himself, there can be few social thinkers whose

fate has been to be so persistently misunderstood as Durkheim. In his own day Durkheim's theoretical writings were regarded by most critics as embodying an unacceptable metaphysical notion of the "group mind". Some recent sympathetic accounts have largely dispelled this sort of mis-interpretation but have supplanted it with one which places virtually the whole emphasis upon Durkheim's functionalism. In this book, I have sought to rescue Durkheim as a historical thinker. Durkheim always emphasised the crucial significance of the historical dimension in sociology, and I believe that an appreciation of this leads to quite a different assessment of Durkheim's thought from that which is ordinarily given. Durkheim was not primarily concerned with "the problem of order", but with the problem of the changing nature of order in the context of a definite conception of social developments' (Giddens 1971a, p. ix). For further criticisms see Giddens (1977a, which contains a number of essays written during this period).

43. As Giddens notes, 'So far as the "classics" themselves are concerned, *Capitalism and Modern Social Theory* did foster the effect noted by Poggi: it helped to establish the view that Marx, Durkheim and Weber were *the* dominant thinkers whose ideas have shaped modern sociology.' He adds: 'At the time at which I wrote *Capitalism and Modern Social Theory* – amazingly enough, in the light of developments very shortly after – Marx was not widely thought of as one of the thinkers whose work still had to be reckoned with in contemporary sociology. Save among those who explicitly designated themselves as "Marxists", the dominant standpoint was that expressed in Talcott Parsons's *The Structure of Social Action* (1937). According to this view, Marx belonged to the generation before the development of sociology proper, a process initiated by Durkheim, Weber and others at the turn of the present century. Marx, like Comte, was relegated to the pre-history of the discipline. I hope I played some part in dissolving that kind of position' (Giddens 1990b, p. 298). See also Mullan (1987, especially pp. 95–120).

44. For a discussion of the debate, see, *inter alia*, Gouldner (1971), Birnbaum (1971), Habermas (1976) and Sklair (1980).

45. For Weber's influence in Giddens's later writings, see Turner (1992b).

46. Giddens himself claims that Habermas is the theorist from whom he has learnt the most (Giddens 1982, p. 107).

47. That is, Giddens represents the standpoint of a British writer who is part of what Bourdieu terms the dominated fraction of the dominant classes. See Bourdieu (1988). An additional factor which we need to examine is Giddens's social trajectory as a concrete individual. Giddens discusses his social background in Pierson (1998).

48. For a discussion concerning the difficulty of merging the two, see Lukes (1991).

CHAPTER 2

1. Giddens adds that 'what an actor knows as a competent – but historically and spatially located – member "shades off" in contexts that stretch beyond his or her day-to-day activity' (Giddens 1984, pp. 91–2).

2. Thus Giddens writes that 'the rationalisation of action is always bounded, in every sort of historical context; and it is in exploring the nature and persistence of these bounds that the tasks of social science are to be found. As I have proposed … there are three types of circumstances relevant here: unconscious elements in action, practical consciousness, and the unintended consequences of action, all of which combine within the reproduction of social systems' (Giddens 1979, p. 250).

3. Giddens also notes: 'In the case of generalisations in social science, the causal mechanisms are inherently unstable … generalisations in the social sciences are "historical" in character … it means that only the circumstances in which generalisations hold are temporally and spatially circumscribed, depending as they do on definite mixes of intended and unintended consequences of action' (Giddens 1984, pp. 346–7).

4. 'A purely hermeneutic account of the social sciences places out of court the possibility – which is actually a necessity – of analysing social conduct in terms which go beyond those of actors situated in particular traditions, and which are of explanatory significance in relation to them' (Giddens 1976, p. 62).

5. Giddens illustrates this in *Central Problems in Social Theory* by referring to Winch's (1958) discussion of Zande sorcery. Thus: 'Mutual knowledge is the necessary medium of identifying what is going on when a sorcerer places a malicious spell upon an individual in order to procure that person's death. But this is no logical bar at all to critical inquiry into the empirical grounding that can be marshalled to support the validity of the belief-claims held in relation to this practice' (Giddens 1979, p. 252).

6. Giddens states that there is 'a non-contingent relation between demonstrating a social belief to be false and practical implications for the transformation of action linked to that belief. Criticising a belief means (logically) criticising whatever activity or practice is carried on in terms of that belief, and has compelling force (motivationally) in so far as it is a reason for action' (Giddens 1984, p. 340).

7. Giddens's position on ideology recognises the implications of working with a science/ideology opposition, which he argues bears residues from the Enlightenment critique of prejudice. It also implies a break from the belief that ideology must be connected to epistemology, which originates with Mannheim. These implications are borne out in this remark: 'The approach to ideology I shall suggest certainly implies accepting that social science can deliver objectively valid knowledge. But it involves rejecting the line of argumentation according to which the relation between such "valid knowledge" and "invalid knowledge claims" is the defining feature of what ideology is' (Giddens 1979, p. 186).

8. Giddens adds, 'This is related to the dialectic of control' (Giddens 1979, p. 72).

9. 'I don't really think of critical theory in the sense in which you want me to think of it. I think it's first of all dependent upon finding an acceptable mode of theorising relationship between human actors as beings who can make a difference in the world and know what they're doing on the one hand and yet who live in a world which affects them and which has

circumstances and conditions which constrain them, which are beyond their control, not as individuals but as totalities.

I think it demonstratively makes a difference if for example you treat human beings as knowledgeable actors in the sense in which I argue, humans are knowledgeable. It makes a demonstrable difference to the style of social analysis that some people do as compared to the style of social analysis that other people do. If you recognise extension in time and space and the significance of the drift of unintended consequences this has other substantive implications of the kind I was trying to indicate earlier, and indicates that a programmed society, for example, is probably a logical impossibility not just a factual unreality. It's around the core of that that I would group lots of these things not around the traditional normative problems of critical theory' (Bleicher and Featherstone 1982, p. 76).

10. As Giddens states, 'I regard social practices, together with practical consciousness, as crucial mediating moments between two ordinary established dualisms in social theory. One is the dualism of individual and society, or subject and object; the other is the dualism of conscious/unconscious modes of cognition' (Giddens 1979, pp. 4–5).

11. See Wittgenstein (1958) and, in more recent use, the work of Garfinkel (1967) and Polanyi (1967). For a broader overview, see Turner (1994).

12. Giddens briefly mentions sectional interests in his discussion of ideology, though this remains partial and impressionistic. See Giddens (1979, pp. 180–90).

13. The only example Giddens gives is of Paul Willis's (1977) work, *Learning to Labour* (Giddens 1984, pp. 291–2).

14. Again I draw on Barnes (1995, pp. 94–103).

15. Nevertheless, the obverse of this figurational development is also a greater interdependence. See Elias (1978).

16. Thus Giddens writes: 'That is, though I'm sympathetic to realism, for example, especially the so-called "new realism" of Bhaskar, Harre, and others, I don't think of myself as working in any innovative way on epistemological issues, and I try to "bracket" them to some substantial degree. What I'm trying to do is to work on essentially what I describe as an ontology of human society, that is, concentrating on issues of how to theorise human agency, what the implications of that theorising are for analysing social institutions, and then what the relationship is between those two concepts elaborated in conjunction with one another. I think that it is true that any version of social theory presumes some kind of epistemological position, some position with regard to epistemological debates – for example, whether there can be an epistemology in the traditional sense, about which I'm still a bit unsure – but I don't think it either necessary or possible to suppose you could formulate a fully-fledged epistemology ... That's why I think of what I'm doing as rather different from the work of writers like Bhaskar, or even of more important writers like Habermas, who are attempting to round out philosophical questions of that sort much more than I am' (Gregory 1984, p. 124).

17. Notwithstanding Giddens's claim that Habermas is the theorist from whom he has learnt the most (Giddens 1981b, p. 107), there are also

substantial differences in their approaches, which are partly highlighted in Giddens's criticism of Habermas. For Giddens, Habermas's focus on technocratic domination results in the creation of separation of instrumental and communicative action and between technical rules and social norms, which means that he fails to incorporate divergent interests in interaction, confining them to purposive rational action of labour as well as making them difficult to reconnect once separated. It is also divergent in terms of Habermas's formal procedural grounding of an ideal speech situation which for Giddens seems to be desirable not because actors want it to be so but because of the formal structure itself. Significant differences also arise from Habermas's adoption of the Parsonian theory of power as well as his evolutionism. For a more extensive comparison see Livesay's fine paper (Livesay 1985).

18. Giddens also writes: 'It is right to claim that the condition of generating valid descriptions of a form of life entails being able in principle to participate in it (without necessarily having done so in practice) ... But it does not follow from such a conclusion that the beliefs and practices involved in forms of life cannot be subjected to critical assessment – including within this the critique of ideology. We must distinguish between respect for the authenticity of belief, as a necessary condition of any hermeneutic encounter between language-games; and the critical evaluation of the justification of belief. Expressed in less cumbersome fashion, we must differentiate what I call "mutual knowledge" from what might simply be called "common sense"' (Giddens 1984, p. 251).

19. Giddens also notes in relation to reasons and actions, 'once more at the risk of upsetting the more philosophically minded reader, I propose simply to declare that reasons are causes' (Giddens 1984, p. 345).

20. Although Bhaskar's ontology and epistemology are more securely grounded than Giddens's, the former's conception of ideology, which refers to false consciousness, has to be rejected since its presupposes a distinction between the material and the ideal.

21. Throughout, I take the idea of importance of the self-fulfilling prophecy from Barnes.

22. 'It is the self-fulfilling prophecy which goes far toward explaining the dynamics of ethnic and racial conflict in the America of today' (Merton 1957, p. 477). Merton adds: 'As a result of their failure to comprehend the operation of the self-fulfilling prophecy, many Americans of good will (sometimes reluctantly) retain enduring ethnic and racial prejudices. They experience these beliefs, not as prejudices, not as prejudgements, but as irresistible products of their own observation' (ibid., p. 478).

23. Thus Merton writes: 'This [self-fulfilling prophecy] is peculiar to human affairs. It is not found in the world of nature, untouched by human hands. Predictions of the return of Halley's comet do not influence its orbit. But the rumoured insolvency of Millingville's bank did affect the actual outcome. The prophecy of collapse led to its own fulfillment' (Merton 1957, p. 477).

24. I do not, of course, mean this in the technical sense of how people relate to nature.

25. Merton's account is flawed not only as a result of his positivistic beginnings but also due to political determinations. He tends to portray 'human nature' as somehow originally 'good' until it becomes tainted by the 'evil' of false definitions of the situation. This will continue, he believes, until their deliberate institutional controls allay or prevent these 'evil fears' from arising. However, we could also add that the attribution of real and good and unreal and false predicates in describing social situations results from Merton's functionalist-structuralist method, which goes beyond lay actors' phenomenological relations to the underlying latent functions towards which their actions are geared. This discounting of agents' own reasons for acting as they do allows Merton to apply 'false' and 'real' beliefs upon them. Moreover, to argue for a conception of 'false consciousness' implies a position which mistakenly separates the 'ideal' from the 'material'.

26. The development of Wittgenstein's thought from the *Tractatus* to the *Philosophical Investigations* represents an exemplar of both of these standpoints. See Austin (1965) for the constitute role of language and beliefs.

27. Elsewhere Giddens writes: 'The so called "self-fulfilling prophecy", of which Merton and others have written, is a special case of a much more generic phenomenon in the social sciences' (Giddens 1984, p. xxxii).

28. It is in view of the fact that all social actors alter their theories in the light of incoming information that Giddens adumbrates the prescience of rational expectations theory in his characterisation of the knowledge-ability and instability of social actors and their knowledge. See Giddens (1987, ch. 8).

29. In response to the question posed during an interview, 'So how do we then assess the theorist's standpoint, given the possibility of a multiplicity of readings. In what sense is one theory better than another, more objective, or more critical than another, what sort of criteria are to be employed?', Giddens answered: 'The sense in which one theory is better than another has still do, in my opinion, with the facts of the matter. I don't accept that theory is intractable to the facts, it seems to me that there is, as it were, a dialogue between theory and fact which is the basis of the possibility of doing any kind of sociological analysis or political analysis or whatever. I don't accept there are a multiplicity of equally persuasive interpretations of the world, that I don't think is so. I don't think, on the other hand, anyone can any longer suppose that you can just have one that everyone is going to inevitably accept because it demonstrates itself somehow through the facts to be the only one. I don't see there is a choice just between those two alternatives: the real situation we are in is somewhere in the middle. For example, I think I can persuade quite a lot of people that there are strong reasons to be dubious about evolutionary theories, let's say in the light of what we now believe that we know about a wide range of different societies, and that this does have some persuasive force. I don't expect it to have the force of absolute conviction for everybody has some persuasive force. As regards moral and political statements, I think, something of the same thing is true, that is to say, arguments informed by fact and related to

moral ideals which not many people are going to question in the abstract, have a good deal of persuasive power. I don't see that as a programme for grounding critical theory though ... It's all too easy to suppose that it's impossible to do anything until you've got a completely secure base you can go back to and I think you can't have a secure house, either in respect of the facts or in respect of moral critique on the part of the theorist or the analyst. I don't like this measure of shifting sands very much. I think it's more a matter of moving between two households and changing them as you move and as you change the facts of the matter you might change your political interpretation' (Bleicher and Featherstone 1982, p. 74).

30. 'I'm not sure what my views on a critical theory of modern society would look like because I haven't worked it out. To me it depends on what one makes of the residue of socialism particularly in respect of how far socialist programmes and ideals still have some real significance in the modern world ... that socialism still retains some of the traditional ideals of the humane form of society that it was linked with. But I'm not hoping nor anticipating developing some kind of closed epistemological position which is a sort of test from which you can judge, in some sort of infallible way, whether certain things are right to do or not' (Bleicher and Featherstone 1982, p. 75).

31. There are, of course, many forms of relativism, some strong and some weak, often depending on the equivalence postulates they embody. However, we can follow Bhaskar here and talk of the distinction between epistemological relativism and judgemental relativism. See also Barnes and Bloor (1982) and Hesse (1980).

32. Such a personality requires a highly developed superego.

CHAPTER 3

1. Thus Giddens notes: 'I distinguish the reflexive monitoring and rationalisation of action from its motivation. If reasons refer to the grounds of action, motives refer to the grounds which prompt it' (Giddens 1984, p. 6).

2. Giddens states, 'By "critical situations" I mean circumstances of radical disjuncture of an unpredictable kind which affect substantial numbers of individuals, situations that threaten or destroy the certitudes of institutionalised routines' (Giddens 1984, p. 61).

3. 'An agent who does not participate in the dialectic of control, in a minimal fashion, ceases to be an agent' (Giddens 1979, p. 149).

4. '[A]ll power relations manifest autonomy and dependence "in both directions". A person kept thoroughly confined and supervised, as an individual in a straitjacket, perhaps has lost all capability of action, and is not a participant in a reciprocal power-relation. But in all other cases – that is, in which human agency is exercised within a relationship of any kind – power relations are two-way' (Giddens 1979, p. 149).

5. Thus material constraints are constraints 'deriving from the character of the material world and from the physical body' whilst negative sanctions

are constraints 'deriving from punitive responses on the part of some agents towards others' (Giddens 1984, p. 176).

6. '[C]onstraint deriving from the contextuality of action, i.e. from the given character of structural properties', which 'do not operate independently of the motives and reasons that agents have for what they do' (Giddens 1984, p. 181).

7. This theory can also be criticised in terms of its failure to embody agents. According to Smith and Turner, who draw sparingly on the work of Foucault and Mauss, Giddens's theory of the agent fails to address human embodiment and the resistance that agents show to power and constraint (Smith and Turner 1986).

8. This incorporates a shift from a focus on the text vis-à-vis post-structuralism to conversation in everyday life (Giddens 1986).

9. However, whether Giddens explicitly bases his account of subjectivity on this notion, as Wagner implies, is debatable. Thus, Giddens seems to rely on Wittgenstein in discussing the meaning and constitution of social practices and Heidegger for his discussion of timing and spacing (see Chapter 6), without ever really reconciling the two, even though they undoubtedly share certain similarities in outlook. Moreover, even if we accept Wagner's argument that Giddens adopts Heidegger's notion of *Dasein*, this is not the cause of his retreat into a fixed or solipsistic subject, but rather an effect.

10. More generally, accounts of human agency can raise issues of individual responsibility which cross and transcend right–left political divisions.

11. 'The principal basis ... of the efficacy of a system of rules as a whole lies in the moral authority it exercises. Sanctions form only a secondary support' (Parsons 1937, p. 402). Similarly, 'the primary source of constraint lies in the moral authority of a system of rules. Sanctions thus become a secondary mode of enforcement of the rule, because the sanctions are, in turn, dependent on moral authority' (ibid., p 463).

12. However, Giddens at the same time shares many of the assumptions of the Parsonian approach. Thus, both theorists write against the alleged hegemony of 'positivism' and both subscribe to a rarefied Freudianism.

   Moreover, it is clear that Giddens shares much of Parsons's account of action, intentionality and meaning, even though he criticises many of its specific details. An apparently important difference between the two theorists is that Giddens rejects Parsons's division of the 'mental' realm into an ego which acts, and other compartments of the mind which affect the ego. Likewise he rejects a division between the mind (including the ego, the conscience, and so forth) and the body.

13. It also allows stable wants, desires or needs of any kind, conscious or unconscious, to be cited in order to make it so. It is useful to recall how rational choice theorists impute agency (choice) *precisely* in order to engender accounts of action as predictable/controllable, given that Giddens regards the very same imputation as the necessary means for allowing creativity/innovation.

14. As Wittgenstein notes: 'we sometimes wish for a notation which stresses a difference more strongly, makes it more obvious, than ordinary language does, or one which in a particular case uses more strongly

similar forms of expression ... Our mental cramp is loosened when we are shown the notations which fulfil these needs. These needs can be of the greatest variety' (Wittgenstein 1969a, p. 59, cited in Bloor 1983, p. 47).

CHAPTER 4

1. Thus 'neither school of thought is able to grapple adequately with the constitution of social life as the production of active subjects' (Giddens 1976, p. 121). Both 'are alike in according priority to the object over the subject, or in some sense, to structure over action' (Giddens 1979, p. 50). Giddens also notes that 'Functionalism and Structuralism in some part share similar origins and have important features in common. The lineage of both can be traced back to Durkheim as refracted in the former instance through the work of Radcliffe-Brown and Malinowski and in the latter through that of Saussure and Mauss' (ibid., p. 9).

2. 'The use of "structure" in social theory is not necessarily inculpated in the failings of either structuralism or functionalism, in spite of its terminological association with them' (Giddens 1976, p. 120).

3. In *New Rules of Sociological Method* Giddens notes, 'not because society is like a language, but on the contrary because language as a practical activity is so central to social life that in some basic respects it can be treated as exemplifying social processes in general' (Giddens 1976, p. 127).

4. 'The theory of structuration, thus formulated, rejects any differentiation of synchrony and diachrony or statics and dynamics' (Giddens 1979, p. 69).

5. Formulated rules 'that are given verbal expression as canons of law, bureaucratic rules, rules of games and so on', should be taken not as exemplifying rules in general but 'are specific types of rule, which, by virtue of their overt formulation, take on various specific qualities' (Giddens 1984, p. 21).

6. As noted earlier, for Giddens rules and resources exist as memory traces and can be characterised as having a 'virtual existence'. However, it might be inferred that 'allocative' resources such as raw materials, land, and so forth clearly possess a 'real existence' in space-time. But for Giddens, 'their "materiality" does not affect the fact that such phenomena become resources, in the manner in which I apply the term here, only when incorporated within the process of structuration. The transformational character of resources is logically equivalent to, as well as inherently bound up with the instantiation of, that of codes and normative sanctions' (Giddens 1984, p. 33).

7. For a critique of Giddens's misuse of Derrida's notion of *différance* see Dallmayr (1982, p. 20).

8. The interpretations of Wittgenstein by Baker and Hacker are relevant here: see Bloor (1992).

9. 'All social reproduction is grounded in the knowledgeable application and reapplication of rules and resources by actors in situated social contexts: all interaction thus has, in every circumstance, *to be*

contingently "brought off" by those who are party to it' (Giddens 1979, p. 114; my italics).

10. See also the insightful critique of Giddens by Callinicos (1989). Giddens also fails to indicate how rules are learned in order for them to be generalisable by actors in the first place. That is, he fails to confront 'why and how, this knowledge is generalisable'. Wittgenstein states: 'How do I explain the meaning of "regular", "uniform", "same" to anyone? – I shall explain these words to someone who, say, only speaks French by means of the corresponding French words. But if a person has not yet got the concepts, I shall teach him to use the words by means of examples and by practice' (Wittgenstein 1958, pp. 82–3). In addition, with regard to rule-following, it is imperative to explain the motivation or springs behind actors following rules. The criterion Giddens posits in relation to this crucial question is far from satisfactory. For Giddens, most actors are unconsciously motivated to follow rules in order to maintain 'ontological security'. However, to accord 'ontological security' such a crucial role in motivating actors to follow rules is surely unwarranted. By employing such a conception Giddens systematically neglects any notion of socially generated interests as motivating factors.

11. Wittgenstein also writes, 'Following a rule is analogous to obeying an order. We are trained to do so; we react to an order in a particular way. But what if one person reacts in one way and another in another to the order and training? Which one is right?' (Wittgenstein 1958, p. 82).

12. Justification ends not in truth or reason, but in 'an ungrounded way of acting' (Wittgenstein, cited in Bloor 1983, p. 162).

13. This argument is put forward most convincingly by Kripke. As he notes the example of the concept of addition that he gives: 'Those who deviate are corrected and told (usually as children) that they have not grasped the concept of addition. One who is an incorrigible deviant in enough respects simply cannot participate in the life of the community and in communication' (Kripke 1982, p. 92).

14. 'And hence also "obeying" is a practice. And to think one is obeying a rule is not to obey a rule. Hence, it is not possible to obey a rule "privately": otherwise thinking one was obeying a rule would be the same thing as obeying it' (Wittgenstein 1958, p. 81).

15. 'The word "agreement" and the word "rule" are related to one another, they are cousins' (Wittgenstein 1958, p. 86).

16. 'The application of the concept "following a rule" presupposes a custom' (Wittgenstein 1978, p. 322). 'To obey a rule, to make a report, to give an order, to play a game of chess, are customs (uses, institutions)' (Wittgenstein 1958, p. 81). It is for this reason that Giddens is mistaken when he asserts that institutions simply feature as backdrops to individual action for Wittgenstein. On the contrary, they are integral to the whole process of action.

17. Wittgenstein is readily seen as a cultural conservative, though this can, I think, be stretched to include his style of thought as a conservative thought-style. See Bloor (1983, pp. 161–81). For an attempt to map his cultural and political conservatism see Janek and Toulmin (1996). See

also Nyiri (1976, 1982). For Spengler's influence see von Wright (1982) and Bloor (1992).

18. This is not to say that Wittgenstein was against individual responsibility: this is evident as a central ethic throughout his life. See Janek and Toulmin (1996) and Monk (1990). For his conservative political values, see Wittgenstein (1980a). For a criticism of his politics, see Anderson (1962, p. 151).

19. Wittgenstein does not maintain that actors always follow rules blindly, only in some cases. However, the latter is a condition of possibility for the former.

20. 'I consider Wittgenstein's later philosophy to be exceptionally important for current problems in social theory, but not in ways in which that philosophy has characteristically been understood by the "post-Wittgensteinians"' (Giddens 1979, p. 4).

21. 'Not withstanding the great interest of Wittgenstein's later philosophy for the social sciences in respect of the relations between language and Praxis, we rapidly come up against its limits in respect of the theorisation of institutions. Institutions certainly appear in Wittgensteinian philosophy, and in a rather fundamental way ... But as expressed in forms of life, institutions are analysed only in so far as they form a consensual backdrop against which action is negotiated and its meanings formed. Wittgensteinian philosophy has not led towards any sort of concern with social change, with power relations, or with conflict in society' (Giddens 1979, pp. 49–50). In addition, whilst criticising Wittgenstein's consensual approach to rules, Giddens notes that 'most rule-systems must not be assumed to be like this. They are less unified; subject to chronic ambiguities of "interpretation", so that their application or use is *contested*, a matter of *struggle*'' (Giddens 1976, p. 124).

22. 'Here it is of the greatest importance that we all, or the majority of us agree in certain things. I can, e.g., be quite sure that the colour of this object will be called "green" by far the most human beings who see it' (Wittgenstein 1978, s. VI, p. 39). And again: 'If language is to be a means of communication there must be agreement not only in definitions but also (queer as this may sound) in judgments' (Wittgenstein 1958, p. 88).

CHAPTER 5

1. '[N]either time nor space have been incorporated into the centre of social theory; rather, they are ordinarily treated more as "environments" in which social conduct is enacted' (Giddens 1979, p. 202).

2. For Giddens, space had also been neglected in social theory, but for different reasons: 'The fact that the concept of social structure ordinarily applied in the social sciences – as like the anatomy of a body or the girders of a building – has been so pervaded by spatial imagery, may be another reason, together with the fear of lapsing into geographical determinism, the importance of space itself has rarely been sufficiently emphasised in social theory' (Giddens 1979, p. 206).

3. 'All social life occurs in, and is constituted by, intersections of presence and absence in the "fading away" of time and the "shading off" of space' (Giddens 1984, p. 132).

4. '[S]tructural practices of social systems "bind" the temporality of day-to-day life-world to the *longue durée* of institutions, interpolated in the finite span of existence of the individual human being' (Giddens 1981a, p. 28).

5. Giddens states: 'One of the reasons for using the term "locale" rather than "place" is that properties of settings are employed in a chronic way by agents in the constitution of encounters across space and time' (Giddens 1984, pp. 118–19).

6. In contradistinction to Goffman, Giddens argues that '[t]he differentiation of front and back regions by no means coincides with a division between the enclosure (covering up, hiding) of aspects of the self and their disclosure (revelation, divulgence)' (Giddens 1984, p. 126). Rather, they seem to refer to spatial settings or regions, such as tea rooms or toilets on shop floors, which are spatially severed from the 'main' sites of interaction.

7. Lockwood (1964) distinguishes between 'social integration', which examines how individuals in a social system produce the actions necessary to maintain that system, from 'system integration', which considers how the functioning of various parts of the system, in terms of institutions, secures the persistence of the system.

8. By drawing on and modifying Goffman's typology of the contours of interaction, Giddens posits various modes of interaction. These include: gatherings, social occasions, unfocused interaction, focused interaction and encounters (or face-engagement).

9. 'I try to show how an analysis of motivation, as developed in relation to routinisation and the unconscious, can bring out the systematic character of Goffman's work more fully. Goffman's emphasis on trust and tact strikingly echoes themes found in ego psychology' (Giddens 1984, p. xxiv).

10. 'By "distanciation" here I mean to get at the process whereby societies are "stretched" over shorter or longer spans of time and space' (Giddens 1981a, p. 90).

11. The concepts of social and system integration have to be understood in terms of the structuring of interaction in time-space through mediation/transformation. The most basic sense of mediation, Giddens tells us, is that involved in the 'binding' of time and space themselves, the very essence of social reproduction. All social interaction involves mediation in so far as there are always 'vehicles' that carry social interchanges across spatial and temporal gaps. Thus in societies of high presence-availability where face-to-face interaction occurs, the mediating vehicles are those supplied by the faculties of physical presence. However, in system integration, where communication takes place with an absent other, writing and other media of communication (for example, the telephone and mechanised modes of transportation) can bind and mediate much greater distances of time and space.

12. According to Giddens, Marx tended to merge two independent sets of phenomena when discussing the possibility of revolution: the

relationship of exploitation of the bourgeoisie and proletariat and a revolutionary consciousness would follow from a knowledge of exploitation. In contrast Giddens posits a tripartite division between class identity, class conflict and revolutionary consciousness. Hence he makes a distinction between 'class awareness' and 'class consciousness'.

13. 'I define class-divided societies as "a society in which there are classes, but where class analysis does not serve as a basis for identifying the basic structural principle of organisation of that society"' (Giddens 1981a, p. 7).

14. 'The power-centre that is the city, has as its nucleus, both physically and socially, the theocratic order of the temple' (Giddens 1981a, p. 101).

15. For Giddens, 'Surveillance' involves two things: 'the collation of information relevant to state control of the conduct of its subject population, and the direct supervision of that conduct' (Giddens 1981a, p. 5).

16. 'I want to argue that the origins of surveillance, as a phenomenon of capitalism linked strongly, but not specifically, to the state, is directly bound up with the formation of the nation-state; and that in turn, the European state system was the platform from which the world economy of capitalism was launched and sustained' (Giddens 1984, p. 169).

17. Drawing on Foucault, Giddens argues that surveillance as the capacity for the storage of authoritative resources is a key feature of modern states. According to Giddens, the 'insulation of economy from polity involves ... the extrusion of the means of violence from the principle axis of class exploitation, the capital/wage relation' (Giddens 1981a, p. 1). Thus surveillance replaces violence within modern societies. However, the associated pacification within the state becomes simultaneously displaced onto violence between nation-states.

18. '... the most radical disjuncture of relevance in modern history ... as distinctive a transition in human cultural development as the wheel or any other technical innovation' (Giddens 1984, p. 123).

19. Giddens contrasts the nation-state with traditional states and their transitional replacement absolutist states.

20. For Giddens, society has two meanings or senses: a bounded system and a social association in general. (See also Giddens 1984, p. 165.)

21. By 'circuits of reproduction', Giddens is referring to the 'clearly defined "tracks" of processes which feed back to their source, whether or not such feedback is reflexively monitored by agents in specific social positions. When Marx uses the term "circuits of capital" he seems to have something of this sort in mind; however, I want to refer to actual conditions of social reproduction, while Marx sometimes uses the term in reference to what I have called structural sets' (Giddens 1984, p. 192).

22. However, Giddens adds that both the conditions and the outcomes of situated interaction often stretch far beyond the confines of those situations.

23. For Giddens, transformation and mediation are 'the two most essential characteristics of human social life' (Giddens 1981a, p. 53). Transformation capacity forms the basis of human action through the notion that the agent 'could always do otherwise', whilst at the same

time connecting domination to power. Mediation expresses the variety of ways in which interaction is made possible across space and time.

24. It is at this level of analysis, Giddens argues, that we can understand Marx's account of the key structural relations involved in the capitalist system of production which make up a structural set: private property – money – capital – labour contract – profit.

25. 'Structural principles are principles of organisation implicated in those practices most "deeply" (in time) and "pervasively" (in space) sedimented in society … The analysis of structural principles is closely bound up with questions of how societies should be typified or characterised' (Giddens 1981a, pp. 54–5).

26. In tribal societies incorporating hunter-gatherer bands and settled agricultural communities, the dominant structural principle operates along an axis between kinship and tradition. In class-divided societies, including city-states, ancient empires and feudal societies, the dominant axis relates urban areas to rural hinterlands or the city to the countryside. Lastly, class societies are organised according to structural principles relating state institutions to economic institutions.

27. Mapped upon these forms of collective groups are varieties of unintended consequence stretching beyond the recursive effects of the duality of structure. In tribal societies marked by associations, system reproduction can be conceived of as homeostasis in which causal loops operate 'blindly'. Here, circular causal relations pertain whereby change in one item initiates a sequence of changes affecting others which eventually return to the original item that initiated the sequence. In class-divided societies where organisations exist there occurs self-regulation through selective 'information feedback'. These, in contrast to homeostasis, usually promote some form of directional change. Finally, in modern capitalist societies, social movements characterised by reflexive self-regulation persist.

28. Giddens goes on to distinguish contradiction from conflict: 'If contradiction refers to an antagonistic relation between structural principles the conflict concerns the antagonism between actors and groups. By conflict I mean actual struggle between actors or groups, however such struggle may be carried on or through whatever sources it may be mobilised' (Giddens 1984, p. 198). Although distinct concepts referring to dissimilar domains, conflict and contradiction tend to coincide since contradictions often express themselves through the 'main fault lines' in the structural constitution of social systems.

29. The emergence of state-based societies simultaneously stimulates the emergence of secondary contradictions. For Giddens, the central secondary contradiction in modern societies is between the drive towards the internationalisation of capital and the internally bounded consolidation of nation-states. Thus as nation-states consolidate centralised power, drawing into their ambit various aspects of social activity, they concurrently instigate the development of ties and connections which cut across territorial borders.

30. Giddens in part echoes these earlier caveats by identifying four levels at which research can be carried out. These include (a) hermeneutic

elucidation of frames of meaning, (b) investigation of context and form of practical consciousness (the unconscious), (c) identification of the bounds of knowledgeability, and (d) specification of institutional orders. The methodological 'insertion' of the research investigator into whatever material is the object of study can be made at any one of the four levels indicated.

31. 'Most forms of social theory have failed to take seriously enough not only the temporality of social conduct but also its spatial attributes. At first sight, nothing seems more banal or uninstructive than to assert that social activity occurs in time and in space. But neither time nor space have been incorporated into the centre of social theory; rather, they are ordinarily treated as mere "environments" in which social conduct is enacted' (Giddens 1979, p. 202).

32. As Gregory notes, 'For the most part, structuration theory has been directed towards the elucidation of systems of interaction, and Giddens has displayed little interest in location. He constantly talks about locales whose settings are drawn upon by actors and emphasises their substantially given character. This is how actors routinely encounter locales in the conduct of everyday life, no doubt, but any genuinely critical theory must go beyond these mundanities to show how particular places and spaces are produced' (Gregory 1989, p. 208).

33. As Friedland correctly points out in his review of *The Nation-State and Violence*, 'Despite Giddens' disclaimers about the dialectic of control, that to be human is to have power, the historical panorama is dominated by agents of the state – policemen, scribes, soldiers, kings – whose expanding means of surveillance first crush and then codify a malleable population. Indeed, the human subject is barely visible' (Freidland 1987, p. 41).

34. 'Routinisation of social relations is the mode in which the potentially corrosive effects of anxiety are contained. The familiar is reassuring' (Giddens 1979, p. 128).

35. '"Continuity" is actually a more useful term by which to examine the relation between stability and change in society than words like "persistence" are: for continuities exist through the most radical and profound phases of social transformation' (Giddens 1979, p. 216).

36. Such a conception is highlighted in Giddens's remarks concerning routine and tradition: 'routine is founded in tradition, custom or habit' (Giddens 1984, p. 86). And again: 'Routine is closely linked to tradition in the sense that tradition "underwrites" the continuity of practices in the elapsing of time' (Giddens 1979, p. 220).

37. Giddens writes: 'Any influences which corrode or place in question traditional practices carry with them the likelihood of accelerating change' (Giddens 1979, p. 220).

38. According to Giddens, the ontological security of tradition is undermined by three sets of transformations by the capitalist social form: (a) the commodification of labour through its transformation into labour power as a medium for the production of surplus-value, (b) the transformation of the 'time-space paths' of the day through an emphasis upon a defined sphere of 'work' physically separate from the household, and (c) the commodification of urban land, resulting in the 'created space' or habitat of

the majority of the population in developed capitalist societies (Giddens 1981a, pp. 10–11).

39. '[I]f routine is such an important feature in the continuity of social reproduction, we can approach an account of the sources and nature of social change in the industrialised societies through attempting to indicate the conditions under which the routinised character of social interaction is sustained or dislocated. Routine is strongest when it is sanctioned, by tradition: when "reversible time" is invoked in connecting past and present in social reproduction. Although the term "traditional society" may often be used in an umbrella-like way to cover any kind of society short of those which have become fully industrialised, the hold of tradition is clearly likely to be firmest in the smaller more isolated types of society' (Giddens 1979, p. 219).

40. This applies in particular to Willis's *Learning to Labour* (1977), which concerns working-class reproduction through education and not the duality of structure.

41. In *New Rules of Sociological Method*, Giddens writes: 'This study is only intended as one part of a more embracing project. This latter involves three overlapping concerns. One is to develop a critical approach to the development of nineteenth-century social theory and its subsequent incorporation as the institutionalised and professionalised "disciplines" of "sociology", "anthropology" and "political science" in the course of the twentieth century. Another is to trace out some of the main themes in nineteenth-century social thought which became built into theories of the formation of the advanced societies, in both Marxist and non-Marxist works, and to subject these to critique. The third is to elaborate upon, and similarly to begin a reconstruction of, problems raised by the – always troubling – character of the social sciences as concerned with, as a "subject-matter", what those "sciences" themselves presuppose: human social activity and intersubjectivity. This book is proposed as a contribution to the last of these three. But any such discussion bursts the bounds of this sort of conceptual container, and has immediate implications for work in the other areas. As a single project, they are tied together as an endeavour to construct a critical analysis of the legacy of social theory of the nineteenth and early twentieth centuries for the contemporary period' (Giddens 1976, p. 7).

42. The difference between the two approaches is analogous to the distinction between Husserl's work and Schutz's immersion into the life-world or Heidegger's opening of ontological brackets. This is particularly surprising given that Giddens believes all social life to be contingent and contextual whilst simultaneously failing to delineate how concepts apply in particular contingent circumstances.

43. In Wittgensteinian terminology there is a 'craving for generality'. 'The tendency to look for something common in all entities which we commonly subsume under a general term. We are inclined to think that there must be something common to all games, say, and that this common property is a justification applying the general term "game" to the various games; whereas games form a family the members of which have family likenesses ... The idea of a general concept being a common

property of all its particular instances connects up with other primitive, too simple, ideas of the structure of language. It is comparable to the idea that properties are the ingredients of things that have the properties; e.g. that beauty is an ingredient of all beautiful things as alcohol is of beer and wine, and that we could have pure beauty unadulterated by anything that is not beautiful' (Wittgenstein 1969a, p. 17).
44. A contrasting position is to be found in Bryant and Jary (2001b).

CHAPTER 6

1. According to Giddens, the invention of the mechanical clock in the eighteenth century was fundamental in creating a uniform, empty time which allowed such a precise zoning of the day. This, in turn, involved an emptying and subsequent 'zoning' of space, which became 'phantasmagoric' as locales became more and more influenced by distant social influences and directly substitutable for one another.
2. For Giddens, although modernity is inherently globalising so that time-space distanciation becomes stretched in a process which links the local with the global through disembedding, this disembedding may become complemented by a process of re-embedding in which disembedded social relations are pinned down.
3. '[S]elf-identity becomes a reflexively organised endeavour. The reflexive project of the self which consists in the sustaining of a coherent, yet continuously revised biographical narrative, takes place in the context of multiple choice as filtered through abstract systems' (Giddens 1991, p. 5).
4. For Giddens, living in modernity is a contradictory and tension-provoking experience in terms of certain fundamental dilemmas which need to be resolved in order to preserve a coherent narrative of self-identity. The first dilemma is that between unification versus fragmentation; the second, powerlessness versus appropriation; the third, authority versus uncertainty; and the fourth, personalised versus commodified experience.
5. 'A creative involvement with others and the object-world is almost certainly a fundamental component of psychological satisfaction and the discovery of "moral meaning". We do not need to resort to an arcane philosophical anthropology to see that the experience of creativity as a routine phenomenon is a basic prop to a sense of personal worth and therefore to psychological health. Where individuals cannot live creatively, either because of the compulsive enactment of routine, or because they have been unable to attribute full "solidity" to persons and objects around them, chronic melancholic or schizophrenic tendencies are likely to result' (Giddens 1991, p. 41).
6. 'In all cultures, social practices are routinely altered in the light of ongoing discoveries which feed into them. But only in the era of modernity is the revision of convention radicalised to apply (in principle) to all aspects of human life, including technological intervention in the material world' (Giddens 1990a, p. 29).

7. 'The reflexivity of modernity actually subverts reason, at any rate where reason is understood as the gaining of certain knowledge. Modernity is constituted in and through reflexively applied knowledge, but the equation of knowledge with certitude has turned out to be misconceived. We are abroad in a world which is thoroughly constituted through reflexively applied knowledge, but where at the same time we can never be sure that any given element of knowledge will not be revised' (Giddens 1990a, p. 39).

8. Giddens uses the term 'modernity' for the first time during the mid-1980s in *The Nation-State and Violence* (1985), but there it had a different meaning, referring to the distinction between three 'organisational clusters'. No mention is made of risk, trust, wholesale reflexivity or globalisation, which only later become central features of this concept.

9. Thus material constraints are constraints 'deriving from the character of the material world and from the physical body' whilst negative sanctions are constraints 'deriving from punitive responses on the part of some agents towards others' (Giddens 1984, p. 176).

10. Some of these orientations may, of course, be misrecognised (as Bourdieu (1977) uses the term).

CHAPTER 7

1. Giddens's reading of Marx in *Capitalism and Modern Social Theory* is not only anti-Soviet but belies a humanist interpretation. Hence he characterises Marx's discussion of alienation as a fundamental component of Marx's theory. He also approvingly cites Marx's early conception of communism as an 'exciting and brilliant formula' (Giddens 1971a, p. 17). In *Capitalism and Modern Social Theory*, Giddens's account of Marx is more sympathetic, detailed and accurate than it will later become in his three-volume critique; for example, he states that Marx 'rejects a unilinear viewpoint' (ibid., p. 23), a position he later charges Marx with in *A Contemporary Critique of Historical Materialism* (1981a). In part, this reflects the ascendant position which Marxism held within the academy as well as Giddens's own political sympathies.

2. According to Giddens, there have been four major responses to these circumstances on the level of theory, each of which represents an attempt to depart from the premises involved in structural-functionalism. These are embodied in conflict theory, the sociology of knowledge, ethnomethodology, and Marxist theory, all of which he argues are inadequate.

3. 'Taken together, the conjunction of the rise of social democracy, the megacorporations and oligopoly, and state planning, constitutes a linked series of changes which, while they cannot be accurately represented as "post-capitalism", are of significant nature. In referring generically to the capitalism of the-post-war period, therefore, I shall make use of the somewhat graceless terms "neo-capitalism" and "neo-capitalist society"' (Giddens 1973, p. 164).

4. Marshall distinguishes three forms of citizenship in the modern state: the civil, the political and the social. The civil element refers essentially to legal rights such as the freedom of speech and right to own property; the political aspect to the rights of every member to participate in the exercise of political power; and the social to the rights of everyone to enjoy a certain minimum standard of living. For Marshall, each of these three rights has developed at a different rate and served as the platform for the development of the others. Civil freedoms in the eighteenth century, political in the nineteenth century and social in the twentieth century.

5. In comparing what he calls state socialism with capitalism, Giddens defines the latter thus: '"State socialism", as I employ the notion here, refers to any economic order in which the means of production is formally socialised in the hands of the state. This implies that the state assumes directive control of economic life, and that consequently the ultimate criteria regulating production are determined by political decisions. Such a situation does not preclude, of course, the continued existence of private property in the means of production in certain sectors, nor does it entail (if this were conceivable at all) the abandonment of "market mechanisms" altogether' (Giddens 1973, p. 155).

6. Furthermore, this form of repressive organisation within state socialism is unlikely to undergo any liberalisation or social change. What little change may occur, Giddens argues, will not be in the direction of a democratic Yugoslavian model of 'market socialism', but will instead tend towards a tightening of political control. 'In any case, it is unlikely that any other Eastern European country will lean so far as Yugoslavia in the direction of "market socialism". The most probable course of development of the state socialist societies, in the near future at least, will be one veering from the re-taxation of political controls over the economic order back to the reimposition of a tight hierarchy of political command' (Giddens 1973, p. 253).

7. 'There is a form of political response to the rationalisation which does not attempt to discredit rationality as an overall cultural ethos, and which, very profoundly is based upon acceptance of this ethos; it is a response which is part of Marxism as well as other forms of socialism and anarchism ... it depends upon the premise that "rationalisation", in the sense of the rational transmutation of the cultural ethos, provides men with the understanding necessary to control "rationalisation" in the sense of the dominance of technical rationality in social life' (Giddens 1973, p. 277).

8. 'The weaknesses in the respective views established by Marx and Weber on class structure in relation to the state are complementary. In the Marxian conception, political "power" exists only in so far as it "translates" the coercive asymmetry of class relationships, in Weber's discussion, on the other hand, any (rationalised) form of authority system involving the coordination of the activities of men within the political and economic order necessarily furthers the subordination of the mass to the dictates of a few. In retrospect, it seems quite evident that just as Marx drew too heavily upon the "class principle", Weber overstated the significance of the "bureaucratic principle"' (Giddens 1973, pp. 125–6).

9. See Chapter 5, note 41.

10. Giddens had already briefly discussed some of these issues in his *Studies in Social and Political Theory* (1977a).

11. In an essay on Marcuse, Giddens writes: 'No one today, however committed a socialist he or she might be, should complacently accept the idea that socialism (in whatever forms it is conceived of) inevitably extends the range of human freedoms' (Giddens 1981d, p. 161). For Giddens, the fundamental problem in Marcuse's work is precisely that the 'domination of persons will cede place to the administration of things, as the foundation of free society' (ibid.). In another essay Giddens (1981c) repeats many of these themes. Additionally, he argues: 'it is correct to speak of the exhaustion of Western social and political thought in current times', particularly in reference to Marxism and liberalism. However, he adds: 'There is no need to release hold of "modernism" yet, to renounce the ideals of the Enlightenment as false gods to be replaced by a brutish acquiescence in the reality of power' (ibid., p. 225).

12. Giddens notes his position in an interview with Bleicher and Featherstone in 1982: 'What I'm trying to do is to produce what I call a deconstruction of historical materialism. I do not think it's any good in trying to remedy the mistakes in Marx's materialist conception of history and bring it up to date and produce something of the same form as, for example, Habermas claims to be doing. I deliberately use the term deconstruction instead of reconstruction of historical materialism' (Bleicher and Featherstone 1982, p. 63).

13. Giddens summarises the contradictory social and political position he occupies in a book review in the early 1980s: 'We are ... faced with an increasingly deadlocked capitalism, an ossified state-socialism, impotent New Left theorising and a seemingly exhausted social democracy' (Giddens 1981e, p. 308). In an interview with Derek Gregory in 1984, he states: 'In the contemporary world we are between capitalism and socialism in two senses, and any discussion of normative political theory must be concerned with both. In the shape of the actually existing socialist societies, socialism is a reality, part of the power-bloc system that tenuously controls the anarchy of the world nation-state order. It no longer is plausible, if it ever was, to say that they are not really socialist at all or that their insufficiencies have nothing to do with shortcomings of Marxist thought in general. On the other hand, if socialist ideals retain any validity, we are between capitalism and socialism in the sense that such ideals seem capable of much more profound development than has been achieved in any society to date ... Marx thought he discerned a real movement of change – the labour movement – that would provide history's solution to the anarchy of the capitalist market and the degradation of work. But where is the dialectical process that will transcend the political anarchy that threatens us all with imminent destruction? So far as I can see, there, is none in view. Every existing form of world organization at the moment seems impotent in the face of the monopoly of violence in the hands of nation-states. There is no sense in not admitting that today we stand at the outer edge of the precipice of history. Our existence now is unique in an eerie way. After

a half a million years of human history, we are the first human beings whose individual lifespans might terminate with that of the whole of humankind. Has the cunning of reason here deserted us?' (Gregory 1984, p. 124).

14. 'The tension that Durkheim diagnosed between ideals of equality and directive control of economic activity constantly resurfaces in the history of socialism' (Giddens 1994a, p. 56).

15. Hayek's arguments on epistemology may have been influenced by both Wittgenstein, who was his uncle, and Schutz, who was his teacher. Both influences emphasise the practical aspect of knowledge.

16. The anti-Marxist tradition of criticism, from Bohm-Bawerk through to von Mises and Hayek, aimed at reinstalling free market economic ideology in the context of the rise in socialism expressed through the Austrian labour movement and Austro-Marxism. As Anderson (1992b, pp. 271–3) notes, Austrian economics was always marked by an emphasis on realism, stressing uneven time, imperfect knowledge and cyclical imbalance. It became the most conservative school in modern economics. Interestingly, the emphasis on the tacit knowledge is something shared by both the Hungarian philosopher of science Michael Polanyi (Karl's brother) and Hayek drawing on an interpretation of another Austrian, Wittgenstein (Hayek's uncle), which discloses the importance of looking at the social and cultural context of the Austro-Hungarian empire under Franz Josef in understanding their thought and the contradictions it attempted to resolve. See Janek and Toulmin (1996). Anderson, in his discussion of the 'white emigration', argues that 'England was not an accidental landing-stage on which these intellectuals found themselves unwittingly stranded. For many it was a conscious choice, as the antithesis of everything they rejected. Namier, who was most lucid about the world from which he had escaped, expressed his hatred of it most deeply. He saw England as a land built on instinct and custom, free from the ruinous contagion of Europe – general ideas. An emphasis on the dismissal of general ideas was shared by all' (Anderson 1992a, p. 63).

17. The term 'doxic' is derived from Bourdieu. He writes: 'schemes of thought and perception can produce the objectivity that they do produce only by producing misrecognition of the limits of the cognition they make possible, thereby founding immediate adherence' (Bourdieu 1977, p. 164).

18. As Weber notes at the end of *The Protestant Ethic*: 'No one knows who will live in this cage in the future, or whether at the end of this tremendous development entirely new prophets will arise, or there will be a great rebirth of old ideas and ideals, or if neither, mechanised petrification, embellished with a sort of convulsive self-importance. For of the last stage of this cultural development, it might well be truly said: "specialists without spirit, sensualists without heart; this nullity imagines that it has attained a level of civilisation never before achieved"' (cited in Bernstein 1986, pp. 190–1). For a longer discussion, see Mitzman (1970).

19. This was particularly in terms of the greater efficiency and the less protracted nature of the contradiction between formal and substantial rationality which was to be found in market economies. They represented

the best of possible economic systems. Moreover, for Weber, it was not the ownership of private property which was important but the control of entrepreneurial positions.

20. For Weber's ambiguous moral/political relation to socialism, see Mommsen (1974).

21. For Giddens's generally uncritical relationship to methodological individualism, see his *The Constitution of Society* (1984, pp. 207–26).

22. There is a long literature here but see, especially, Habermas (1981), Brubaker (1984) and Mouzelis (1975). For an overview, see Beetham (1996).

23. Sayer argues that the concept of the iron cage attributed to Weber by Parsons is somewhat unfortunate. 'A better choice of analogy might be the shell on a snail's back: a burden perhaps, but something impossible to live without, in either sense of the word' (Sayer 1991, p. 144).

CHAPTER 8

1. Fabians such as Beatrice and Sidney Webb and Liberals such as Dahrendorf have all held directorship positions (Smith 1998).

2. Giddens accompanied Blair on a trip to the US where they met with Bill Clinton, who was also pursuing a Third Way version of politics which aimed for a global reconstitution of the centre left.

3. 'This book began life some fifteen years ago, as the planned third volume of what I then termed a "contemporary critique of historical materialism". The third volume was never written, as my interests moved away in somewhat different directions. The present work is based on the ideas I sketched for the third volume, but also draws extensively on concepts I developed in subsequent published writings' (Giddens 1994a, Preface).

4. Tradition defended in the traditional way, for Giddens, constitutes a form of fundamentalism, that is, a refusal to dialogue in the face of reflexivity.

5. However, although Giddens argues that conservatism has collapsed or become self-contradictory, he still believes that some of its key ideas should be retained. 'We should all become conservatives now, I shall argue – but not in the conservative way' (Giddens 1998, p. 49). He also states: 'traditions in some guises and in some contexts, surely do need to be defended today, even if not in the traditional way. Traditions need to be saved, or recovered ... in so far as they provide generalisable sources of solidarity' (ibid., p. 48).

6. Although the term 'third way', which arose at the turn of the century, was used by a number of right-wing groups in the 1920s, it was later taken up by social democrats in the late 1940s. Following the Second World War, it was used by the Swedish to refer to programmatic renewal and more recently by Bill Clinton and Tony Blair to characterise their political policy.

7. For a further discussion of Giddens's politics see, *inter alia*, his 'Brave New World: The New Context of Politics' (Giddens 1994e).

8. This, along with generational change and changing economic forms, such as the decline of blue-collar work and the large-scale entry of women into the workforce, have all led to a shift in values.

9. However, governments still retain a large degree of economic and cultural power over their citizens. For Giddens the notion of 'governance' is a more useful way to refer to administrative and regulating capacity of the government.

10. Giddens gives the example of cancer: 'The risks of contracting cancer are likely to be minimised if the following lifestyle practices are observed: not smoking; avoiding undue exposure to strong sunlight; following certain diets rather than others; avoiding toxic substances at work; making use of early detection procedures' (Giddens 1994a, p. 154).

11. 'Inclusion refers in its broadest sense to citizenship, to the civil and political rights and obligations that all members of society should have, not just formally but in their real lives. It also refers to opportunities and to involvement in public space' (Giddens 1998, pp. 102–3).

12. A further measure would be through 'improving the quality of public education, sustaining a well resourced health service, promoting safe public amenities, and controlling levels of crime' (Giddens 1998, pp. 107–8).

13. As Giddens notes, 'The dynamic sectors of the economy today are in finance, computers and software, telecommunications, biotechnology and the communications industries. The telecommunications industry in the US employs more people than the car and car parts industries combined. Measured in terms of annual turnover, the health and medical industry in the US is bigger than oil refining, aircraft and car production, logging, steel and shipping put together' (Giddens 2000, p. 69).

14. The one exception being Islam.

15. Since the price level in any economy is set by the money supply and the stimulation of demand only generates a greater anticipation of price rises, a strict control of the money supply is necessary in order to control inflation. A rein on the latter forms the foundation of any stable economy, albeit at the expense of unemployment, which follows a natural rate of increase.

16. Nonetheless, Giddens does make this claim: 'socialism and communism have passed away, yet they remain to haunt us. We cannot just put aside the values and ideals that drove them, for some remain intrinsic to the good life that it is the point of social and economic development to create. The challenge is to make these values count where the economic programme of socialism has become discredited' (Giddens 1998, pp. 1–2). Yet he goes on to state: 'For Marx, socialism stood or fell by its capacity to deliver a society that would generate greater wealth than capitalism and spread that wealth in more equitable fashion. If socialism is now dead it is precisely because these claims have now collapsed' (ibid., p. 4).

17. His defence is not without its problems. See Anderson (1998, p. 231). For Anderson, Bobbio defends his concepts at a theoretical level rather than fully examining the empirical political forces that shape and inflect them.

18. It is also true that political affiliations based on ethnic or regional identification have, in many places, further disrupted the neat symmetries implied by a one-dimensional political spectrum.

19. The notions of left and right were European inventions following the French Revolution (Hobsbawm 2000, p. 95).

20. Hobhouse often emphasised the reciprocal obligations between individuals and governments. And Toynbee emphasised that governments should not undermine personal responsibility. However, Giddens supplements these arguments on freedom by drawing on Sen's work on 'social capability. So that policies aimed at augmenting equality should be focused on the capability set – the overall freedom a person has to pursue his or her well-being' (Giddens 2000, p. 88).

21. As Carling (1999) notes, capitalism is consistent with autonomy on a superficial level as personal freedom. However, autonomy on a deeper level as self-determination, requires a parity of access to resources. Capitalism may be consistent with formal democratisation of the state. However, a vast amount of empirical evidence demonstrates that it often prevents the wider democratisation of society.

CHAPTER 9

1. 'In Ancient Greece, there was no independent word for society or individual. For Aristotle, there exists no separate term for society and the distinctions between community and society and state and society are not in evidence' (Frisby and Sayer 1986, p. 14).

2. 'In the Aristotelian concept of space, as in the Thomistic idea of the community, each thing had its own place in the order of nature and tended to return to it: heavy bodies fell in order to reach the centre of the earth, light bodies rose because the natural place for them was above. Things were spoken to and judged by space, were told what to do and where to go, in exactly the same way as men were judged and directed by the community, and the language of space was basically, the language of God' (Goldmann 1964, p. 31).

3. As Williams notes: 'The growth of capitalism, and the great social changes associated with it, encouraged certain men to see "the individual" as a source of economic activity, by his "free enterprise". It was less a matter of performing a certain function within a fixed order than of initiating certain kinds of activity, choosing particular directions' (Williams 1961, p. 92).

4. '"Community" reached the same stage of development in the seventeenth century, and "State" had reached this stage rather earlier, having added to its two earlier meanings – the condition of the common life, as now in "state of the nation"; the signs of a condition or status, as in "the King's state" – the sense of the "apparatus" of the common life, its framework or set order. Thus we see the terms of relationship separating out, until "individual" on the one hand, "society", "community", and "state" on the other, could be conceived as abstractions and absolutes' (Williams 1961, pp. 93–4).

5. This argument and the arguments that follow draw heavily on the work of Lucien Goldmann (see Goldmann 1964, 1977).

6. According to Elias (1978, p. 18), the roots of the dichotomy are based on a particular way of experiencing oneself brought on during the Civilising Process: 'Ultimately the roots of the dichotomy lie in a particular way of experiencing oneself, a way which has been characteristic of wider and wider circles of European society since the Renaissance ... It leads them to believe that their actual "selves" somehow exist "inside" them; and that an invisible barrier separates their "inside" from everything "outside" – the so-called "outside world".' This, he argues, is compounded by our prevailing way of forming words and concepts so that they reify and dehumanise social structures. For an elaboration of these ideas, see Elias (1991). Alternative explanations of individualisation are also found in Durkheim (1933) and corresponding essays in Bellah (1973).

7. In philosophy, Descartes, Leibniz, and Spinoza, Kant and Fichte. In politics, the whole liberal tradition begins with the individual and his/her rights with a minimal 'society' to ensure these rights. Thus for Hobbes and Locke the individual is the starting point and the abstraction of the bare human being as a separate entity is ordinarily taken for granted. See MacPherson (1962).

8. In referring to Giddens's adoption of individualism, it may be useful to distinguish some versions of it. This has usefully been done by Lukes (1973), who distinguishes individualism according to: (1) a moral principle, (2) autonomy and self-direction, (3) privacy, (4) self-development, and (5) on a different logical status, as abstractly given. Giddens centrally incorporates the first, second, fourth and fifth aspects of the above typology of individualism, and touches upon the third. He draws upon these conceptions largely in reaction to the situation of individuals in state socialism. The first conception refers to the moral principle of the supreme and intrinsic value or dignity of the individual human being and largely against individual interests being sacrificed to the collective. The second conception, in which an individual's thoughts and actions are his own, is revealed in his dialectic of control and the ability of the individual to always do otherwise. The fourth conception of self-development, which derives from Romanticism, is intrinsic to the whole of Giddens's thought referring to forms of exploitation and the dehumanising of individuals in market society to man's relation to the created environment. The fifth conception pictures individuals as abstractly given, in terms of interests and wants, purposes and needs.

9. However, the fact that the historical genesis of these concepts has been noted does not necessarily mean they are 'wrong' or false. Rather, the argument is that their emergence leads to a number of difficulties in trying to reconcile the two concepts.

10. On Heidegger's politics, see Rorty (1990), Bourdieu (1991), Safranski (1998) and Wolin (1998).

11. My analysis of this Marxist aspect of social beings as well as many other insights draws heavily on Derek Sayer's exemplary work and interpretation of Marx (see Sayer 1983, 1987).

12. Marx puts this well: 'Because Mr Proudhon posits on the one hand eternal ideas, the categories of pure reason, and, on the other man and his practical life which, according to him, is the practical application of these categories, you will find in him from the very outset a dualism between life and ideas, between soul and body – a dualism which occurs in many forms. So you now see that the said antagonism is nothing other than Mr Proudhon's inability to understand either the origin or the profane history of the categories he has deified' (Marx 1846b, p. 12).

Bibliography

Abrams, P., Deem, R., Finch, J. and Rock, P. (eds) (1980) *Practice and Progress: British Sociology 1950–80*, London: Allen & Unwin.

Adorno, T. and Horkheimer, M. (1944) *The Dialectic of the Enlightenment*, 3rd impression, London: Verso.

Alexander, J. (1995) *Fin de Siecle Social Theory: Relativism, Reduction and the Problem of Reason*, London: Verso.

Althusser, L. (1968) *For Marx*, London: New Left Books.

Anderson, P. (1962) 'Origins of the Present Crisis' in *English Questions*, London: Verso, 1992.

Anderson, P. (1977) *Considerations on Western Marxism*, London: Verso.

Anderson, P. (1983) *In the Tracks of Historical Materialism*, London: Verso.

Anderson, P. (1992a) 'Components of the National Culture' in *English Questions*, London: Verso.

Anderson, P. (1992b) 'A Culture in Contraflow' in *English Questions*, London: Verso.

Anderson, P. (1992c) 'Norberto Bobbio' in *Zone of Engagement*, London: Verso, pp. 87–129.

Anderson, P. (1998) 'A Sense of Left', *New Left Review* 231: 73–81.

Anthias, F. (1999) 'Theorising Identity, Difference and Social Divisions' in M. O'Brien, S. Penna and C. Hay (eds) *Theorising Modernity: Reflexivity, Environment and Identity in Giddens' Social Theory*, London: Longman.

Archer, M. (1982) 'Morphogenesis versus Structuration: On Combining Structure and Action', *British Journal of Sociology* 33(4): 455–83.

Austin, J. (1965) *How to Do Things with Words*, New York: Oxford University Press.

Barnes, B. (1977) *Interests and the Growth of Knowledge*, London: Routledge & Kegan Paul.

Barnes, B. (1982a) *T.S. Kuhn and Social Science*, London: Macmillan.

Barnes, B. (1982b) 'On the Extension of Concepts and the Growth of Knowledge', *Sociological Review* 30: 23–44.

Barnes, B. (1987) 'Concept application as a Social Activity', *Critica* 19.

Barnes, B. (1988) *The Nature of Power*, Cambridge: Polity Press.

Barnes, B. (1991) 'How Not to Do the Sociology of Knowledge', *Annals of Scholarship* 8(3): 321–35.

Barnes, B. (1993) 'How to Do the Sociology of Knowledge', *Danish Yearbook of Philosophy*, vol. 28.

Barnes, B. (1994) 'Cultural Change – The Thought-Styles of Mannheim and Kuhn', *Common Knowledge* 3: 65–78.

Barnes, B. (1995) *The Elements of Social Theory*. London: UCL Press.

Barnes, B. (2000) *Understanding Agency*, London: Sage.

Barnes, B. and Bloor, D. (1982) 'Relativism, Rationalism, and the Sociology of Knowledge' in M. Hollis and S. Lukes (eds) *Rationality and Relativism*, Oxford: Blackwell.

Bauman, Z. (1989) 'Hermeneutic and Modern Social Theory' in D. Held and J. Thompson (eds) *Social Theory of Modern Societies: Anthony Giddens and His Critics*, Cambridge: Cambridge University Press.

Beck, U. (1988) *Risk Society: Towards a New Modernity*. London: Sage.

Beck, U., Giddens, A. and Lash, S. (eds) (1994) *Reflexive Modernisation: Politics, Tradition and Aesthetics in the Modern Social Order*, Cambridge: Polity Press.

Beetham, D. (1996) *Bureaucracy*, Buckingham: Open University Press.

Bellah, R. (1973) *Emile Durkheim on Morality and Solidarity*, Chicago, IL: University of Chicago Press.

Benton, T. (1999) 'Radical Politics – Neither Left nor Right?' in M. O'Brien, S. Penna and C. Hay (eds) *Theorising Modernity: Reflexivity, Environment and Identity in Giddens' Social Theory*, London: Longman.

Berger, P. and Luckmann, T. (1966) *The Social Construction of Reality*. Harmondsworth: Penguin.

Berger, P. and Pullman, S. (1966) 'Reification and the Sociological Critique of Conciousness', *New Left Review* 35: 56–71.

Bernstein, R.J. (1986) 'The Rage Against Reason', *Philosophy and Literature* 10(2).

Bernstein, R.J. (1989) 'Social Theory as Critique' in D. Held and J. Thompson (eds), *Social Theory of Modern Societies: Anthony Giddens and His Critics*, Cambridge: Cambridge University Press.

Bertillson, M. (1984) 'The Theory of Structuration: Prospects and Problems', *Acta Sociologica* 27: 339–53.

Bhaskar, R. (1979) *The Possibility of Naturalism*, Brighton: Harvester.

Birnbaum, N. (1971) 'The Crisis in Marxist Sociology' in *Towards a Critical Sociology*, New York: Oxford University Press.

Bleicher, J. and Featherstone, M. (1982) 'Historical Materialism Today: An Interview with Anthony Giddens', *Theory, Culture & Society* 1(2): 63–77.

Bloch, M. (1965) *Feudal Society*, London: Routledge & Kegan Paul.

Bloor, D. (1973) 'Wittgenstein and Mannheim on the Sociology of Mathematics', *Studies in the History and Philosophy of Science* 4(2): 173–91.

Bloor, D. (1983) *Wittgenstein: A Social Theory of Knowledge*, London: Macmillan

Bloor, D. (1992) 'Left and Right Wittgensteinians' in A. Pickering (ed.) *Science as Practice and Culture*, Chicago, IL: University of Chicago Press.

Bloor, D. (1997) *Wittgenstein: Rules as Institutions*, London: Routledge.

Bobbio, N. (1996) *Left and Right*, Cambridge: Polity Press.

Bottomore, T. (1990) *The Socialist Economy*, London: Harvester Wheatsheaf.

Bottomore, T. and Rubels, M. (1963) *Karl Marx: Selected Writings*, London: Penguin.

Bourdieu, P. (1977) *Outline of a Theory of Practice*, Cambridge: Cambridge University Press. Originally published in France in 1972.

Bourdieu, P. (1984) *Distinction: A Social Critique of the Judgement of Taste*, London: Routledge.

Bourdieu, P. (1988) *Homo Academicus*, Cambridge: Polity Press.

Bourdieu, P. (1991) *The Political Ontology of Martin Heidegger*, Cambridge: Polity Press.

Bourdieu, P. (2000) *On Television and the Media*, London: Pluto Press.

Bourdieu, P. and Wacquant, L. (1992) *An Introduction to Reflexive Sociology*. Cambridge: Polity Press.

Brasher, S. (1997) 'Influences: Anthony Giddens', *New Statesman* 10 (31 January): 32.

Brenner, R. (1998) 'Uneven Development and the Long Downturn', *New Left Review* 229: 1–264.

Brubaker, R. (1984) *The Limits of Rationality*, London: Routledge.

Bryant, C. and Jary, D. (eds) (1991) *Giddens' Theory of Structuration: A Critical Appreciation*, London: Routledge.

Bryant, C. and Jary, D. (eds) (1997) *Anthony Giddens: Critical Assessments*, 4 vols, New York: Routledge.

Bryant, C. and Jary, D. (2001a) *The Contemporary Giddens: Social Theory in a Globalising Age*, Basingstoke: Palgrave, now Palgrave Macmillan.

Bryant, C. and Jary, D. (2001b) 'The Uses of Structuration Theory: A Typology', *The Contemporary Giddens: Social Theory in a Globalising Age*, Basingstoke: Palgrave, now Palgrave Macmillan.

Callinicos, A. (1989) 'Anthony Giddens – A Contemporary Critique' in A. Callinicos (ed.) *Marxist Theory*, Oxford: Oxford University Press.

Callinicos, A. (1999) *Social Theory*, Cambridge: Polity Press.

Callinicos, A. (2001) *Against the Third Way*, Cambridge: Polity Press.

Carling, A. (1999) 'New Labour's Polity', *Imprints* 3: 214–83.

Clark, J., Modgil, C. and Modgil, S. (eds) (1990) *Anthony Giddens: Consensus and Controversy*, London: Falmer Press.

Clegg, S. (1989) *Frameworks of Power*, London: Sage.

Clegg, S. (1992) 'How to Become a Famous British Social Theorist', *Sociological Review* 40: 576–93.

Cohen, I. (1989) *Structuration Theory: Anthony Giddens and the Constitution of Social Life*, London: Macmillan.

Collins, R. (1979) *Credential Society*, New York: Academic Press.

Collins, R. (1985) *Weberian Sociological Theory*, Cambridge: Cambridge University Press.

Collins, R. (1986) *Max Weber: A Skeleton Key*, London: Sage.

Collins, R. (2000) *The Sociology of Philosophies: A Global Theory of Intellectual Change*, Cambridge, MA: Harvard University Press.

Condorcet (1795) *Sketch for a Historical Picture of the Progress of the Human Mind*.

Craib, I. (1992) *Anthony Giddens*, London: Routledge.

Csikszentmihalyi, M. (1992) *Flow: The Psychology of Happiness*, London, Rider.

Dahrendorf, R. (1958) *Class and Conflict in Industrial Society*, Stanford, CA: Stanford University Press.

Dallmayr, F. (1982) 'The Theory of Structuration: A Critique' in A. Giddens (ed.) *Profiles and Critiques in Social Theory*, London: Macmillan.

Davidson, D. (1980) *Essays on Actions and Events*, Oxford: Oxford University Press.

Dawe, A. (1970) 'The Two Sociologies', *British Journal of Sociology* 21(2): 207–18.

Dawe, A. (1978) 'Theories of Social Action' in T.B. Bottomore and R. Nisbet (eds) *A History of Sociological Analysis*, New York: Basic Books.

De Certeau, M. (1984) *The Practice of Everyday Life*, Berkeley, CA: University of California Press.

Devine, P. (1988) *Democracy and Economic Planning*, Cambridge: Polity Press.

Durkheim, E. (1933) *The Division of Labour*, New York: Free Press.

Durkheim, E. (1976) *The Elementary Forms of Religious Life* (ed. R. Nisbet), London: Allen & Unwin.

Durkheim, E. and Mauss, M. (1963) *Primitive Classification*, London: Cohen & West.

Eagleton, T. (1991) *Ideology*, London: Verso.

Eccleshall, R. (1986) *British Liberalism: Liberal Thought from the 1640s to 1980s.* New York: Longman.

Elias, N. (1978) *What is Sociology?*, London: Hutchinson.

Elias, N. (1987) *Involvement and Detachment*, Oxford: Blackwell.

Elias, N. (1991) *Society of Individuals*, Oxford: Blackwell.

Elias, N. (1994) *The Civilising Process* (2 vols), Oxford: Blackwell.

Foster, R. (2001) *Enlightenment: Britain and the Creation of the Modern World*, London: Penguin.

Foucault, M. (1982) 'The Subject and Power' in H.L. Dreyfus and and P. Rabinow, *Michel Foucault, Beyond Structuralism and Hermeneutics*, Brighton: Harvester Press.

Foucault, M. (1991) 'Questions of Method' in G. Burchell, C. Gordon and P. Miller, *The Foucault Effect*, Hemel Hempstead: Harvester Wheatsheaf.

Freidland, R. (1987) 'Giddens' Golden Gloves', *Contemporary Sociology* 16: 41.

Frisby, D. and Sayer, D. (1986) *Society*, London: Routledge.

Gallie, W. (1955) 'Essentially Contested Concepts', *Proceedings of the Aristotelian Society* 56: 167–98.

Garfinkel, H. (1967) *Studies in Ethnomethodology*, Englewood Cliffs, NJ: Prentice Hall.

Gay, P. (1977) *The Enlightenment: An Interpretation. Vol. 1: The Rise of Modern Paganism; Vol. 2: The Science of Freedom*, New York: Norton.

Gellner, E. (1992) *Reason and Culture*, Oxford: Blackwell.

Giddens, A. (1964) 'Suicide, Attempted Suicide, and the Suicidal Threat', *Man: A Record of Anthropological Science* 64. 115–16 (art. 136).

Giddens, A. (1965a) 'George Simmel', *New Society* 4(112): 24–5.

Giddens, A. (1965b) 'Suicide', *British Journal of Sociology* 16: 164–5.

Giddens, A. (1965c) 'The Suicide Problem in French Sociology', *British Journal of Sociology* 16: 3–18.

Giddens, A. (1965d) 'Theoretical Problems in the Sociology of Suicide', *Advancement of Science* 21: 522–6.

Giddens, A. (1966) 'A Typology of Suicide', *Archives europeenes de Sociologie* 7: 276–95.

Giddens, A. (1968a) 'George Simmel' in T. Raison (ed.), *Founding Fathers of Sociology*, London: Penguin.

Giddens, A. (1968b) '"Power" in the Recent Writings of Talcott Parsons', *Sociology* 2: 257–72.

Giddens, A. (1970a) 'Marx, Weber and the Development of Capitalism', *Sociology* 4: 289–310.

Giddens, A. (1970b) 'Recent Works on the History of Social Thought', *Archives europeenes de sociologie* 11: 130–42.

Giddens, A. (1970c) 'Recent Works on the Position and Prospects of Contemporary Sociology', *Archives europeenes de sociology* 11: 143–54.

Giddens, A. (1971a) *Capitalism and Modern Social Theory: An Analysis of the Writings of Marx, Durkheim and Weber*, Cambridge: Cambridge University Press.

Giddens, A. (1971b) 'Durkheim's Political Sociology', *Sociological Review* 19: 477–519.

Giddens, A. (1971c) 'The "Individual" in the Writings of Emile Durkheim', *Archives Europeans de Sociologie* 12: 210–28.

Giddens, A. (1972a) 'Elites', *New Society* (series on Social Stratification) 22(258): 389–92 (art. 7).

Giddens, A. (1972b) 'Elites in the British Class Structure', *Sociological Review* 20: 345–72.

Giddens, A. (1972c) 'Four Myths in the History of Social Thought', *Economy and Society* 1: 357–85.

Giddens, A. (1973) *The Class Structure of the Advanced Societies*, London: Hutchinson.

Giddens, A. (1974) 'Elites in the British Class Structure' in P. Stanworth and A. Giddens, *Elites and Power in British Society*, Cambridge: Cambridge University Press.

Giddens, A. (1976) *New Rules of Sociological Method*, London: Hutchinson.

Giddens, A. (1977a) *Studies in Social and Political Theory*, London: Hutchinson.

Giddens, A. (1977b) 'Functionalism apres la lutte', *Studies in Social and Political Thought*, London: Hutchinson.

Giddens, A. (1978) 'The Prospects for Social Theory Today', *Berkeley Journal of Sociology* 22: 201–23.

Giddens, A. (1979) *Central Problems in Social Theory: Action, Structure and Contradiction in Social Analysis*, London: Macmillan.

Giddens, A. (1981a) *A Contemporary Critique of Historical Materialism, Vol. 1: Power, Property and the State*, London: Macmillan.

Giddens, A. (1981b) 'Durkheim, Socialism and Marxism' in A. Izzo et al. (eds) *Durkheim*, Rome: Institute of Sociology. Reprinted in *Profiles and Critiques in Social Theory*, London: Macmillan, 1982.

Giddens, A. (1981c) 'From Marx to Nietzsche? Neo-Conservatism, Foucault and the Problems in Contemporary Political Theory' in *Profiles and Critiques in Social Theory*, London: Macmillan, 1982.

Giddens, A. (1981d) 'The Improbable Guru: Re-Reading Marcuse' in *Profiles and Critiques in Social Theory*, London: Macmillan, 1982.

Giddens, A. (1981e) Contribution to a Review Symposium on U. Himmelstrand, G. Ahrne and L. Lundberg, *Beyond Welfare Capitalism: Issues, Actors and Forces in Societal Change*, London: Heinemann, 1981, *Acta Sociologica* 25: 308–13.

Giddens, A. (1982) (ed.) *Profiles and Critiques in Social Theory*, London: Macmillan.

Giddens, A. (1983) 'Four Theses on Ideology', *Canadian Journal of Political and Social Theory* 7, pp. 18–21.

Giddens, A. (1984) *The Constitution of Society*, Cambridge: Polity Press.

Giddens, A. (1985) *The Nation-State and Violence*, Cambridge: Polity Press.

Giddens, A. (1986) 'Action, Subjectivity and the Constitution of Meaning', *Social Research* 53: 529–45.

Giddens, A. (1987) *Social Theory and Modern Sociology*, Cambridge: Polity Press.

Giddens, A. (1989) 'A Reply to My Critics' in D. Held and J. Thompson (eds), *Social Theory of Modern Societies: Anthony Giddens and His Critics*, Cambridge: Cambridge University Press.

Giddens, A. (1990a) *The Consequences of Modernity*, Cambridge: Polity Press.

Giddens, A. (1990b) 'Structuration Theory and Sociological Consensus' in J. Clark, C. Modgil and S. Modgil (eds) *Anthony Giddens: Consensus and Controversy*, London: Falmer Press.

Giddens, A. (1991) *Modernity and Self-Identity*, Cambridge: Polity Press.

Giddens, A. (1992) *The Transformation of Intimacy: Sexuality, Love and Eroticism*, Cambridge: Polity Press.

Giddens, A. (1994a) *Beyond Left and Right*, Cambridge: Polity Press.

Giddens, A. (1994b) 'What's Left for Labour?', *New Statesman and Society* 7(322) (30 September): 37–40.

Giddens, A. (1994c) 'Agenda Change', *New Statesman and Society* 7(323) (7 October): 23–5.

Giddens, A. (1994d) 'Out of the Red', *New Statesman and Society* 7(324) (14 October): 22–4.

Giddens, A. (1994e) 'Brave New World: The New Context of Politics' in D. Milliband (ed.) *Reinventing the Left*, Cambridge: Polity Press.

Giddens, A. (1996) 'There is a Radical Centre', *New Statesman and Society* 9(432) (29 November): 18–19.

Giddens, A. (1998) *The Third Way: The Renewal of Social Democracy*, Cambridge: Polity Press.

Giddens, A. (2000) *The Third Way and Its Critics*, Cambridge: Polity Press.

Goffman, E. (1961) *Asylums*, Harmondsworth: Penguin.

Goldmann, L. (1964) *The Hidden God: A Study of Tragic Vision in the Pensees of Pascal and the Tragedies of Racine*, London: Routledge & Kegan Paul.

Goldmann, L. (1968) *The Philosophy of the Enlightenment: The Christian Burgess and the Enlightenment*, London: Routledge & Kegan Paul.

Goldmann, L. (1971) *Kant*, London: New Left Books.

Goldmann, L. (1977) *Lukacs and Heidegger*, London, Routledge & Kegan Paul.

Goodman, N. (1978) *Ways of Worldmaking*, Indianapolis: Hacket Publishing.

Gouldner, A. (1955) 'Metaphysical Pathos and the Theory of Bureaucracy', *American Political Science Review* 49.

Gouldner, A. (1971) *The Coming Crisis of American Sociology*, London: Heinemann.

Gregory, D. (1984) 'Space, Time and Politics in Social Theory: An Interview with Anthony Giddens', *Environment and Planning D: Society and Space* 2: 123–32.

Gregory, D. (1989) 'Presences and Absences: Time Space Relations and Structuration Theory' in D. Held and J. Thompson (eds) *Social Theory of Modern Societies: Anthony Giddens and His Critics*, Cambridge: Cambridge University Press.

Gregson, N. (1989) 'On the (Ir)Relevance of Structuration Theory to Empirical Research' in D. Held and J. Thompson (eds) *Social Theory of Modern Societies: Anthony Giddens and His Critics*, Cambridge: Cambridge University Press.

Habermas, J. (1975) *Legitimation Crisis*, Boston, MA: Beacon Press.

Habermas, J. (1976) *Theory and Praxis*, Boston, MA: Beacon Press.

Habermas, J. (1981) *The Theory of Communicative Action* (2 vols), Boston, MA: Beacon Press.

Hall, S. (1998) 'The Great Moving Nowhere Show', *Marxism Today* (November/December): 9–14.

Hampson, N. (1968) *The Enlightenment*, Harmonsworth: Penguin.

Harding, S. (1996) 'Standpoint Epistemology (A Feminist Version): How Social Disadvantage Creates Epistemic Advantage' in S. Turner (ed.) *Social Theory and Sociology*, Oxford: Blackwell.

Hardt, M. and Negri, A. (2000) *Empire*, Cambridge, MA: Harvard University Press.

Harvey, D. (1990) *The Condition of Postmodernity*, Oxford: Blackwell.

Hawthorne, G. (1976) *Enlightenment and Despair: A History of Sociology*, Cambridge: Cambridge University Press.

Hay, C. (1999) *The Political Economy of New Labour*, Manchester: Manchester University Press.

Hayek, L. von (2000) *The Road to Serfdom*, London: Routledge.

Hayes, S. (1993) 'Structure and Agency and the Sticky Problem of Culture', *Sociological Theory*: 55–72.

Heidegger, M. (1978) *Being and Time*, Oxford: Blackwell.

Hekman, S. (1990) 'Hermeneutics and the Crisis of Social Theory: A Critique of Giddens' Epistemology' in J. Clark, C. Modgil and S. Modgil (eds) *Anthony Giddens: Consensus and Controversy*, London: Falmer Press.

Held, D. and Thompson, J. (eds) (1989) *Social Theory of Modern Societies: Anthony Giddens and His Critics*, Cambridge: Cambridge University Press.

Heritage, J. (1984) *Garfinkel and Ethnomethology*, Cambridge: Polity Press.

Hesse, M. (1980) 'The Strong Thesis of Sociology of Science' In *Revolutions and Reconstructions in the Philosophy of Science*, Brighton: Harvester.

Hirst, P. and Thompson, J. (1999) *Globalisation in Question*, Cambridge: Polity Press.

Hobsbawn, E. (2000) *The New Century*, London: Little Brown.

Holton, R. and Turner, B.S. (1989) *Max Weber on Economy and Society*, London: Routledge.

Hutton, W. (2001) 'Introduction' in C. Bryant and D. Jary (eds) *The Contemporary Giddens: Social Theory in a Globalising Age*, Basingstoke: Palgrave, now Palgrave Macmillan.

Janek, A. and Toulmin, S. (1996) *Wittgenstein's Vienna*, Chicago, IL: Elephant Paperbacks.

Kalberg, S. (1979) 'Max Weber's Types of Rationality', *American Journal of Sociology* 85: 1145–79.

Kant, I. (1996) 'An Answer to the Question: What is Enlightenment?' in H. Reiss (ed.) *Kant: Political Writings*, Cambridge: Cambridge University Press.

Kant, I. (1997) *Critique of Pure Reason*, Cambridge: Cambridge University Press.

Kilminster, R. (1991) 'Structuration as a World-View' in C. Bryant and D. Jary (eds) *Giddens' Theory of Structuration: A Critical Appreciation*, London: Routledge.

Kilminster, R. (1998) *The Sociological Revolution*, London: Routledge.

Kripke, S. (1982) *Wittgenstein on Rules and Private Language: An Elementary Exposition*, Oxford: Blackwell.

Krishna, D. (1974) 'The Self-Fulfilling Prophecy and the Nature of Society', *American Sociological Review* 36: 1104–7.

Lange, O. and Taylor, F. (1938) *On The Economic Theory of Socialism*, Minneapolis: University of Minnesota Press.

Layder, D. (1981) *Structure, Interaction and Social Theory*, London: Routledge & Kegan Paul.

Layder, D. (1985) 'Power, Structure and Agency', *Journal for the Theory of Social Behaviour* 15(2): 131–49.

Lemert, C. (1997) *Social Things*, Boston, MA: Rowman and Littlefield.

Livesay, J. (1985) 'Normative Grounding and Praxis: Habermas, Giddens and a Contradiction within Critical Theory', *Sociological Theory* 3: 66–76.

Lockwood, D. (1956) 'Some Remarks on the Social System', *British Journal of Sociology* 7: 134–46.

Lockwood, D. (1964) 'Social Integration and System Integration' in G.K. Zollschan and W. Hirsch (eds) *Explorations in Social Change*, London: Routledge & Kegan Paul.

Lowith, K. (1982) *Karl Marx and Max Weber*, London: Allen & Unwin.

Loyal, S. and Barnes, B. (2001) 'Agency as a Red-Herring in Social Theory', *Philosophy of Science* 31(4): 507–24.

Lukacs, G. (1971) *History and Class Consciousness*, London: Merlin.

Lukes, S. (1973) *Individualism*, Oxford: Blackwell.

Lukes, S. (1974) *Power: A Radical View*, London: Macmillan.

Lukes, S. (1991) 'Equality and Liberty: Must they Conflict?' in D. Held (ed.) *Political Theory Today*, Oxford: Blackwell, pp. 48–68.

MacPherson, C.B. (1962) *The Political Theory of Possessive Individualism*, Oxford: Oxford University Press.

Mandel, E. (1986) 'In Defence of Socialist Planning', *New Left Review* 159: 5–37.

Manicas, P. (1980) 'The Concept of Social Structure', *Journal for the Theory of Social Behaviour* 10: 65–82.

Manis, J. and Meltzer, B. (eds) (1967) *Symbolic Interaction: A Reader in Social Psychology*, Boston, MA: Allen & Bacon.

Mannheim, K. (1960) *Ideology and Utopia*, London: Routledge & Kegan Paul.

Mannheim, K. (1982) *Structures of Thinking*, London: Routledge & Kegan Paul.

Mannheim, K. (1986) *Conservatism: A Contribution to the Sociology of Knowledge*. London: Routledge & Kegan Paul.

Marcuse, H. (1964) *One Dimensional Man*, London: Routledge & Kegan Paul.

Marshall, T.H. (1973) *Citizen and Social Class*, Westport, CT: Greenwood Press.

Marx, K. (1843) 'Critique of Hegel's Rechtphilosophie', Introduction, *Collected Works [CW]* 3, Moscow: Progress Publishers.

Marx, K. (1844) *Economic and Philosophical Manuscripts*, CW 3.

Marx, K. (1846a) *The German Ideology*, CW 5.

Marx, K. (1846b) 'Letter to Annenkov' in D. Sayer, *Karl Marx Reader*, London: Routledge.

Marx, K. (1857) *Grundrisse: Foundations of the Critique of Political Economy* (trans. M. Nicolaus), London: Allen Lane.

Marx, K. (1858a) *Grundrisse*, CW 28.

Marx, K. (1858b) General Introduction to the *Grundrisse*, CW 28.

Marx, K. (1970) 'Theses on Feuerbach II', in *The German Ideology* (ed. C.J. Arthur), London: Wishart.

Marx, K. (1976) *Capital* Vol. 1, Harmondsworth: Penguin.

Marx, K. and Engels, F. (1844) *The Economic and Philosophical Manuscripts*, Marx and Engels *Collected Works*, vol. 3, London: Wishart.

Merton, R. (1949) *Society and Social Structure*, Glencoe, IL: Free Press.

Merton, R. (1957) *Social Theory and Social Structure*, Glencoe, IL: Free Press.

Mills, C.W. (1959) *The Sociological Imagination*, Harmondsworth: Penguin.

Mitzman, A. (1970) *The Iron Cage*, New York: Knopf.

Mommsen, W. (1974) *The Age of Bureaucracy: Perspectives on the Political Sociology of Max Weber*, Oxford: Blackwell.

Monk, R. (1990) *Wittgenstein: Portrait of a Genius*, London: Cape.

Mouzelis, N. (1975) *Organisation and Bureacracy*, London: Routledge & Kegan Paul.

Mouzelis, N. (1999) 'Exploring Post-Traditional Orders: Individual Reflexivity, "Pure Relations" and Duality of Structure' in M. O'Brien, S. Penna and C. Hay (eds) *Theorising Modernity: Relexivity, Environment and Identity in Giddens' Social Theory*, London: Longman, pp. 83–97.

Mullan, B. (1987) 'Anthony Giddens' in *Sociologists on Sociology*, London: Croom Helm.

New, C. (1994) 'Agency and Social Transformation', *Journal for the Theory of Social Behaviour* 24(3): 187–205.

Nisbet, R. (1967) *The Sociological Tradition*, London: Heinemann.

Nyiri, J. (1976) 'Wittgenstein's New Traditionalism' in 'Essays on Wittgenstein', *Acta Philosophica Fennica* 28(1–3): 503–12.

Nyiri, J. (1982) 'Wittgenstein's Later Work in Relation to Conservatism', in B. McGuinness (ed.), *Wittgenstein and His Times*, Oxford: Blackwell.

Outhwaite, W. (1990) 'Agency and Structure', in J. Clark, C. Modgil and S. Modgil (eds) (1990) *Anthony Giddens: Consensus and Controversy*, London: Falmer Press.

O'Brien, M., Penna, S. and Hay, C. (eds) (1999) *Theorising Modernity: Reflexivity, Environment and Identity in Giddens' Social Theory*, London: Longman.

Parsons, T. (1937) *The Structure of Social Action*, New York and Glencoe, IL: Free Press.

Parsons, T. (1967) *Sociological Theory and Modern Society*, New York: Free Press.

Pierson, C. (1998) *Conversations with Anthony Giddens*, Cambridge: Polity Press.

Pleasants, N. (1999) *Wittgenstein and the Idea of a Critical Social Theory*, London: Routledge.

Poggi, G. (1990) 'Anthony Giddens and "The Classics"' in J. Clark, C. Modgil and S. Modgil (eds) *Anthony Giddens: Consensus and Controversy*, London: Falmer Press.

Polanyi, K. (1944) *The Great Transformation: The Political and Economic Origin of Our Time*, Boston, MA: Beacon Press, 2002.

Polanyi, M. (1967) *The Tacit Dimension*, London: Routledge & Kegan Paul.

Porpora, D.V. (1989) 'Four Concepts of Social Structure', *Journal for the Study of Social Behaviour* 19: 195–212.

Porpora, D. (1993) 'Cultural Rules and Material Relations' *Sociological Theory* 11: 212–19.

Porter, R. (2000) The Enlightenment: Britain and the Creation of the Modern World, London: Penguin.

Quine, W.V. (1951) 'Two Dogmas of Empiricism', Philosophical Review 60: 20–43.

Remmling, G. (1973) Towards the Sociology of Knowledge, London: Routledge & Kegan Paul.

Rex, J. (1961) Key Problems in Sociological Theory, London: Routledge & Kegan Paul.

Ringer, F. (1998) Max Weber's Methodology: The Unification of the Cultural and Social Sciences, Cambridge, MA: Harvard University Press.

Roberts, M. (1995) 'Beyond Revisionism: New Labour', Radical Philosophy 73: 13–22.

Rorty, R. (1990) Essays on Heidegger and Others, Cambridge: Cambridge University Press.

Rorty, R. (1993) 'The Reification of Language' in C. Guignon (ed.), The Cambridge Companion to Heidegger, Cambridge: Cambridge University Press.

Rubinstein, D. (1986) 'The Concept of Structure in Sociology' in M. Wardell and S. Turner (eds) Sociological Theory in Transition, London: Allen & Unwin.

Rustin, M. (1995) 'The Future of Post-Socialism', Radical Philosophy 74: 17–27.

Ryle, G. (1954) 'Knowing How and Knowing That', Aristotelian Society Proceedings 46: 1–16.

Safranski, R. (1998) Martin Heidegger: Between Good and Evil, Cambridge, MA: Harvard University Press.

Saunders, P. (1989) 'Space, Urbanism and the Created Environment' in D. Held and J. Thompson (eds) Social Theory of Modern Societies: Anthony Giddens and His Critics, Cambridge: Cambridge University Press.

Sayer, D. (1983) Marx's Method. Brighton: Harvester.

Sayer, D. (1987) The Violence of Abstraction, Oxford: Blackwell.

Sayer, D. (1989) Readings from Karl Marx, London: Routledge.

Sayer, D. (1990) 'Reinventing the Wheel: Anthony Giddens, Karl Marx and Social Change' in J. Clark, C. Modgil and S. Modgil (eds) Anthony Giddens: Consensus and Controversy, London: Falmer Press.

Sayer, D. (1991) Capitalism and Modernity: An Excursus on Marx and Weber, London: Routledge.

Scheler, M. (1980) Problems of a Sociology of Knowledge, London: Routledge & Kegan Paul.

Schumpeter, J. (1987) Capitalism, Socialism and Democracy, London: Allen & Unwin.

Seidman, S. (1983) Liberalism and the Origins of European Social Theory, Oxford: Blackwell.

Sewell, W. (1992) 'A Theory of Structure: Duality, Agency and Transformations', American Journal of Sociology 98: 1–29.

Shaw, E. (1994) The Labour Party since 1979: Crisis and Transformation, London: Routledge.

Sklair, L. (1980) 'Sociologies and Marxisms: The Odd Couples' in P. Abrams, R. Deem, J. Finch and P. Rock (eds) Practice and Progress: British Sociology 1950–1980, London: Allen & Unwin.

Smith, D. (1998) 'Anthony Giddens and the Liberal Tradition', British Journal of Sociology 49(4).

Smith, J. and Turner, B.S (1986) 'Contructing Social Theory and Constituting Society', *Theory, Culture & Society* 3(2): 125–33.

Stanworth, P. and Giddens, A. (1974) *Elites and Power in British Society*, Cambridge: Cambridge University Press.

Studholme, M. (1997) 'From Leonard Hobhouse to Tony Blair: A Sociological Connection?', *Sociology* 31(3): 531–47.

Taylor, C. (1982) 'Rationality' in M. Hollis and S. Lukes (eds) *Rationality and Relativism*, Oxford: Blackwell.

Taylor, C. (1989) *The Social Sources of the Self*, Cambridge: Cambridge University Press.

Thompson, E.P. (1968) *The Making of the English Working Class*, Harmondsworth: Penguin.

Thompson, E.P. (1979) *The Poverty of Theory*, London: Merlin.

Thompson, J. (1989)'The Theory of Structuration' in D. Held and J. Thompson (eds) *Social Theory of Modern Societies: Anthony Giddens and His Critics*, Cambridge: Cambridge University Press.

Thompson, J. (1995) *The Media and Modernity*, Cambridge: Polity Press.

Turner, B. (1992a) 'Ideology and Utopia in the Formation of an Intelligentsia: Reflections on the English Cultural Conduit' *Theory, Culture & Society* 9: 183–210.

Turner, B. (1992b) 'Weber, Giddens and Modernity', *Theory, Culture & Society* 9(2): 141–6.

Turner, S. (1994) *The Social Theory of Practices: Tradition, Tacit Knowledge and Presuppositions*, Cambridge: Polity Press.

Urry, J. (1982) 'Duality as Structure: Some Critical Issues', *Theory, Culture & Society* 1(2): 100–6.

Urry, J. (1991) 'Time and Space in Giddens' Social Theory' in C. Bryant and D. Jary (eds) (1991) *Giddens' Theory of Structuration: A Critical Appreciation*, London: Routledge.

Voltaire (1733) *Lettres philosophiques ou Lettres anglaises*.

Wagner, G. (1993) 'Giddens on Subjectivity and Social Order', *Journal for the Theory of Social Behaviour* 23(2): 139–55.

Wainright, H. (1994) *Arguments for a New Left: Answering the Free Market Right*, Oxford: Blackwell.

Weber, M. (1971) 'Socialism' in *Max Weber: The Interpretation of Social Reality* (ed. J.E.T. Eldridge), London: Michael Joseph.

Wellmer, A. (1985) 'Reason, Utopia, and the Dialectic of Enlightenment' in R.J Bernstein (ed.) *Habermas and Modernity*, Cambridge, MA: MIT Press.

Williams, R. (1961) *The Long Revolution*, London: Pelican.

Williams, R. (1976) *Keywords*, London: Fontana.

Williams, R. (1977) *Marxism and Literature*, Oxford: Oxford University Press.

Willis, P. (1977) *Learning to Labour*, Aldershot: Ashgate.

Winch, P. (1958) *The Idea of Social Science and its Relation to Philosophy*, London: Routledge & Kegan Paul.

Wittgenstein, L. (1958) *The Philosophical Investigations*, Oxford: Blackwell.

Wittgenstein, L. (1969a) *The Blue and Brown Books*, Oxford: Blackwell.

Wittgenstein, L. (1969b) *On Certainty*, Oxford: Blackwell.

Wittgenstein, L. (1978) *Remarks on the Foundations of Mathematics*, Oxford: Blackwell.

Wittgenstein, L. (1980a) *Culture and Value*, Oxford: Blackwell.

Wittgenstein, L. (1980b) *Remarks on the Philosophy of Psychology*, Vol. 1, Oxford: Blackwell.

Wolin, R. (1998) *The Heidegger Controversy*, Cambridge, MA: MIT Press.

Wright. E.O. (1989) 'Models of Historical Trajectory: An Assessment of Giddens' Critique of Marxism' in D. Held and J. Thompson (eds) *Social Theory of Modern Societies: Anthony Giddens and His Critics*, Cambridge: Cambridge University Press.

Wright, G.H. von (1982) 'Wittgenstein in Relation to His Time' in B. McGuinness (ed.), *Wittgenstein and His Times*, Oxford: Blackwell.

Wright-Mills, C. (1940) 'Situated Actions and Vocabularies of Motive', *American Sociological Review* 5: 904–13.

Wright-Mills, C. (1959) *Society and Social Structure*, Glencoe, IL: Free Press.

Index

Compiled by Sue Carlton